CHIEF O'NEILL'S SKETCHY RECOLLECTIONS OF AN EVENTFUL LIFE IN CHICAGO

CHIEF O'NEILL'S

SKETCHY RECOLLECTIONS

OF AN EVENTFUL LIFE IN CHICAGO

FRANCIS O'NEILL

EDITED BY ELLEN SKERRETT AND MARY LESCH | FOREWORD BY NICHOLAS CAROLAN

BRANDON

First published in Britain and Ireland in 2008
by Brandon
an imprint of Mount Eagle Publications
Dingle, Co. Kerry, Ireland, and
Unit 3, Olympia Trading Estate, Coburg Road, London N22 6TZ, England

10 9 8 7 6 5 4 3 2 1

ISBN 978-086322-378-5

Mount Eagle Publications / Sliabh an Fhiolair Teoranta
receives support from the Arts Council / An Chomhairle Ealaíon.

First published in the United States of America by Northwestern University Press
Printed in the United States of America

For John Lesch and
Mary Wade

CONTENTS

A NOTE ON THE TEXT

MARY LESCH

My earliest memories of my family include an awareness of Francis O'Neill, my great-grandfather. He died in 1936 before I was born, but he had a significant importance in my father's family. My father, Frank Mooney (named after his grandfather), spent half of his childhood from the ages of four to sixteen in the O'Neill home. My father's family, the Mooneys, lived at 836 East Fifty-second Street, just a few blocks away from the O'Neill house at 5448 South Drexel Boulevard. After Rogers O'Neill died on February 13, 1904, my father spent more and more time with his grandparents and his aunts. My father was probably a distraction from their grief over Rogers's sudden death and a hope for the future.

The stories I was told about Francis O'Neill were not about the Irish music, his musical skill, or his adventures in the police department. I heard about his love of nature, of his vast knowledge of plants and trees, and of his interest in farming. Eventually I learned about his library and his focus on Irish history and Irish music. Our family's bookshelves always included several volumes on Irish history that had been part of Francis O'Neill's library. I knew he had donated his books to the University of Notre Dame before he died. In 1983 I had an opportunity to browse through the stacks of his donated volumes; today his books are in the Special Collections section of the Hesburgh Library at the University of Notre Dame and are available to scholars by request. In preparing for the publication of this book, Ellen Skerrett and I were the recipients of a Cushwa Center for the Study of American Catholicism grant which enabled us to study his books at Notre Dame. As he describes in his reflections, his library has been judiciously chosen book by book in two specific areas: topics concerning Ireland and Irish music.

His early travels around the world were marvelous stories for me which cast him in a very heroic or romantic role. I was an adult before I understood that he had been superintendent of police in Chicago and that he had published eight books on traditional Irish music. In 1975 I found a handwritten section of his memoir that had been stored in our garage. In his flourishing penmanship, which was fairly easy to read, he told the story of building his first house in Bridgeport and needing mortar to finish his chimney. His quest to finish his chimney led him to depend on his neighbors who were immigrants from other countries. O'Neill concluded that this was a wonderful country where people, regardless of their national origin, take time to help one another.

Twenty years later when my Aunt May, O'Neill's last surviving child, died, my cousin Jim Mooney discovered a typed version of O'Neill's memoir. The expanded recollection did include the wonderful story about the mortar. It is this memoir which is the basis of this book.

This is a view of Bantry, Ireland, as it looked a hundred years ago. In the distant hills in the upper right is the convent of the Sisters of Mercy, built in 1862 and later sketched by O'Neill. (Courtesy of myhometown.ie)

O'NEILL FAMILY TREE

John O'Neill
1801–67
m. Catherine O'Mahony
1812–1900

Philip	Mary	John	Michael*	Catherine	Michael*	(Daniel) Francis**
b. 1835	b. 1836	b. 1838	b. 1841	b. 1843	b. 1845	1848–1936
						m. 1870
						Anna Rogers
						1846–1934

John*	John*	Mary	Francis	Julia	Anne	Philip	Rogers	Caroline	Mary
1871–71	1872–76	1873–76	1875–79	1879–1971	1890–1964	1882–85	1886–1904	1881–1968	1888–1990
				m. 1900				m. 1913	
				James Mooney				Daniel Crowe	
				1875–1960				1870–1942	

Frank	Julia	William	Mary	Philip	James
1900–85	1915–80	1905–84	1910	1908–37	1904–44
m. 1941		m. 1949	m. 1953	m. 1936	m. 1932
Marjorie		Rosemary	Thomas	Mary	Jeanne
Glavin		Burke	Wade	Slusser	Adams
1904–78		1908–89	1902–92	1912–94	1912–2002

Mary
b. 1942
m. 1966
John Lesch
b. 1940

James
b. 1934
m. 1957
Doris Mohr
b. 1936

Philip
b. 1943

Katherine
b. 1985

Julianna	John	Thomas	Mary	Julia	James
b. 1967	b. 1971	b. 1977	b. 1958	b. 1959	b. 1961
m. 1993		m. 2004		m. 2004	m. 1984
Paul Mann		Anne Crosby		Bernard	Susan
b. 1966		b. 1978		Goulding	Kaiser
				b. 1959	b. 1963

Lauren	Eleanor	Caroline	Bridget
b. 1996	b. 1999	b. 2007	b. 2006

Katherine	James	Patrick
b. 1987	b. 1990	b. 1992

---

* It was a common practice to use the name of a deceased child in naming a newborn sibling.

** Francis O'Neill was baptized Daniel Francis. When he immigrated to the United States he dropped the name Daniel and used the names Francis or Frank.

Even with this detailed record of a written memoir, newspaper clippings, official police reports, published books, and personal scrapbooks, the essence of O'Neill the person remained elusive to me. I knew my father admired him and was in awe of his knowledge of flora. But I could not remember what my dad knew about O'Neill as a man. Was he nice? Was he fun? Did he talk to people or did he prefer to read in his library? My aunt Mary Wade, who lives in Ocean Springs, Mississippi, has been my direct link to O'Neill the person. According to Mary, O'Neill was indeed a scholar, but he was also a gregarious man engaging the company of people of all ages. Mary remembers that he enjoyed having his grandchildren climb all over him. In his retirement he spent his winters in Ocean Springs, and Mary recalls that O'Neill would call her, her sister, and her brothers to come with him to the movies. As they walked along, O'Neill invited all of the children they passed to join them. When your grandchildren remember you as fun-loving and generous, you have left a worthy legacy.

Because this memoir is an original document, we wanted to preserve the manner in which O'Neill wrote and the order in which he recorded his life events. Therefore, only very light editing has been done to the memoir, and all extracts from O'Neill's reports have been reproduced in their original style.

FOREWORD

*The Influence of Francis O'Neill
on Irish Traditional Music*

NICHOLAS CAROLAN

It is hard, if not impossible, to imagine what Irish traditional music might be like today if Francis O'Neill had not lived. What long musical processes have been set in motion by musicians learning tunes from his publications for over a century now, directly and indirectly? What changes have been brought about in local repertory in all parts of Ireland and the Irish diaspora? What might composers of Irish traditional music have created if the O'Neill collections had not been part of their intellectual and emotional landscapes? What melodies, especially those of dance music, might have vanished from the body of Irish music to be forgotten forever? What would the national repertory now be?

As the driving force of a group of more than fifty musical collaborators—most notable among them James O'Neill—Francis O'Neill gathered from oral and printed sources some twenty-six hundred pieces of Irish music. More important in terms of influence, he made these pieces (and information about many of them) universally available in eight book publications over two decades, at a time when there were few similar publications in existence. His published work in music has been exerting an influence for longer now than the life span of any musician, and it has been exerting that influence through many channels: the volumes themselves and their many editions and reprintings; the manuscripts that were copied from them; the commercial and field sound recordings and other printed collections that drew on them; the mass media of radio, television, and the Internet that have amplified their effects enormously; and, of course, the living oral tradition.

And there are other aspects to the musical influence of Francis O'Neill: the self-esteem and national pride that his sumptuous publications engendered in traditional musicians; the boost his publications gave to the spread of music literacy among them; the now universally used tune versions and titles that he and his circle created; the enormous reservoir of melodies he provided for professional musicians and arrangers; the information he put into circulation as a historian and as a collector of oral history; the example he gave to other collector-publishers and music historians.

O'Neill's was the greatest individual influence on the evolution of Irish traditional dance music in the twentieth century. His contribution has become a permanent although constantly changing component of the bloodstream of the music, and it is one that is accordingly increasing in effect in the new century rather than disappearing with the passage of time.

Nicholas Carolan, director of the Irish Traditional Music Archive in Dublin, Ireland, is shown here at ITMA headquarters holding a copy of his biography of O'Neill, A Harvest Saved. *Carolan is considered to be the foremost authority on Irish traditional music. (Photograph by Mary Lesch)*

ACKNOWLEDGMENTS

Verifying the details of Francis O'Neill's life in Chicago and finding photographs to complement his 1930s memoir has been a challenging and exciting collaboration. We are indebted to our friend William R. Currie for introducing us to the world of Celtic music and helping us understand the significance of O'Neill's publications. It was Bill who led us to Noel P. Rice, noted Irish musician, director of the Academy of Irish Music, and president of the Irish American Heritage Center. We are particularly grateful to Noel for being our expert source on Irish music in Chicago in the twentieth and twenty-first centuries. Noel was always able to answer our research questions with an astonishing immediacy. He made our work easier, and he helped us develop a broader understanding of Irish music and its place in Irish culture.

Our sincere gratitude to Northwestern University Press for seeing the value in O'Neill's recollections and agreeing to publish them and for historian Perry R. Duis's enthusiastic support. We want to thank our acquisitions editor, Henry Carrigan, and his predecessor, Sue Betz, as well as Nora Gorman, sales and marketing coordinator. We also want to thank Serena Brommel, senior project editor at the press, for guiding us through the editing process. Thank you to Greta Polo for her handsome design and to the art, layout, and production staff who have worked so diligently to bring out this book.

Mary Wade, Francis O'Neill's granddaughter, is the only person we could find who knew Chicago's celebrated chief of police when he was alive. In addition to sharing her memories of him, she has been invaluable in corroborating our research with rare family documents and reconstructing the O'Neill family tree. We are especially grateful to James L. Mooney, O'Neill's great-grandson, who found the typed manuscript of O'Neill's memoir.

James T. McGuire has been a help to us in sharing his unpublished work on James O'Neill and Selena O'Neill. We have also benefited enormously from Michael Precin's painstaking research and family archival material on Selena O'Neill.

Our deep thanks to Timothy Matovina, director of the Cushwa Center for the Study of American Catholicism at the University of Notre Dame, and Kathleen Sprows Cummings, associate director, for the generous research travel grant in 2005 to prepare an appendix of the rare books in the Francis O'Neill Collection in the Hesburgh Library. We are also grateful to Sara B. Weber, reading room supervisor and digital project coordinator, Department of Rare Books and Special Collections, Hesburgh Library; Ben Panciera, rare books librarian and curator for special collections; George Rugg, curator for special collections; and Joe Ross, rare book cataloger. Senior library assistant Rita D. Erskine graciously filled many requests for paging rare volumes in preparation for our research trips, and Marilyn Bierwagen, senior library assistant, kindly provided us with copies of the card catalog of the O'Neill Collection. We also thank Wendy Clauson Schlereth, director of the University of Notre Dame Archives, and William Kevin Cawley, archivist and curator of manuscripts, for their assistance in tracing O'Neill's correspondence with the University of Notre Dame.

We are indebted to Nicholas Carolan, the author of *A Harvest Saved* and the director of the Irish Traditional Music Archive in Dublin for his thoughtful assessment of O'Neill's impact on Irish music today. Another Dubliner who has been tireless in his efforts to rekindle the memory of O'Neill's accomplishments is Harry Bradshaw, who has recently retired from his position as a broadcast journalist for RTE Radio in Ireland.

Catherine Mulhall was our go-to person in Ireland when we needed verification of facts and added details. No inquiry on our part was too trivial for Catherine; she enthusiastically brought us solutions and answers to all of our questions. Catherine organized a committee of volunteers in Tralibane to erect two monuments in honor of O'Neill: a plaque at the crossroads and a statue overlooking the valley. The committee members are Liam Barrett, John Collins, Catherine Mulhall, Cecelia Wilcox, Mary Kate O'Sullivan, Kathleen Cadogan (rest in peace), Gordon Shannon, Nora Cremin, and Tim McCarthy, president. We are grateful to Catherine for all of her kindnesses to the Lesch family, including many meals at her house and many guided tours of Tralibane. We also thank Timothy O'Brien, a cousin of Catherine's and a cousin of O'Neill's who has generously offered his time to assist us in our research and has introduced us to friends and neighbors of the O'Neill family. We want to give a special thanks to Father John Paul Hegarty, P.P., of Mayfield, Cork, Ireland, for sending us the biographical data on Canon Sheehan.

We are grateful to Len Aronson, retired producer at WTTW in Chicago, whose program "Chicago Stories, Francis O'Neill" sparked interest in O'Neill that eventually led to the publication of this book. We also want to thank Mike Dooley, retired detective of the Chicago Police Department for collecting thousands of signatures in support of the publication of the O'Neill memoir.

So many historians, archivists, and librarians have been very generous to us, but above all we want to thank John E. Corrigan for sharing his vast knowledge of Chicago Irish history and providing us with citations from his database relating to Francis O'Neill and Irish culture. Chicago historians Suellen Hoy, Ann Durkin Keating, and Rima Lunin Schultz offered critical support for our project, and Irish scholars Emmet Larkin and Caoimhin MacAoidh helped us develop unexplored facts of O'Neill's life. We are also grateful to Richard D. Barrett for his invaluable assistance at the National Archives and the Library of Congress in Washington, D.C. Claretian archivist Malachy R. McCarthy generously spent hours searching the *Boston Pilot* for ads that convinced Francis O'Neill to move to Edina, Missouri, and he graciously answered research questions and provided last-minute image scans. And we remain particularly grateful for Joan A. Radtke's help in telling Francis O'Neill's story at the Hibernian lecture at the University of Notre Dame on November 18, 2005.

We also want to recognize Julie A. Satzik, assistant research archivist, Archdiocese of Chicago's Joseph Cardinal Bernardin Archives and Records Center; Reverend Louis P. Rogge, O. Carm., Carmelite Provincial Archives; Jerry O'Sullivan, retired captain of the Chicago Police Department; Lesley Martin, Chicago History Museum Research Center; Ray Gadke, reading room manager, Regenstein Periodicals and Microforms Department, University of Chicago Library; and Debbie Damolaris, librarian at the University Club of Chicago. Lorrie Vodden, archivist of the Catholic Diocese of Peoria, helped us verify the date of Francis O'Neill's marriage to Anna Rogers at Holy Trinity parish in Bloomington, Illinois.

We want to thank Francis J. Clarke III for lending us *O'Neill's Irish Music: 400 Choice Selections Arranged for Piano and Violin* and for sharing family material related to his grandfather, Irish immigrant Francis J. Clarke, who joined the Chicago Police Department as a musician in 1907. Christine Colburn of the Preservation and Special Collections Department of the University of Chicago Library was especially helpful in providing us with scans of images in time to meet our publication deadline, as were Robert Medina and Bryan McDaniel of the Rights and Reproductions Department of the Chicago History Museum.

We are deeply grateful to Chicago Public Library commissioner Mary Dempsey for the many complimentary Xeroxes from Chicago's historic newspapers that aided us in annotations. William Cliff and Tamara Shkundina, library clerks, generously assisted us in the microfilm room at Harold Washington Library, and Morag Walsh and Teresa G. Yoder of the Special Collections Department of the Harold Washington Library provided invaluable help in finding images and information about early Chicago.

We are indebted to Paul Lane of Photo Source in Evanston, Illinois, for his photographic skill. He performed magic with rare O'Neill photographs and turned them into handsome scans. We also thank Jennifer A. Riforgiate for her help editing and scanning pictures and for photographing the rich O'Neill material culture which included police batons, commemorative badges, and police stars.

Thank you to Brendon and Siobahn McKinney, owners of the Chief O'Neill Pub for their generosity to us. John Daly, director of the Irish American Heritage Center, has been very supportive of our work with this book and remains a wonderful resource.

To all of our friends and family who have helped us over the years we offer our sincere gratitude.

INTRODUCTION

ELLEN SKERRETT

Francis O'Neill's memoir, written in Chicago in 1931 when he was eighty-three years old, provides a rare glimpse of the world Irish immigrants encountered—and embraced—after the Great Fire of 1871. Young Irish men had helped build the city since its incorporation in 1837, digging the Illinois and Michigan Canal; laying railroad track; working in the stockyards and steel mills. Irish women worked as domestics, and their small wages, sent back to Ireland, enabled sisters and brothers to make the long journey out. The Chicago they discovered and claimed for themselves was among the fastest-growing cities in the United States, with thousands of German-born residents and transplanted New England Yankees. And as the city continued to grow and expand, the Irish presence remained unmistakable, especially in the realm of politics, municipal government, and religion. In neighborhoods throughout Chicago, church steeples and parochial schools symbolized the dividends of Irish investment in urban life.

Unlike many Irish immigrants born in 1848 during the Great Famine, O'Neill came from a prosperous farming family in Tralibane, County Cork, and had excelled as a student at the national schools in Dromore and Bantry, where he studied Latin, Greek, and mathematics. But his aspirations to attend the School of Design in Cork "met with no favors at home," and he sought employment as a teacher with the Christian Brothers in Blackrock. When he missed Bishop William Delany "by fifteen minutes," O'Neill's fate was sealed: he left Ireland in 1865 at age sixteen and spent the next four years traveling the world as a sailor. His adventures from Alexandria, Egypt, to Japan and the Hawaiian Islands and the West Indies profoundly shaped his outlook on life. O'Neill was an "educated seam[a]n," whose pursuit of literature on long voyages became the stuff of legend. When his ship docked

xix

in a foreign port, he would "drop overboard unobtrusively with a package of books tied on top of my head and swim to a vessel several hundred yards away." His passion for collecting continued on dry land, and by 1898, O'Neill had amassed a library of fifteen hundred volumes that was considered to be among the largest private collections of Irish literature in the United States. In 1931, he donated it to the University of Notre Dame in South Bend, Indiana, a "magnificent gift" that has continued to attract scholars from all over the world (see the list in the back of this book).[1]

While his travels made him cosmopolitan, O'Neill remained painfully aware that the life of a sailor was one of "enforced slavery," and his experience working with African Americans left a deep impression. While loading freshly cut pine in Brunswick, Georgia, in 1866, a Negro stevedore "showed such consideration for my youth" that the memory remained fresh in O'Neill's mind when he was in a position to hire African American policemen in Chicago. Indeed, *Broad Ax* publisher Julius F. Taylor regularly praised O'Neill as a "race man" and devoted considerable space to his books on Irish music.[2]

Although O'Neill's well-deserved reputation as the police chief who "saved Irish music" has received scholarly attention in recent years, equally fascinating is his thirty-two-year career in the Chicago Police Department. *Chief O'Neill's Sketchy Recollections of an Eventful Life in Chicago* is primarily a police memoir, a vivid behind-the-scenes look at the attractions of law enforcement for a bright, ambitious, English-speaking immigrant. Despite his classical education, it took O'Neill more than a month of tramping on Chicago streets in 1871 to land his first job as an unskilled laborer "trucking dressed hogs and pounding ice." Decades could not dim his memory of waiting in the cold outside the Kent and Hutchinson packinghouse with scores of other hopeful workers. At the last minute, by linking arms with four Germans, he got the job, but the monthly wage of less than fifty dollars provided little chance to save for a home with his new bride, Anna Rogers, who was expecting their first child. The story of how the O'Neills became homeowners in the wake of the Great Fire of October 8–9, 1871, offers a new perspective on the development of the Bridgeport neighborhood by entrepreneurs who appropriated "unguarded" lumber and helped each other transform simple wooden boxes into respectable five-room cottages.

O'Neill continued to seek better employment on the Chicago and Alton Railroad and then in the shipping department of John V. Farwell and Company, but he found his advancement stymied because he did not belong "in

favored organizations," nor did he enjoy "the backing of friends and relatives." Little wonder that he set his sights on the Chicago Police Department,
where an Irish immigrant could earn a thousand dollars a year. However, the
work was often dangerous because officers had to patrol large areas of the city
alone, and the "copper" on the beat often confronted boys as well as men
who carried pistols and did not hesitate to shoot.[3]

Despite glowing recommendations from his employers and a member of
Congress, however, O'Neill found his application ignored. Finally, through
the intervention of alderman William Tracey, O'Neill joined the "long blue
line" of officers on July 12, 1873. Only six weeks earlier, he had become a
naturalized citizen, swearing to support the U.S. Constitution and "absolutely and entirely renounce and abjure all allegiance and fidelity to every
Foreign Prince, Potentate, State or Sovereignty . . . [especially to] the Queen
of Great Britain & Ireland." From the day O'Neill joined the Chicago police
force, he battled political pull and the interference of local aldermen and
championed civil service reform. His introduction to the dangers of police
work came after just one month on the job, when he was shot by a thief at
Clark and Monroe streets downtown on August 17, 1873. O'Neill's response
showed the restraint that came to be a distinguishing characteristic of his
career: he used his wooden baton to disarm his attacker and "prevent[ed] the
Pinkerton [watch]man from blowing out the burglar's brains." The next day
he was "promoted for conspicuous bravery by the Board of Police and Fire
Commissioners from probationer to regular patrolman."[4]

As a patrolman and later desk sergeant at the Deering Street station at
2913 South Loomis Street, O'Neill became a familiar figure in Bridgeport, then
one of the busiest police districts in the city. Although he lived in the neighborhood and was known by name as well as by face, O'Neill suffered no illu-
sions about the popularity of policemen. One of the most celebrated murder
trials in Chicago's history ended with the hanging of Christopher Rafferty
on February 27, 1874, for killing police officer Patrick O'Meara in Mary
O'Brien's Bridgeport saloon. Thousands gathered for the funeral of Rafferty
at Nativity Church and followed the hearse to the Northwestern Depot on
Kinzie Street for the cemetery train to Calvary in Evanston. The outpouring
of affection for Rafferty, argued the *Chicago Tribune*, provided proof that
"the uneducated Irish masses have very small sympathy with policemen, . . .
forgetting that, in the United States, the officer of the law is the servant of the
people, not of the despot." Finley Peter Dunne's famous literary character,
"Mr. Dooley," spoke for many Chicagoans when he asked the question in

1897, "How is it that whin a fireman dies th' whole city mourns an' whin a polisman dies all annywan says is: 'Who's th' first iligible on th' list?'"[5]

As O'Neill's memoir confirms, throughout his long career, he resisted political "pull" and suffered the consequences, being transferred from station to station. According to the *Chicago Tribune*, he became a "modern pariah, with his hand against every precinct boss and every precinct boss' hand against him." Yet O'Neill's intelligence and competence could not be ignored: as former chief clerk to general superintendent Austin J. Doyle for nine years, his reports combined accuracy with clear penmanship, a legacy of his national school days in Ireland. He also understood the value of original documents and the need for a department archive, saving letters between the mayor and city department heads "in pigeonholes entirely apart from ordinary correspondence in the vault."[6]

Although O'Neill ranked first among thirty police lieutenants and captains with a score of 99.8 percent on the civil service exam in 1898, his impressive accomplishment did not immediately translate into a promotion. In fact, when Mayor Carter Harrison II finally appointed him superintendent of police on April 29, 1901, Chicago newspaper editors were caught by surprise, along with many of the city's aldermen. Yet when O'Neill's name was read out at the city council chambers, "cheers broke out in the galleries, which were packed with visitors." In a move symbolic of his plans to restore the luster of the Chicago Police Department, the new superintendent sent out the traditional five-pointed star "to the nickel-plater" to be trimmed and burnished. He described the police department as "rank with factions and infested with political discord" and promised the people of Chicago "to begin at once to eradicate these elements," adding that "I did not seek this position, and therefore consider myself under obligations to no one but the Mayor."[7]

With his trademark bluntness, O'Neill told the *Chicago Daily News*, "Every new chief of police as far back as I can remember begins his reign by stating that he is going to divorce politics from the police force." As a former assistant to the superintendent, O'Neill knew from experience that aldermen tried to influence hiring decisions because their constituents expected it. While he hoped that civil service would ultimately prevail, the new superintendent remained confident that "with the material at hand Chicago can be policed as well as any city in the world."[8]

Shortly before he was reappointed superintendent for a second term in 1903, O'Neill reflected on the challenges police officers faced in making arrests and bringing offenders to justice. He recalled his own experience back in 1895 chasing the notorious robber Mickey Shevlin as he jumped from an Indiana Avenue electric car. Despite accompanying Shevlin in a patrol wagon and personally booking him at the Stanton Avenue station, when O'Neill showed up at police court the following morning, he discovered that "the disorderly conduct charge had mysteriously disappeared" and that Shevlin had been released on a straw bond. "There I was, a police captain, unable to secure the enforcement of law against a thief, and merely because of unwarranted and criminal interference." In O'Neill's view, a good honest police officer found himself importuned at every turn because "everybody he arrests is a son of some one, a brother-in-law of some one, or at least a friend of some one."[9]

O'Neill's career in the Chicago Police Department encompassed some of the city's—and the nation's—most volatile labor battles, from the great railway strike of July 1877 to the May 4, 1886, protest meeting at Haymarket Square in which eight police officers were killed and sixty wounded; the Pullman railroad strike in July 1894; the City Railway strike of 1903; and the packinghouse strike of July 1904. In keeping with the spirit of his memoir, *Chief O'Neill's Sketchy Recollections of An Eventful Life in Chicago*, O'Neill views these events from the perspective of a police officer whose duty is to maintain order among strikers and their sympathizers and protect property. His report on the 1894 railroad strike is full of eyewitness detail and corroborates Illinois governor Peter Altgeld's assessment that federal troops sent by President Grover Cleveland "accomplished nothing." In addition to criticizing soldiers who fired into crowds, killing and wounding strikers at Forty-ninth and Loomis, O'Neill also singled out "timid railroad employees and officials" who believed exaggerated reports of "intimidation, pin pulling, switch throwing, and assaults."[10]

As superintendent of police, O'Neill made many innovations, including new police badges that incorporated "the City Seal in the center and with copper numbers brazed on the nickel surface" that could be easily read. He introduced standardized blank forms which not only saved stationery but also promoted efficiency and developed "a comprehensive new Book of Rules and Regulations governing the Department of Police." And he continued to write his own reports in an engaging, narrative style. Not content merely to record the number of officers and arrests they made, O'Neill used the department's annual reports to document the headline-breaking cases solved by detectives and patrolmen and to recount the challenges posed by labor strikes, large and small. His 1903 report (included later in this book) contains a heartrending account of the Iroquois Theater disaster of December 30 in which more than six hundred people, mostly women and children, were killed when scenery caught fire and shot "tongues of flame" into the auditorium. Rushing to the scene, O'Neill joined policemen and firemen who worked "steadily and solemnly" to carry the bodies of the dead, "with only lanterns to partially dispel the gloom amid smoke and steam."

O'Neill was no stranger to death. As a police officer who rose steadily through the ranks, he had seen his share of violent murders and mourned the deaths of officers killed in the line of duty. But like many families in nineteenth-century Chicago, the O'Neills experienced the loss of five of their ten children to epidemics, "the two oldest passing to eternity in one

When Chicago Daily News *artist Thomas A. O'Shaughnessy arrived on the scene of the tragic Iroquois Theater fire on December 30, 1903, he found Chief O'Neill holding a lantern as Bishop Peter J. Muldoon anointed victims. O'Neill described the scene of bodies at the exits of the second balcony as resembling "a field of timothy grass blown flat by the wind and rain of a summer storm."* (Chicago Daily News, *December 30, 1903*)

day." Yet the family's move from working-class Bridgeport to middle-class Hyde Park could not insure the lives of the remaining O'Neill children. The "angel of death" returned, claiming the last surviving son, eighteen-year-old Rogers O'Neill, in 1904. Out of deference to his wife, Anna, O'Neill never again played music in their home at 5448 South Drexel Boulevard.[11]

As his memoir makes clear, O'Neill grew up with the sound of Irish music and "dancing at the crossroads," but this rich legacy nearly disappeared entirely as a result of famine and eviction. Walking his beat in Bridgeport or traveling on the streetcars, O'Neill would hear familiar tunes whistled by immigrant newcomers, and he spent a lifetime—and a small fortune—publishing these melodies. Although his vision and persistence made it possible for later generations to play and appreciate Irish traditional music, at the time of his death in 1936, O'Neill thought his life's work on behalf of Irish culture had been a failure. He lamented that Catholic parishes did not hire talented musicians for their theatrical productions and that there was little reason for the children and grandchildren of Irish immigrants to devote years "to acquire an art so little appreciated. Better learn ragtime and piano pounding, which gets both money and applause."[12]

While the memory of Irish music and dancing fueled Francis O'Neill's passion for collecting, his day job as a police officer provided him with a unique opportunity to describe the growth and development of the Chicago Police Department in the thirty-five years after the Great Fire of 1871. *Chief O'Neill's Sketchy Recollections of An Eventful Life in Chicago* makes a compelling case for the attractions of police work—and urban life—for the Irish in the United States, and it contributes to Francis O'Neill's enduring reputation as a scholar and historian of Chicago.

NOTES

1. Francis O'Neill began his education at the National School in Dromore and completed his studies at the Bantry National School. For a lengthy description of his library, see "O'Neill's Fine Books," *Chicago Chronicle*, February 20, 1898. See especially the correspondence between Francis O'Neill and Reverend Charles L. O'Donnell, C.S.C., September 18, 1931 and September 28, 1931, University Libraries of Notre Dame, Department of Special Collections. Also O'Neill to O'Donnell, October 1931, and O'Donnell to O'Neill, November 10, 1931, Records of President Charles O'Donnell, box 6, folder 91, Archives of the University of Notre Dame; O'Donnell to O'Neill, October 2, 1931, box 6, folder 92, Archives of the University of Notre Dame.

2. In an editorial after the teamsters' strike of 1905, Julius Taylor praised O'Neill for hiring "between five and six hundred colored men" as special police officers and insisting that Chicago lumber merchants and businessmen had "no right to dictate to the city as to the color or the nationality of the men it selected to guard or to protect their property." "Chief O'Neill and the Colored Policemen," *Broad Ax*, June 17, 1905. We are grateful to Suellen Hoy for this citation as well as the *Broad Ax* articles on O'Neill's music books: October 24, 1903; October 31, 1903; August 21, 1915.

3. According to the *Chicago Tribune*, March 7, 1873, "there are only two policemen to every mile, and their beats are such that they can meet each other but once in three hours." Even if the officers succeeded in making arrests, they were "a mile-and-a-half from the station." When police officers arrested Paddy Connors on Blue Island Avenue near Taylor Street, for example, he allegedly shouted to his friends to use their revolvers "to shoot the dirty devils," *Chicago Tribune*, March 19, 1873.

4. Thanks to the digitization of the *Chicago Tribune* by the ProQuest Historical Newspapers initiative, we have been able to document that Francis O'Neill was shot on August 17, 1873, not August 12, as was reported in subsequent news accounts and biographical entries. See *Chicago Tribune*, August 18, 1873, and *Chicago Inter Ocean* August 18, 1873. The legal document "Frank R. O'Neill" signed on May 23, 1873, acknowledged that he had "arrived in the United States a minor" and that he had lived in the United States for seven years, three in the state of Illinois. Thanks to Julius Machnikowski, assistant archivist at the Circuit Court of Cook County, for his assistance in obtaining O'Neill's naturalization papers.

5. While acknowledging the dangers of solitary patrols and the impact police shootings had on morale, the *Chicago Tribune* on August 21, 1873, editorialized: "Policemen do not use their pistols enough. There is nothing so demoralizing to these brutal cowards as the death of two or three of their number, and the knowledge that a policeman can shoot as well as they." The quote on Irish attitudes toward policemen appears in the account of Christopher Rafferty's funeral, "Dust to Dust," *Chicago Tribune*, March 2, 1874. See especially Finley Peter Dunne's column on Chicago policemen versus firemen, originally published in the *Chicago Evening Post*, August 7, 1897, with notes and comments by Charles Fanning, ed., *Mr. Dooley and the Chicago Irish: The Autobiography of a Nineteenth-Century Ethnic Group* (Washington, D.C.: Catholic University of America Press, 1987), 110–12.

6. "A Gallery of Local Celebrities, Francis O'Neill," *Chicago Tribune*, August 25, 1901.

7. See "Fit to Be Captains," *Chicago Chronicle*, February 1, 1898, for the ranking of Chicago police lieutenants and captains based on the civil service exam. For information on civil service in Chicago, see A. N. Waterman, ed., *Historical Review of Chicago and Cook County* (Chicago: Lewis Publishing Company, 1908), 1:112–16. See also "Captain O'Neill Chief of Police," *Chicago Tribune*, April 30, 1901; "O'Neill to Clean Force," *Chicago Chronicle*, May 1, 1901; and "Pledge of the New Chief," *Chicago American*, April 30, 1901.

8. "Blow at Politicians," *Chicago Daily News*, April 30, 1901.

9. Francis O'Neill, "Why the Laws of Chicago Cannot Be Properly Enforced," *Chicago Inter Ocean*, February 8, 1903. For biographical information on Mickey Shevlin and the Shevlin gang, see "Chief Badenoch Defies Goggin," *Chicago Tribune*, December 12, 1895.

10. In an address at Cooper Union, New York, and reported in the *New York Times* of October 18, 1896, Altgeld asserted that the federal troops in Chicago during the Pullman Strike "did no good . . . instead of overawing the mob or exerting an influence for good, their presence added to the excitement and served as an irritant, and instead of suppressing rioting it will be noticed that it did not begin until after their arrival and then grew steadily, and on the 6th [July 1894], the worst day, instead of suppressing they accomplished nothing."

11. Anna and Francis O'Neill's first born, John Francis, died ten days after his birth on November 12, 1871. Their second and third children, John Francis and Mary Catherine, both died on August 26, 1876. Francis, age four, was buried on August 2, 1879; Philip Anthony, age two, was buried on January 2, 1885; Rogers F. O'Neill, age eighteen, died on February 13, 1904. The daughters who survived were Julia Ann Mooney (1879–1971); Caroline O'Neill Crowe (1881–1968); Mary O'Neill (1888–1990); and Anne O'Neill (1890–1964). According to the *Chicago Inter Ocean*, April 13, 1904, Francis O'Neill designed the mausoleum in Mount Olivet Cemetery in Chicago where he is buried with his wife, Anna, and son, Rogers. The O'Neill children who died between 1871 and 1885 are all buried in Calvary Cemetery in Evanston, Illinois.

12. Francis O'Neill to Reverend Seamus O'Floinn, October 15, 1918, in Francis O'Neill correspondence, University of Notre Dame, Department of Special Collections.

CHIEF O'NEILL'S SKETCHY RECOLLECTIONS OF AN EVENTFUL LIFE IN CHICAGO

EARLY YEARS
1848–1866

An octogenarian who has led an adventurous life on sea and land, and circumnavigated the globe before attaining his majority, may be privileged to review the leading episodes and events of a checkered career. When the days of our prime are past and the currents of emotion have subsided, old age finds some compensation in the pleasures of memory. This sketchy narrative, written reluctantly at the urgent solicitation of old-time friends, makes no claim to merit but faithful adherence to facts.

My birth on August 28, 1848, a famine year, could hardly have been a joyous event in the already large family of my parents, John O'Neill and Catherine O'Mahony (Klenach). Our townland, Tralibane, was three miles southeast of Bantry, an historic seaport town in West Cork. I had learned to read long before being able to walk that distance and made rapid progress at the Bantry National School, notably in mathematics, in spite of incidental difficulties at home. Tallow candles and dogwood splinters were the only illuminants in farmhouses in those days, kerosene lamps being then unknown. Neighbors came in nightly to learn the news from the Crimean War. After reading the newspapers for the benefit of all, my father interpreted the story to those who spoke only the Irish language. Crowded out from the candles, I contrived to study my tasks, or lessons, by the fitful light of the turf fire on the hearth.

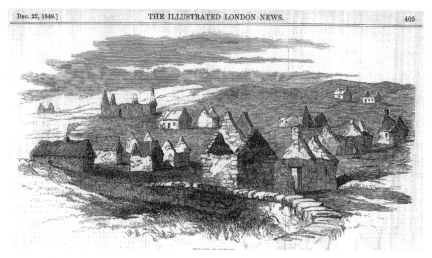

Many Irish villages never recovered from the effect of the Great Famine of 1848, and haunting images of deserted cabins soon became familiar features in British journals. The rich tradition of music and dance that Francis O'Neill remembered from his youth in Tralibane was virtually extinguished as fiddlers and pipers died or emigrated. (Illustrated London News, *December 22, 1849*)

At the age of twelve I was appointed junior monitor and two years later was advanced to senior monitor. In both cases those ages were reported as fourteen and sixteen, respectively, to the Commissioners of Education at Dublin. Not yet sixteen, I sat in with aspirants for promotion from various school districts and passed an examination for teacher successfully.

O'Neill's birthplace and childhood home as it appears today in Tralibane, West Cork, Ireland. (Photograph by Mary Lesch)

Fair day in Bantry, the larger town adjacent to O'Neill's birthplace, occurred once a month and provided Irish families with the opportunity to sell and trade livestock. According to Noel P. Rice, particular festivals were also celebrated, such as the harvesting of apples or gooseberries. (Courtesy of Catherine Mulhall)

Drawing and sketching engrossed every available moment of those years. One day the parish priest, Canon Sheehan, came upon me unexpectedly as I was sketching the new convent which crowned a picturesque mound overlooking the town of and bay of Bantry. His proposition to send me to the School of Design in Cork met with no favor at home. Crops and cattle, not art, were their perennial problem. Of this I had practical experience in the tillage fields in summer when others of my class were enjoying their vacations.

Debarred by my youth from any prospect of obtaining a position as schoolteacher for several years, and with no other outlet in view for goading ambition, I decided to challenge the Fates in a wider field of human endeavor.

In formulating a plausible excuse for leaving home, I was encouraged in the belief that I could obtain a position as teacher in the school ships, *Hawk* and *Hastings,* of the English Navy, anchored in Queenstown Harbor. With one pound of my own salary in my pocket, I bravely set out on top of the mail coach, bound for the city of Cork, one morning early in the month of April 1865, Queenstown, or Cobh, being my destination.

The gold-braided naval officer to whom I presented my application and credentials courteously informed me that the infrequent appointment of

As a child in the 1850s, O'Neill would have accompanied his parents to the weekly market day in Bantry, helping them sell or trade their wares. (Courtesy of Catherine Mulhall)

After the Great Famine of 1848, traditions such as "dancing at the crossroads" nearly disappeared as a result of death, emigration, and the hostility of Irish priests to such festive gatherings of young men and women. The memory of these dances inspired O'Neill to preserve and collect Irish music when he settled in Chicago in 1870. (Courtesy of Catherine Mulhall)

A GRATEFUL CONGRECATIONS TRIBUTE TO THE MEMORY
OF
THE Rᵗ Rᵉᵛᵒ Mᵒʳ SHEEHAN. P. P. V C
WHO FOR TEN YEARS RULED IN HONOUR THIS PARISH
OF Sᵗ PATRICK'S AND AMONG MANY WORKS OF ZEAL
AND PIETY BUILT THIS CHURCH AT HIS SOLE EXPENSE
BORN MARCH 25ᵗʰ 1810
DIED JUNE 27ᵗʰ 1887

The Convent of Mercy sketched by Francis O'Neill before he left Ireland in 1865 was one of Bantry's newest buildings, designed by architect S. F. Hynes. At the time this photo was taken in November 2006, the Sisters of Mercy had received news their convent would soon close. (Photograph by Mary Lesch)

O'Neill's parish priest, Canon George Sheehan, was an enthusiastic supporter of the Cork School of Design where Francis hoped to continue his passion for drawing and sketching. Sheehan ministered to the spiritual needs of famine survivors in Saint Patrick's parish in Mayfield, Cork, and, shortly before his death, he financed Saint Joseph Chapel, which was dedicated on October 6, 1881. (Courtesy Catherine Mulhall and Reverend John Paul Hegarty, P.P.)

teachers was not within his jurisdiction. Another shock awaited me when refused enlistment as a seaman, the maximum age in times of peace being sixteen years, and I was several months past that.

Depressed but not defeated, a faint hope led my lagging footsteps to the Butter Market in the city of Cork, to which our farm firkins were consigned. The trip was fruitless and a waste of time.

ALMOST A CHRISTIAN BROTHER

Disappointed in obtaining expected employment and penniless, I called on Bishop Delaney at his residence at Blackrock, five miles from the city on the picturesque banks of the river Lee. After looking over my credentials, the kindly prelate offered me a position as teacher with the Christian Brothers, at whose school I was to meet him later that day. This was by no means the future I had hoped for, yet under the circumstances it was acceptable, so I walked back to the city and inquired my way to the North Monastery. When I arrived there, weary and footsore, imagine my dismay when informed that His Grace had been there but had gone again. And so I missed the vocation of a Christian Brother by fifteen minutes, owing to the distance I had to walk.

With all my cherished designs frustrated, there came the determination to get away from Ireland, anywhere, by any means, and as soon as possible.

After cheerless weeks of diligent effort, friendless and penniless, Captain Watson of an English vessel—the barque *Anne*—agreed to take me with him to Sunderland, England, but according to the admiralty laws, no one could be carried free. I should pay a fare, or he should pay me for service. As I had no money, the humane captain paid me—three shillings—when we arrived at his destination.

ARRIVED IN ENGLAND

Locating a cheap lodging house in Narrow Flag Lane, patronized by peddlers, ballad singers, and other human drift, I resumed my daily rounds among the shipping. Waiting for a chance at the stove (in common use for all), to roast a herring to season a bun for such times as I could eat, relieved the monotony at the lodging house.

The last penny of scanty three shillings being gone, I was obliged to sell, for sixpence, my cherished flute, and later, one by one, my precious books, in order to live, before I succeeded in shipping as an apprentice seaman on the brig *Jane Duncan* bound for Alexandria, Egypt.

From the deck of the ship the shorelines of Portugal and Spain, the Rock of Gibraltar, and other scenes on the Mediterranean are fascinating, especially when seen for the first time by a novice in travel. Weary migrating birds avail themselves of the opportunity for resting on passing ships occasionally, and no doubt many such migrants, encountering storms or losing their sense of direction in flying to or from the African coast, drop into the sea from exhaustion.

ALEXANDRIA, EGYPT

At the time of which I write (1865–66) there were no piers or docks at Alexandria, so that the process of loading or unloading a cargo was slow and primitive. Coal had to be hoisted out of the holds of vessels in tubs and dumped into a chute leading to a scow moored alongside.

Every morning I sculled ashore for a gang of so-called Arab laborers who filled the coal tubs for the ship's crew to "jump out" and return them to shore each evening. Those laborers were all faithful Mohammedans, regardless of their complexions, which ranged from light brown to jet-black Nubians.

Probably observing a religious fast, they accepted such food as was given to them but never ate a bite until after sundown ashore.

Even a soldier on sentry not far from our anchorage laid down his gun at intervals and, facing in the direction of Mecca, prostrated himself a number of times before seizing his gun and resuming his duties.

Invariably chosen to scull the captain ashore and either wait for his return at the landing or accompany him on various missions, I had an opportunity to see much of Oriental life in this truly cosmopolitan city.

A visit to the ancient Necropolis west of the city, then and for some years before being excavated, presented a serious subject for philosophic contemplation. It appears that passageways, seven or eight feet wide and ten feet deep, had been cut out of the solid sandstone rock. On either side, two tiers of receptacles, or pigeonholes, large enough for a coffin or human body, had been chiseled out of the rock. Ages of irresistible drifting sand from the Libyan Desert gradually overwhelmed this ancient burial place. In the nineteenth century it was commercialized. Sand, gravel, fragments of pottery, human bones, skulls, and even jaws with teeth still in their sockets were loaded and conveyed to ships in the harbor for ballast in their voyage to some other port for a cargo.

HARBOR OF ODESSA IN THE BLACK SEA

When the *Jane Duncan* reached the anchorage opposite Odessa, Russia's principal port in the Black Sea, her two hundred tons of ballast, including scattered fragments of human remains, were hoisted out of the hold and dumped overboard. What Egyptian mother, nursing and fondling her babes and crooning them to sleep, could have imagined that a thousand or more years later their bones would find a final resting place at the bottom of the Black Sea?

Before leaving Egypt, it may be well to relate that when accompanying Captain Andersen to a ship chandler store at Alexandria, I solved an accounting problem in dispute between the captain and ship chandler. This so impressed the latter that he wanted to employ me, but the nature of my contract with the ship would not permit of my leaving and becoming an Egyptian — in the land of the pharaohs.

THE ARCHIPELAGO AND DARDANELLES

The scenery in sailing through the Archipelago to the Dardanelles, and thence through the Sea of Marmara to Constantinople on the voyage to Odessa, was delightful and impressive. On not a few of the rocky islets of the Archipelago, among which the ship's course had to be cautiously threaded, ruined temples to forgotten gods were occasionally glimpsed, and the desire to land and explore them was ever present, and even hoped for.

Shipwrecks, such as the Duncan Dunbar *(shown here in 1865), remained a perennial threat to crews and passengers alike. When the* Minnehaha *was shipwrecked off Baker Island, O'Neill swam to shore with a pet monkey clinging to his neck. (*Illustrated London News, December 2, 1865*)*

So strong is the outward current through the strait of the Dardanelles — the only outlet to the immense accumulation of waters pouring into the Black Sea from the great rivers of southern Russia and eastern Europe — that sailing vessels require the aid of powerful tugboats to pass beyond its influence.

In passing the city of Constantinople either way to the Black Sea or return, all ships are required to stop and report to the authorities for clearance papers. In all four stops, I rowed the captain ashore and awaited his return at the landing, all of which added to my experience with and among Orientals.

Forbidding and cheerless is the Black Sea, or Euxine of the ancients, as compared with other waters. Not an island in its great expanse of 175,000 square miles to break the monotony.

NUDE BATHING AT ODESSA

Odessa occupies an elevated plateau of southern frontage with wide terraced stairways leading to the strand. A pier projects a few hundred feet out from shore, where boats from ships anchored out in deep water may land their occupants.

The return cargo of the *Jane Duncan* was linseed or flaxseed, a decidedly slippery freight in rough sailing. Being liable to shift when a ship lists to one side, linseed must fill the hold to the deck, and with a view to leave no space for shifting, Russian women, as well as men, with hand scoops are employed to fill every space possible, as they crouch on their sides close under the deck to do so.

At the dinner hour both sexes enjoy their coarse fare together, after which the men undress, climb onto the ship's rail, and plunging head foremost into the sea, swim about for a little while. Absolutely unabashed, the men climb back to the deck and put on their dusty clothes without disconcerting the other sex in the least. And this happened every day until the vessel was loaded.

In keeping with this unconcern in regard to nudity was the indiscriminate bathing of men and women of all ages and sizes, which I witnessed one Sunday forenoon while awaiting the captain's visit ashore. Young men and women paired, and entirely nude, swam away and disported themselves as they saw fit, and altogether they seemed unconscious of sex. There was one exception, however: an aged woman who led a child into shallow water held one open hand to shade her abdomen.

The return voyage to England was uneventful. After lying at anchor in Falmouth Harbor awaiting orders, the *Jane Duncan* sailed for Hull, the chief shipping port of Yorkshire, to which the cargo was consigned. There being no further use for their services, the entire crew was paid off, excepting the first mate, Mr. West, and myself.

NEARLY KILLED

Captain Andersen's wife came down from Sunderland to meet him, and as the distance between the two ports was but a day's sail, a tugboat was chartered to tow the brig to her home port. Now here's where I came near to ending my life.

As the vessel—high out of the water without cargo or ballast—was being towed into the river, with the captain at the wheel talking to his wife, he either misconstrued or misunderstood the pilot's order, and the vessel headed for the stone wharf. Realizing that a collision was imminent, I seized a cork fender and jumping to the bow handed it to the mate. Before I could jump backward she struck, crushed in her timbers, and hurled me to the wharf. When I regained consciousness, I was in the marine hospital, labeled "compound fracture of the cranium," the scars of which are quite distinct on my forehead to this day.

SECOND VOYAGE

When the brig was ready to sail again, I was given the choice of going with her or remaining at Sunderland until the next voyage. Venturing to go, on the assurance that I would not be required to do any work until fully recovered, I soon found out that the ship owner's promise meant nothing to the new crew.

We had no sooner put out to sea than a heavy gale was run into, and while I contrived to keep from being pitched out of my bunk, only persuasion of one member of the watch saved me from being dragged out of it by one or two others who could not see why a boy should be permitted to occupy a dry bunk while other bunks were leaky. In the general turmoil inevitable in a storm at sea in a small ship, a sick boy with bandaged head is liable to be forgotten, and had it not been for the generosity of one young sailor who shared with me the remnant of a fruitcake his girlfriend had given him, I would have fared badly indeed.

After a storm there comes calm, and so it came in this instance. Fine weather followed, and though not being robust enough for ordinary seaman's work, I was obliged to earn my living by standing at the wheel and steering the ship eight hours a day for a few weeks. A two-hour "trick at the wheel," which requires judgment and concentration, is all that is ordinarily expected of any man, as a seaman's time is divided into four-hour shifts day and night, except a dogwatch of two hours daily to alternate the reliefs. Fortunately I was a good helmsman, and skill in that capacity was brought into service later on other ships and under a different flag.

KYUSTENDIL, BULGARIAN SEAPORT

Our destination on this voyage was Kyustendil on the Black Sea again, Bulgaria's only seaport. Old Roman remains of ancient occupation lay scattered about on the high ground inland from the town. A gravity railway brought trainloads of Indian corn down to the wharf for shipment, a convenience which shortened our stay at that port.

Sheepskin coats and sheepskin caps were almost universally worn by peasants and middle class. Only persons of wealth or prominence wore cloth coats with the red fez skullcap, or tarboosh, after the Turkish fashion.

THE BOSPORUS

The passage through the Bosporus which connects the Black Sea with the Sea of Marmara and is twenty miles long is no less interesting than the Dardanelles or Hellespont, but it is of an entirely different character. Rugged hills, some crowned with ruined castles, rise abruptly from both shores, while picturesque bays indent the hillsides. One of them, called Beikus, or Bighouse Bay on the Asiatic side, is a favorite anchorage for ships awaiting orders. At a favorable opportunity, I swam ashore just to be able to say truthfully that I was once on the continent of Asia.

The mansions of the wealthy, hailing from various places, by no means few, may be seen on the wooded slopes of both sides of this torrential strait for its entire length.

During his travels around the world to such exotic ports as the Bosporus, O'Neill was constantly on the lookout for new reading material. His punishment for swimming to another vessel with a pile of books on his head involved climbing "aloft at five o'clock every morning . . . [to] scrape the masts and pulley blocks" of the sailing ship. (Courtesy of the Library of Congress, Prints and Photographs Division, Abdul Hamid II Collection, LC-USZ62-81042)

BOWLING GREEN ON THE CLYDE

With a cargo of corn, the *Jane Duncan* reached Bowling Green, a small port on the river Clyde, not far from Glasgow, Scotland, in April 1866 and, according to custom, paid off the crew, except the first mate and two apprentices — the present writer and Fred, a Belgian, who spoke four languages besides a fair command of English.

On learning that our ship had changed owners and that a new captain would take command, Fred and I determined to get away, not considering ourselves to be under any further obligations in the changed conditions. The scheme was both difficult and dangerous, and anything which would awaken suspicion of our purpose must be avoided. Fortunately we had a few shillings given us by the crew when leaving. To travel in any direction in sailor's garb would lead to certain detection eventually, so wearing all the clothing we could put on, and with an extra pair of shoes stuffed into the pockets of our coats, we sneaked ashore at dusk and sauntered carelessly along the highway toward Glasgow. Seeing a boatman pulling across the Clyde from the other side, we hastened down the bank to meet him. It was dark when he landed us at the stub end of a country road at the south side of the river. Three miles inland we entered a town where we secured lodgings for the night. As a precaution to ensure our honesty, we were locked in. In fact, we had no desire to be seen outside until the locomotive whistle warned us of the approach of a train bound for Greenock, from whence a steamboat sailed daily for Liverpool. Keeping in seclusion, and avoiding the vicinity of the wharf to the last possible moment, we crossed the gang plank to the deck of the steam packet and, once out on the water, breathed freely.

ESCAPED TO LIVERPOOL

Finding ourselves in Liverpool next morning, we lost no time in finding a sailors' boardinghouse. Before we could map out a plan for the next move, in struts a shipping master and picks out my chum, Fred, for a voyage to the East Indies in a full-rigged clipper ship, and away they went. Oh, how I envied the Belgian's luck! A voyage to China or the East Indies was an ambition cherished for many a day, and here was the chance almost within my grasp. Little time had elapsed for regrets or hopes when, as abruptly as in Fred's case, I was engaged for a trip on the packet ship *Emerald Isle* to New York City.

ASSISTANT STEWARD ON SHIP *EMERALD ISLE*

On the second day out, I was detailed as assistant steward, my duty being the distribution of provisions to the passengers during the voyage, which lasted five weeks. It may be worthy of note that I was paid for coming to America and therefore not an emigrant; that I landed without a coat to my back, having been a victim of thieves; and that I formed acquaintances on that trip that I have been matrimonially associated with for more than half a century.

Fred's path and mine diverged at Liverpool over sixty years ago. He sailed east, I sailed west, and we never met again. So ends the story of my adventures since leaving the old farm, until I crossed the Atlantic and resumed a seaman's life under the Stars and Stripes.

SAILING UNDER THE AMERICAN FLAG

1866–1869

After landing in New York from the *Emerald Isle* packet ship, I was piloted to 66 Oliver Street, a sailors' boardinghouse, by shipmate John Brennan. This place was kept by a Dane who had an Irish wife and bore a good name. This is mentioned because of unpleasant experiences in later times.

SAILORS ENSLAVED BY SHIPPING LAWS

At this juncture it may be well to explain that sailors have no choice of shore quarters on account of shipping conditions. Only from sailors' boardinghouses will ship captains hire a crew. While a sailor's money lasts, the boarding boss is not interested in his welfare, and not before he is in debt for his board does the boss find him a ship. Depending on the length of the voyage, one month's or two months' wages are advanced. You never get the money, but you have the amount to your credit with the boarding boss, who, after deducting any board due him, accompanies you to the outfitting store and permits you to select whatever you please to the extent of your balance, at the sailor's prices, from which the boss obtains a commission. You are completely plucked before going on board the ship, and in debt to the amount of the wages advanced. Forty-eight hours after you have sailed, the boarding boss goes to the shipping office and collects your advanced wages, for which he guarantees your safe delivery on the ship's deck. All this looks like an imposition, and it is; but what is the cure for it? Should the sailor be financially independent and able to pay his way, he would not be hired without assurance that he would not change his mind, and if paid advance money, he probably would get drunk or leave town. The boarding boss is his bondsman in more senses than one, and this is why a sailor seldom escapes from his enforced slavery. There is but one way out of it, and that is to get away from all shipping associations promptly after being paid off. That is just what I had to do eventually.

BRUNSWICK, GEORGIA

My next voyage was on the schooner *Louisa Anne*, bound for Brunswick, Georgia, to be loaded with yellow pine lumber destined for St. Croix, West Indies. Now a prosperous city, Brunswick at that time—1866—consisted of a sawmill and less than half a dozen houses built among the pines adjoining a navigable bayou. The well-nigh tropical temperature in that latitude in the month of August, coupled with the strenuous labor of piling dimension lumber fresh cut from the raft into the ship's hold, overcame all but three of the crew. The Negro hired to work with me showed such consideration for my youth—just eighteen—which the memory of it had never failed to react favorably in my dealings with his race ever after.

TROPICAL HURRICANE

We ran into a hurricane soon after sailing out into the open sea. I was sent to the helm, while others manned the pumps day and night, without rest, and the deck load, braced and chained as it was, yielded to the violence of the waves which dashed over it. Lumber cargoes will not sink but because of their exposure to wind and waves are liable to be torn away, with danger or death to the crew. When the deck load had been removed at St. Croix, three ratholes were discovered, into which water poured into the hold during the storm and kept the pumps in constant operation while the storm lasted.

CATCHING AN EAGLE

A pair of eagles circled our ship high in the air one evening a few days later off the coast of Florida. As it grew dark, one of them lit on the lee topgallant yardarm, and the other was lost sight of in the darkness. I was at the wheel, and when relieved at eight bells, I determined to catch our visitor by climbing aloft on the weather side slowly and carefully. Not until I had reached the jaws of the yard did the eagle display any uneasiness. Keeping perfectly still when he did, and only resuming a sliding motion on the footrope, as the vessel rolled on a high wave, I had come pretty close, when deeming it unsafe to tarry longer, the eagle, peering in my direction, straightened up and spread his wings to fly. 'Twas then or never with me, so holding on to the yard with my right hand I grabbed him under the wing with the left and swung him upside down between the yard and my breast. It was a desperate venture sitting on a footrope swung loosely under the yard high up in the rigging, from which a fall would result disastrously. Fed on rats and canned meat, our trophy was taken alive to our destination, but how the captain disposed of him has been forgotten.

So abundant are fish in West Indian waters that in their eagerness to seize anything edible in the kitchen waste from the galley thrown overboard, they actually jostle one another out of the water. They are much more brilliantly colored than their relatives in the temperate zone. Accompanied by a guide, I explored along the coast where tamarind trees and coconut palms grow wild, almost down to the shore.

IRISH SUGAR PLANTERS

The sugar planters whose homes are located high up on the mountainsides are mostly of Irish ancestry, I was informed, being the descendants of the Irish shipped by Cromwell's orders to the English plantations in Jamaica, Barbados, etc., in the seventeenth century.

CAPTURING A CAT

After dismissing the guide on our return to town about dusk, I noticed a cat sitting in an open window of the second story of a small house, facing into a room. Remembering how the rats had almost sunk us, I decided to attempt the capture of this cat, if possible, for the ship. Climbing up a few feet in the rough stone wall, I grabbed the tail, which hung invitingly down, swung him out, and, holding the terrified tom at arm's length, ran for the boat landing with all speed possible. In his frantic gyrations, suspended by the tail, he hooked a claw into my knee, and instantly four sets of them, reinforced by his teeth, were buried in my flesh. The wharf being in sight when this happened, I hung on. I had him, and he certainly had me, as we tumbled into the waiting boat together. Then both let go; but as the cat dreaded the water more than captivity, we got him safely on board.

Her cargo being unloaded, the *Louisa Anne* sailed for the Ragged Islands, a coral group whose only export was coarse salt obtained from shallow ponds by evaporation from the fierce tropical sunlight. Conical piles of salt awaiting transportation furnished a return cargo, but the means of getting such loose stuff aboard were crude in the extreme. Mat baskets without handles were the only means of transferring the salt from a lighter to a stage, slung on the ship's side, and from that by another man to the gangway, where a third man dumped the basket of salt into the hold. The crew of the lighter was pure black Negroes, not the least savage of them being the preacher.

VOYAGE TO JAPAN

After the West Indian voyage, I was back again at Reid's boardinghouse, 66 Oliver Street, intent on shipping for a long voyage to foreign countries this time. The opportunity soon came, and it was to Yokohama, Japan, on the full-rigged ship *Minnehaha* of Boston.

The voyage across the Atlantic and doubling the Cape of Good Hope, late in the year 1866, was without incident worthy of remark, except that Captain Burleigh, a native of Cape Cod, Massachusetts, turned out to be a bully and a tyrant who exercised his autocratic powers by assaulting whoever happened to be at the wheel when he strode the afterdeck. Never once did I relieve a helmsman without finding traces of blood on the wheel. Being personally expert in that line of duty, I had escaped his violence for a long time. One stormy day as the compass swung around from the tossing of the ship, the captain shouted, "Nothing to windward." As I ventured to say, "She's a little to the lee now, Sir," he rushed at me, grabbed me by the throat, and bent me backwards, with the command, "Don't talk back to me!" In this outburst, he spilled no blood, but not long after, I saw the day when his innate cowardice was abjectly displayed.

After passing the volcanic peaks of St. Paul and Amsterdam islands far out in the Indian Ocean, strong gales drove us away from our course toward Australia, but we eventually entered through the straits of Sunda, into the Java Sea. This body of water is subject to daily calms, but being shallow, the anchorage could be had anywhere, when steering was impractical for lack of headway. So torrid was the temperature that tar oozed out between the planks, and both decks and hull had to be wetted down twice daily, and canvas awnings were stretched between the masts to shade the decks and render life endurable to the white men.

One day all hands were ordered on the lookout for reefs indicated on navigation charts. Some took their posts aloft on maintops and crosstrees. Others paraded on the forecastle or perched on the bowsprit and jibboom — all scanning the sea ahead for indications of a break in the water covering submerged reefs or rocks. A brisk breeze had stirred up whitecaps or foam in all directions along about noon, when without warning the keel grated on the reef all had been trying to locate, and the *Minnehaha*, checked in her momentum, was held fast with her bow resting on the reef.

RAN ON A REEF

In the excitement which followed, Captain Burleigh's voice changed from harsh to pleading, portions of the rigging snapped at the shock were repaired, and with the sails flat every swell of the surf gradually eased the ship astern off the reef and into deep water. Fragments of the keel which came to the surface looked alarming, but a test of the pump well showed only little chance of leakage. The anchor was dropped, however, and a call for divers was sent to Batavia, the capital of Java, to determine the extent of the damage. Two Malayan divers without any apparatus whatever examined the bottom and reported that the voyage might continue. The bullying captain, whose spirit was crushed, went ashore with the divers for hospital treatment, and first mate Hickman took command.

CHINESE PIRATES

In those days every ship in the Chinese or Japanese trade was equipped with cannon or a howitzer and a stand of carbines with ammunition to repel a possible attack by Chinese pirates that infested those waters. The China Sea, like the Java Sea, is subject to calms as well as typhoons. A large sailing vessel is helpless in a calm, while a Chinese junk, though rigged with a lateen sail, can be propelled with oars. Most of the large crew of a pirate junk remains out of sight below decks until approaching their intended prey. Suddenly they appear, hurling stupefying stinkpots onto the ship's deck, clamber abroad, and with long knives attack all who oppose them.

During one of those calms, a day or two after entering the China Sea, a suspicious-looking junk in the distance was seen to be rowing in our direction. The plan for such a contingency was promptly set into action. Seaman Thomson, a Russian who had served in the American Navy, took charge of the cannon mounted on the poop deck, and every able seaman was armed with a carbine ready for use. A breeze which sprang up in the meantime bore us away before the junk, whether pirate or commercial, came within a mile of us.

YOKOHAMA, JAPAN

The sights witnessed while entering the harbor of Yokohama were a revelation. Japanese sampans, with crews wearing only straw hats and breechcloths, came to meet us for trading purposes long before our ship dropped anchor. The crew consisted of five or seven, all sculling standing up and facing the bow or the direction in which they were going. The odd man at the stern did the steering. Our astonishment was by no means lessened on seeing clumsy four-wheeled carts heavily loaded with stone, moving along the public streets propelled by four almost nude men—two in front in a yoke pulling and two in the rear with shoulders against stout stakes, pushing. Keeping step in unison, they repeated two alternate words, as sailors do when hoisting. Their only food being seafood and rice, no wonder living in Japan was cheap.

UNLOADING CARGO

As at Alexandria, Egypt, our cargo of coal had to be unloaded by the same primitive methods—just a tubful at a time. So as to verify the waybills, every tubful was weighed on a small Fairbanks scale on the deck. The present writer was assigned to keep the tallies for the ship, and a Chinese Mandarin did the same for the steamship company to which the cargo had been consigned. Another of my special assignments was the measuring in square feet of the lumber used in the construction of bulkheads to prevent the shifting of the cargo in heavy winds when the ship was listing to one side.

SHORE LEAVE EXPERIENCE

Portuguese sailors who had abandoned a seafaring life for commercial pursuits ashore may be found at all ports on the Pacific. On my first day of shore leave, I patronized one of them who kept a little lunch house convenient to shipping. He treated me to a glass of sake, a native drink distilled from rice. It tasted like sherry wine but took effect much more promptly. Soon my brain was in a whirl, and I was obliged to rest in a bunk for an hour or two before recovering from its effects. It spoiled the day, being my first experience of that nature, but it was by no means so thrilling as to find one's self swimming away off the ship in the midst of a multitude of fish whose contact with me was terrifying. The knowledge that sharks were in the bay so intensified the horror that when I reached the ship's side I was scarcely able to climb aboard.

Though the social customs of the Japanese may seem amazing to a Caucasian, it can be said that in the practice of politeness and fair dealing they compare favorably with the businesspeople of other lands. In lacquer and inlaid cabinet work they are inimitable. Like most others favored by opportunity, I purchased a small cabinet inlaid with multicolored woods and a lady's workbox, both of which I contrived to save through many hazards.

PENALIZED WHILE EXCHANGING BOOKS

Discipline on shipboard in foreign ports must be maintained, and the present writer was once the victim of it. Obviously, reading matter is in great demand among educated seamen on long voyages, consequently the exchange of books between crews while in harbor is effected whenever possible. One Sunday afternoon, when everything was quiet, I dropped overboard unobtrusively with a package of books tied on top of my head and swam to a vessel several hundred yards away. While discussing a trade in the forecastle with our neighbors, a boat arrived from the *Minnehaha* with orders for my immediate return by the way I went. The boat was rowed back, while I was obliged to swim. Such were Captain Hickman's orders. And that wasn't all. I was punished for leaving the ship without permission by having to go aloft at five o'clock every morning for the ensuing week and scrape the masts and pulley blocks until breakfast time. The pursuit of literature under such circumstances has many disadvantages.

One day I noticed the third mate on his return from shore, stupidly groping over the stern, mistaking it for the bow of the ship. He was about to drop into the sea, when I grabbed him and held on until others came to help drag him on board. What I experienced at his hand later was brutality instead of gratitude; and the worst of it was that to resent brutality or injustice is to invite a diet of bread and water in irons.

SAILED FOR HONOLULU

After ten weeks' anchorage in Kanagawa Bay, the good ship *Minnehaha* set sail for Honolulu, the chief port of the Hawaiian Islands, in ballast, but carrying many crates of gorgeous Asiatic pheasants and other Asiatic birds in the care of Japanese attendants, consigned to Queen Emma, then ruler of the kingdom of the Kamehamehas. Within a week we set sail for Baker Island, in the middle of the Pacific, for a cargo of guano, having on board fifty Kanakas, or natives hired to increase the force or relieve others employed in the activities of the shipment. During the voyage those passengers amused themselves in daily contests of strength and agility, outrivaling the best of our crew in physical prowess. To this digression may be added that an old native woman by persistent diving for a couple of hours in six fathoms (thirty-six feet) of water recovered two silver dollars lost by our Chinese cook who slid down the anchor chain one night in the harbor. This coral islet, with its neighbor, Howland Island, flies the American flag, and their value consists in a deposit of the manure of seafowl and their remains, which has accumulated to a thickness of several feet on their entire surface.

BAKER ISLAND

Baker Island, a quarter of a degree north latitude, is almost circular in outline, three miles in circumference, and rises abruptly from the ocean depths to a height of eight or ten feet above high tide. Anchorage being impractical where the plummet records ninety fathoms (540 feet), other means for holding ships in place have been provided. Immense iron buoys or tanks, to each of which are attached three cables diverging like a tripod and held at the bottom by permanent anchors, are suitably located. Hawsers run out from the bow are made fast to the shackles on one buoy, while the stern of the ship is similarly fastened to another. Thus moored a vessel rides as if at anchor in more shallow water.

The human inhabitants of this coral rock were four white men and about 150 Kanakas, or natives of the Hawaiian Islands. Mr. Johnson, whose original home was Wisconsin, was the governor. An Irishman named McSweeney was the boss in charge of the men engaged in digging and shoveling the nauseous mass (guano) into sacks for removal to the beach, where Mr. Lake, an English sailor, directed the crew who transferred the freight to the ship. A German chef did the cooking for the four bosses.

An old white horse pulled a flatcar filled with bags of the guano on movable rails to the beach. Gangs of the Kanakas employed as laborers for specific periods are periodically replaced by others.

WRECKED BY DEEP SEA SWELL

Unloading the seven hundred tons of gravel ballast had not progressed very far when a deep sea swell, following a distant storm, tossed the *Minnehaha* about in an alarming way. To insure greater security, additional hawsers were run out to the buoys at either end. As the ship on the crest of a high wave pitched into the succeeding trough, the unexpected happened; the undershackle of the forward buoy to which the anchor cables were attached snapped. Relieved of their weight, the buoy flew upward and flung high in the air the two men who were fastening the last hawser. Fred, the Belgian, sank, but Brennan, who was a swimmer, reached down where Fred's hat floated and saved him by pulling him up by the hair on his head. There was much excitement, but no confusion, because the customary precaution in anticipation of possible disaster in dangerous waters had not been neglected. All personal property not in actual use had been stowed in a lighter along-side, which when cut loose would drift ashore. Our ship swung against a solid rock with a crash, then was washed onto a ledge by tremendous waves, and eventually she was torn apart during the night by violent waves.

The crew got ashore in boats kept ready for emergencies, except the writer, who collected Jocko, the pet monkey from Java, from his chained imprisonment on deck. When I got back to the ladder, the boats, almost swamped, were some distance away. With my simian friend on my neck, I plunged into the swirling waves and swam to shore.

ROBINSON CRUSOE LIFE

Governor Johnson received the captain and the officers as his guests while he supplied the crew with limited rations of hardtack and drinking water. Shacks, hastily built with driftwood from ancient wrecks, housed the crew. Edibles, generously cast ashore by the sea, were eagerly sought and divided. Fish caught in shallow pools at low tide supplemented our scanty fare from day to day.

The gannets, or boobies, one of the four varieties of seabirds on this island, happened to be rearing their young. Shipwrecked sailors are never fastidious in their choices of food, yet so fishy and rank did their squabs taste, even when doused with vinegar and pepper, that none of us could stomach them. Seabirds are just animated machines for converting fish into flesh, the process having been carried on for ages, yet the product is simply nauseous.

The frigate bird, or man-of-war hawk, shyer than the gannet, selected for a nesting place the bare rocks farthest from human activities. A characteristic not noted by ornithologists is their habit of disgorging a semidigested fish beside their unfledged offspring. The only land bird seen during our stay was a species of curlew. Pelicans, both gray and white, contended for the best roosts on wrecks partly submerged in the sand, while seagulls tirelessly winged their way over the surface of the water scanning for food.

RESCUED WITH OTHERS

Our Robinson Crusoe life had lasted eleven days when the brig *Zoe* came into sight. The *Zoe* had on board the crew of a ship wrecked at Howland Island by the same sea swell. This staunch vessel was annually engaged in conveying workmen to and from Honolulu and the islands with supplies of food and fresh water for their maintenance and those who lived on the islands. Custom-made large water tanks filled the lower half of the hold. Both crews slept on the tanks, which were covered with an old sail. The voyage to Honolulu lasted thirty-four days. The officers were offered the same courtesies accorded them by the governors of Baker Island; they slept in the cabins.

The Captain of the *Zoe* was a white man, but every member of his crew, including the mate and boatswain, was a Kanaka. Every morning a few pounds of hardtack in a bag were given to each mess, which when rationed out among them averaged one and one-half biscuit to each man. Half a pint of a dark beverage called tea was ladled out daily to anyone who preferred it to tank water. Twice a week an allowance of salt meat was distributed with a small potato occasionally to vary the menu. When we arrived at our destination, only three of our crew of twenty-eight men escaped being sent to the marine hospital. The writer fortunately was one of the robust trio, and this is how it happened.

KANAKA MUSICIAN

One of the Kanaka sailors, who had a flute and apparently was proud of his musical accomplishments, regaled us nightly with a hymn tune which he repeated without change while his wind lasted. Being something of a performer on that instrument, I picked it up one evening and rattled off "The Soldier's Joy," "Yankee Doodle," and "The Girl I Left Behind Me." Whatever may have been thought of my performance by others, I won the Kanaka fluter's friendship, for thereafter he shared his daily ration of poi and salmon with me and I gladly let him have my allowance of salt meat. I have no doubt that this incident profoundly influenced my future, for while others were left behind, I was on my way to San Francisco, California, and a new life.

The barque *Comet*, commanded by Captain Abbott, on which I sailed, was a packet ship carrying a mixed cargo, as well as passengers between San Francisco and Honolulu. As an able seaman, I made two round trips on the *Comet* and when in the latter part acted as supercargo checking waybills in the transfer of freight, and incidentally learning a little of the native language.

HAWAIIAN EARTHQUAKE

One evening earthquake shocks not only started the volcano of Mauna Loa on the main island of Hawaii in violent eruption but pushed up a new island in the midst of the waves that rolled inland so high as to destroy villages on shore.

I set out to investigate [Diamond Head] a conspicuous headland (an extinct volcano) on the island of Oahu. An eight-mile walk along the beach from Honolulu brought me to its base. Its seafront is very steep, and being composed of brittle lava rock held together by a growth of vines, its ascent is not unattended with difficulty and danger. From the rim of its bowl-shaped summit, the view repays the effort, and the descent is more easily accomplished on the land's side by a circuitous pathway.

NATIVE RACE VANISHING

Civilization was by no means an unmixed blessing to the Hawaiians, for contemporaneously with the Bible and the white man's religion came the white man's diseases, which the Polynesians cannot withstand. They die out rapidly when brought in contact with Caucasians, degenerate morally, and eventually lose possession of their lands. The native race in the twentieth century is a hopeless minority without property or influence. The process of cooking is obviously distasteful in a tropical climate, and for that reason Chinese restaurants are liberally patronized by all classes in Honolulu.

GAINING A DAY

Before leaving this part of the Pacific Ocean, it may be well to allude to the fact of gaining time in traveling eastward and losing time when going in the opposite direction. Daily observations are made at sea to determine latitude and longitude, and time varies according to the latter. On the *Minnehaha's* voyage from Japan to the Hawaiian Islands, we crossed the 180th degree of longitude east, or west, of the principal meridian at Greenwich, London. This is where changes are made, and our direction being always easterly, we gained so many hours that in order to balance the calendar an extra day, which happened to be Tuesday, was added to our time.

SCANDINAVIAN MONOPOLY OF SHIPPING

With a view to getting into the West Coast trade, I put up with my dunnage at a sailors' boardinghouse in San Francisco, but I soon found out that eastern customs did not obtain here. Day after day as I waited, Scandinavian captains came in and, glancing around, spoke a few words in their language to Scandinavian seamen who, shouldering their bags, walked out silently. The West Coast shipping was practically monopolized by that race.

No wants placarded in a municipal employment office appealed to me, but being bent on seeing the world, I couldn't afford to leave California without seeing more than its seaport. This was in April 1868, and harvesters were wanted at Morley's Ranch in Tuolumne County, distant forty-seven miles by stagecoach from the city of Stockton on the San Joaquin River. I boarded a steamer one evening, woke up on the deck next morning, and contrived to connect with the stage which stopped for lunch at Salter's Ferry on the Tuolumne River. Instead of proceeding to Morley's Ranch, a few miles further, I accepted a job as shepherd from Norman Salter; the flock consisted of eight hundred "mutton sheep," or wethers, reserved for food supply. A Paiute Indian then in charge was impatient to rejoin his tribe in fishing but agreed to show me the range the next day. I never saw him again, so I chanced it alone.

In those days no houses relieved the monotony of the vast extent of billowy treeless open land used mainly for sheep pastures. All settlements were on bottomlands along river courses, where regardless of summer drought the soil retained a certain amount of moisture. Wherever located, all wells had to be drilled to the level of the riverbed to ensure a sufficiency of water.

A SHEPHERD'S LIFE

Late in the evening of my first day, unfamiliarity with the instinct of sheep led me into trouble. Instead of driving them toward home as I thought, they led me unerringly, and my only focus thereafter was to keep the flock from merging into other flocks because there were neither fences nor boundary lines limiting the ranges.

Haying and grain cutting were over in May, and by the middle of June the annual drought, under a blazing sun, not only burned up the pastures but dried up the lagoons. In the last of June, two flocks of about three thousand each were started for pasturage in the Sierra Nevada mountains, feeding as they went and traveling about five miles a day. At night, Bill Anderson, my partner, and I slept on opposite sides of the flock on the bare ground, with no bedding but rough blankets, and our clothes bags for pillows. Anderson, who was a good cook, had breakfast ready long before daylight, for sheep with sharpened appetites scatter out at the gray of dawn but rest in groups under trees in the middle of the day. This intermission gives the shepherds a chance to repair and wash clothing and cook dinner in peace. While mending my torn trousers one day, I was startled by the sudden barking of a large gray squirrel in the tree overhead. Certain the dog would get him when forced to jump down, I climbed up. The squirrel ran into a hollow branch, but when I endeavored to drag him out, I got but the tail from his rump. To leave him in that condition would never do, so procuring a brand from the fire I forced him to come out and jump. The pleasure of my success was turned to horror when I found that a piece of the brand had fallen on my trousers and ruined them beyond repair.

LOST IN THE HILLS

A wagon carrying provisions and tools in charge of an old-time miner who claimed to know every road in the Sierra Nevada met us at intervals, but once his judgment was faulty and we lost our way. Night found us on the summit of a ridge with open woods but no water. There was nothing to be done but keep the flock from scattering in search of water all night. Daylight brought some relief; water was found in a deep gulch not far away. Shouts were heard about ten o'clock, and soon after, White, our guide, approached and told us that stacks of pancakes and bacon awaited us in an abandoned miner's camp half a mile away over the divide. "Scotty" Anderson, preferring rest to food, declined to go but asked me to bring him some food on returning.

The herders of the other flock had reached the camp ahead of me and eaten all that had been cooked by White for four, so mixing a can of batter for pancakes and tasting it, hunger overcame me and I ate it raw! A good meal followed, and with a stack of pancakes and bacon and a bottle of water I returned to my partner, whom I found fast asleep. After eating all I had brought him, he felt strong enough to proceed to the old camp to get something to eat!

CAMPING IN THE WOODS

A month after leaving Salter's ranch found both flocks in a fine secluded valley in the Sierra Nevada range, through which a stream meandered. High ridges timbered with a variety of woods, including the towering sugar pine, framed our territory. A cabin built of boards split by hand from logs was tenanted by the first arrivals, while Anderson and I located at the far end of the valley, lived and slept as we did on the way, and never once were sheltered by a roof while in charge of that flock of sheep and which ended for me on October 9 on the banks of the Tuolumne River in the San Joaquin Valley.

MUSTANG SHEEP

Sheep are proverbially stupid, and no animals are so difficult to drive on a new road, over an obstacle, or across a shallow creek because of their timidity. Atavistic specimens with hair rather than wool are born occasionally. These freaks, sports, or throwbacks, are called mustangs and are usually larger than the average, possess some courage, and are first to lead the way out when the flock is bunched. The deadlock being broken, all unhesitatingly follow. Twice we changed camp because thousands of sheep soon reduced their surroundings to dust with their sharp hoofs and ruined the pasture. The prudence of this change was evidenced by the dollar-a-head premium placed by the butchers on the wethers of our flock as compared with those of the other flock continuously fed at their original location.

RATTLESNAKES

Bears, whose occasional visits were betrayed by their tracks in the dust, caused us no trouble, but the dread of snakes, of which there were at least two poisonous varieties, inspired unremitting caution. Once with poised foot I barely missed stepping on a coiled rattlesnake. At another time, the sniffing of our dog at a hole under a protruding flag led me to believe that a gopher or ground squirrel was at home. I succeeded in raising the flag to an upright position, but no gopher ran out. Instead I was horrified by the sight of a large rattler coiled and ready to strike. Just imagine! Both hands at the hole had been within a few inches of those deadly fangs. Holding him down with a forked stick, Mr. Rattler was soon minus head, skin, and a thirteen-ring rattle. Strange to say, when I returned eight hours later, life still remained in the denuded body.

Just as I was about to bathe in the creek at noon one day, I was placing my shirt on a log which bridged it, when the sight of a large rattler basking in the sun on the log beside instantly changed the program and ended the rattler's life.

HERDER WATKINS'S HOSTILITY

Watkins, the senior of the two men in charge of the other flock, was an irascible Kentuckian, subject to an intermittent ailment which yielded to one particular medicine. Sometimes before that could reach him from Stockton, over one hundred miles away, the necessity for it passed. Having paid for it, Watkins never failed to use it anyway. One morning my partner, Bill Anderson, left camp for a brief visit, as he said, to the other herders. Our flock heading in that direction ran into an area infested with poison laurel, which is fatal to sheep in a few days. Anxious to drive them out of danger, I ran over to Watkins's camp on the other side of the creek to get Anderson to help me. For abruptly breaking in on the party, Watkins became abusive and belligerent. Nothing but blood of "the Irishman" would satisfy his Kentucky pride. As he came toward me with an open knife, I reached around behind a door and, seizing a shotgun I had noticed as I came in, I remarked, "All right, if it is a fight with deadly weapons you want, come on." But he didn't; that unexpected move of mine chilled his bravado. I got my partner away from his prolonged visit, but not before a few of our flock had been poisoned.

A MIRAGE

Such was the condition of the atmosphere on the lower levels after the long summer drought as we approached the plains that the mirage of a large placid lake of irregular shape greeted our astonished vision. A few scattered trees diversified its borders and, like all lakes and lagoons in that region, the margins varying by evaporation were but dimly defined. In my sailing days in the Mediterranean, a mirage on the African coast was by no means a rare sight, but none that I had witnessed was as realistic as that which fascinated us in the San Joaquin Valley. I wondered if by any chance a lake or lagoon of such apparent extent had been heretofore unmentioned or had recently been created. As we gazed in rapt admiration and anticipation of its enjoyment for us and thirsty flocks, the illusion slowly faded and there was nothing left but the wavy, quivering air ascending from the parched brown plain of monotonous reality.

Domestic animals seem possessed of olfactories no less keen than in a wild state, in all that concerns their food and drink. Long before reaching a water supply, our sheep became aware of its existence and raced headlong downhill toward it. They got entirely beyond control, and it was all we could do to keep up with them until we reached a half-dried creek. Even then they ran excitedly up and down from pool to pool drinking until satisfied.

The drive home late in September was accomplished in a week, being all downhill, and as the sheep, well-fed and strong, were eager for salt, they rushed towards the alkali licks at the foothills. So strenuous were our efforts in keeping the flock together in this rapid return from the mountains that on reaching a suitable camping ground one evening, we engaged an Indian and his son to watch the flock all night, so that we might get some rest and sleep. What was left of a slaughtered sheep after our supper was the price paid for the service which they faithfully performed.

STRAYED SHEEP RESTORED TO THE OWNER

Ordinarily flocks are counted twice a year and then only by running them through a narrow passage in single file. Out on the range the herder counts only black sheep, and if one of them is missing, so are many white sheep. In our flock there were eight black sheep, until one day I counted seventeen. We had picked up part of another herd from beyond the ridge, owned by Pat Delaney, who lived on a preempted claim on mineral lands in the foothills. A month later, we separated and returned 666 sheep with the Delaney ear clips to the Delaney ranch.

Concerning our relations with the Chinese on the plains and the Indians in the uplands, it is but justice to them to say that we found them not less kindly and appreciative of fair dealing than the white race.

LIFE ON THE OCEAN WAVES AGAIN

Favored with health, experience, and money, I returned to San Francisco and shipped on the barque *Hannah* bound for Culiacán, Mexico, for a load of logwood consigned to New York. Under the direction of a hunchback mate, she was being prepared for sea by the crew, who slept aboard but ate on shore. After ordering us to breakfast one morning, he disappeared and was succeeded a few days later by a husky Welshman named Jones. On the third day out, the watch below was roused out of their bunks by the mate's stentorian call, "Rouse out and help us get this dead man out of the hold." The corpse proved to be that of the hunchback first mate, who, disappointed at his failure to obtain the promised captaincy of the vessel he had outfitted for the voyage, took poison and crawled back between decks under the cabin and laid down to die. The body, very much bloated, was rolled onto a tarpaulin and lifted to the upper deck. With weights at the feet, it was bound around with canvas, placed on a plank, and slid into the sea as Captain Higgins read the burial service. The weights were insufficient to overcome the buoyancy of the bloated body; the latter, standing upright, sank but halfway and remained bobbing up and down with the waves as the *Hannah* sailed out of sight.

A HURRICANE REEF

This incident made a profound impression on the crew, some of whom would not sit alone on deck at night or descend between decks to get drinking water from the tanks in the daytime with the hatches wide open. But that was nothing compared to what happened later when we ran into a storm off the coast of Lower California, at midnight. Sails were reefed, the hatches were battened down, and as all hands stood around, a violent commotion raged in the empty hold from stem to stern. Under the circumstances there was no access to the hold but through a trapdoor in the cabin floor from which a notched stanchion served as a ladder to the lower deck. One after another the older men refused to obey the boatswain's order to "go below." Much as I disliked the task, I steeled myself to undertake it and, armed with a lighted lantern, I had climbed but halfway down, when whiff! Out went the light as the disturber came thundering toward me. Up I rushed, quicker than I went down. Lowering the lighted lantern to the floor in advance, I followed and barely missed being bowled over by an empty keg that had broken loose from its fastening and was jostled all over the hold by the pitching and tossing of the vessel. The poor mate's ghost, for such the superstitious sailors assumed it to be, when captured and identified promptly ceased its alarming rampage.

CULIACÁN HARBOR, MEXICO

The approach to Culiacán is so shallow that our ship was obliged to drop anchor about six miles from shore, and a crew of eight oarsmen had all they could do against a headwind to pull the captain ashore to report with his papers. Captain and crew were forced to find lodgings in this scattered town overnight; half of the latter was accommodated in the private dwelling of a Portuguese sailor who had married an Indian wife. The Indian wife made excellent coffee, which we sweetened with natural sugar molded in coconut shells. The wealthier classes of the seacoast towns abandon them in the sultry season for more enjoyable inland homes at higher altitudes.

Logwood, from which is derived a purple dye, was brought to our anchorage in lighters and, having been cut into short lengths, was easily loaded. Each day we sat on the forecastle deck at our meals, with baited fishlines hanging over the side; we kept the ship well supplied with fish of a kind we called "grunters" from the sounds they made when pulled on deck.

Mexican houses, such as that occupied by our Portuguese host, are crude and inexpensive. Rough poles or saplings embedded in the ground form the framework on which are woven the walls of interlaced branches like a gigantic basket. The outside is plastered with a sticky mud applied with a shovel. A roof of long-leaved grass or palm extending beyond the walls keeps out the rain—and there you are. Cooking being done under a tree or improvised shade, chimneys are unnecessary. Yet in this sylvan simplicity, people of the tropics may enjoy as much of the essentials of life as their brethren of more civilized countries.

EMERGENCY AT SEA

To seafaring men the direction and force of the wind is a matter of unending concern because wind and weather enter so intimately into all the activities of their daily life at sea. In times of stress and danger, or when indications presage a storm, all hands are ordered on duty to shorten sail or take such other measures as the commander may determine. During such emergencies neither rest nor sleep is considered, and there are occasions when, owing to the rolling and pitching of the ship, cooking has to be abandoned, for utensils could not be kept on the range or stove.

Twice while on the voyage from Japan to Honolulu, Thomson, the Russian previously mentioned, and the writer were ordered by Captain Hickman to take the wheel together on stormy nights. Besides experience, a helmsman needs an alert mind with the faculty of concentration, and it was all we could do at times to hold the wheel when a giant wave dashed against the rudder.

ROUNDING CAPE HORN

Since sailing from Culiacán along the west coast of South America, nothing more thrilling happened than the occasional spouting of a whale or the sight of a school of flying fish skimming the waves to escape their enemies, until we sighted the rugged headlands of Cape Horn, January 1869. In keeping with its reputation for boisterousness, the weather was cold and stormy, although it was summer in southern latitudes at this time. Our ship stood well out to sea when doubling the cape, so as to maneuver against a headwind which beset us for days. In this region, nearly 55° south latitude, the sun did not dip beneath the horizon until long past ten at night, and it was broad daylight again by two in the morning. In the meantime a halo of reflected light dispelled complete darkness.

A SCHOOL OF WHALES

While taking my trick at the wheel one morning when off the Falkland Islands, I felt a jarring shock as if a heavy body had come in contact with the hull. What it may have been remained a mystery until dawn. The fact was that the good ship *Hannah* had run into a school of whales, one of which had in the darkness collided against her side. With daylight came a scene the like of which is seldom witnessed. Spouting whales, scores of them, could be seen in all directions, coming to the surface to breathe and diving again. A sight so unusual attracted all on board. After passing over their feeding grounds, we saw no more of them. Neither had we any exciting experiences during the remainder of the voyage, unless variable winds, calms, and doldrums in the Sargasso Sea can be considered.

CIRCUMNAVIGATED THE GLOBE

The sight of Sandy Hook at the end of a voyage never fails to revive the pleasures of anticipation, and by the time the dock is reached the memories of wrongs and hardships are faded and forgotten.

Having now circumnavigated the globe, March 1869, and seen much of life on sea and land under strenuous conditions since leaving home four years before, I determined to bid farewell to Neptune's domain and leave the future to the Fates on land thereafter.

QUIT SEA LIFE AFTER FOUR YEARS' EXPERIENCE

1869–1905

All of my savings since landing on American soil, June 1866, with wages due when paid off from the barque *Hannah* at New York, March 1869, and a balance grudgingly paid me by the agents of the ship *Minnehaha* (wrecked at Baker's Island), amounted to nearly two hundred dollars. I entrusted my pay to Mrs. Reid, my former host at 66 Oliver Street, for safekeeping the first day on shore, and she kept it literally! When I asked for it a few days later, she put me off with the story that she had used it to pay a pressing bill. Day after day, until my patience was exhausted, she went out ostensibly to collect some money due from steamship agencies without success. With my faith in humanity at low ebb, I proceeded to Erie, Pennsylvania, and went to work with a stevedore gang, where my oldest brother, Philip, was the boss loading coal and unloading iron ore. We were paid by the ton and often worked from daylight to dark when the occasion required it, and though but a youngster among seasoned veterans, I endured the strain.

ATTRACTED TO THE WEST

In those days, it was the ambition of most laborers and wage earners to own a farm. Alluring letters published in the *Boston Pilot* describing the advantages of Knox County, Missouri, attracted considerable attention and so the present writer, the only unmarried member of the gang, agreed to go west to investigate.

Before increasing the distance between me and my money, I went back to New York City hoping to get my money, not without hope of getting it. But I did not. It was the same old story. I was "stung," and in addition to the original loss, I was out of pocket some thirty dollars more in traveling expenses.

Arrived at Edina, the county seat of Knox County, I found that the beauties of the available land in that region of prairie and timber land had not been exaggerated, so while not neglecting the object of my mission, I went to work for a contractor engaged in cutting through a steep hill for a contemplated railway; the wages were $1.75 a day for eleven hours of work from 6:00 A.M. to 6:00 P.M. with one hour for dinner. Less than one-third of those employed came the second day, for the clay was stiff and the temperature was well nigh unendurable.

TAUGHT IN DISTRICT SCHOOL

One Sunday forenoon, a man on horseback called on me at the log house where I boarded on the outskirts of town. Announcing himself as Thomas Broderick, a school director, he stated that he wanted me to take the examination for teacher, as none of the candidates who applied passed a successful examination. This being no part of my program, I consented with reluctance, but declining to avail myself of the week allowed for preparation, I reported to Professor Bostwick the next day. Having had four years' experience as monitor in the Bantry National School, I passed without flaw and, having received a county certificate of competency, was promptly installed in charge of a district school, vacant for some time on account of the scarcity of teachers versed in mathematics.

Several days were spent in the examination and classification of pupils. Everyone wanted to write a business hand, and advanced students wished to limit their studies to mathematics, as that was the subject in which they had failed in previous examinations for teachers. I was soon bombarded with difficult problems to be solved; most of them were found in Robinson's *Higher Arithmetic*. Having triumphantly escaped this trap, for such was its object, advanced pupils from other school districts intent on studying mathematics sought admission.

The result of method, system, and experience in the art of imparting information was soon apparent, and funds were provided to extend the regular term. In the meantime the adjoining district school remained vacant awaiting my release, and I had the pleasure of knowing that three of the advanced pupils who had formerly failed had now obtained teacher's certificates. Between barn dances, well supplied with fiddlers, and hunting, life in Knox County was never monotonous in winter.

TAUGHT THE SCHOOL DIRECTOR

It may be of interest to record that School Director Broderick, a Galway man who could read, write, and speak fluently, confided to me early in our acquaintance that his knowledge of figures was very limited. This deficiency was overcome under my tuition to the extent of keeping accounts and calculating interest and discount, which was all he wanted.

James Kelly, director of another school district, had started out from an Ohio farm with a capital of two hundred dollars, and a team of horses and covered wagon in which his wife and infant son rode. They pioneered with him all the way to Keokuk, Iowa, before the Civil War. Owing to the scarcity of currency among the early settlers, he worked for a bushel of cornmeal a day. At the time of which I write, the original purchase of forty acres had been increased to six hundred acres, well stocked and cultivated.

SAILED ON THE GREAT LAKES

In summertime on a farm, all who are big enough to attend school are strong enough to be useful, so with many pleasant memories and a choice of schools awaiting my return next fall, I left Edina, came to Chicago, and sailed on the Great Lakes during the shipping season of 1870 from Chicago to Buffalo and other ports. Perhaps the most notable circumstance of this experience was the fact that every member of the crew of the barque *Sunnyside* commanded by Captain Patrick Myers could converse in the Irish language.

SUDDEN CHANGE OF PROGRAM

While on my way back to Missouri after the close of navigation on the Great Lakes, I took a stopover in Normal, Illinois, to visit the Rogers family, whose acquaintance I had made on the packet ship *Emerald Isle*, and renewed my friendship with the Rogers family in Brooklyn, New York, after each voyage. The family was preparing to leave, some going south for the winter, others returning to Brooklyn, while one who had bought a home remained. The outcome of this unexpected turn of affairs was that instead of proceeding to Edina, Missouri, to teach school, I married the handsome Anna Rogers on November 30, 1870, and returned to Chicago, while all the rest of the family plan was carried out as originally intended.

FIRST JOB IN CHICAGO

Without relatives or friends it is always difficult to obtain employment, especially in winter. After trudging through snow at six o'clock every morning for a month to the Kent and Hutchinson packinghouse at Twenty-second

Anna and Francis O'Neill's portrait is undated; however, O'Neill descendants and historians believe this photograph was taken shortly after their marriage on November 30, 1870. (Photograph restoration by Paul Lane of Photo Source in Evanston, Illinois; Mary Lesch collection)

and Jefferson streets, I had the good luck of being one of five, among waiting scores of eager men, picked for work in the cellar. How I came to be
"picked" is a story worth telling. The German cellar boss told Superintendent Granger opposite the main office at seven o'clock one morning that
he needed five more men. When told to take them, he faced the crowd,
opened his arms to include the nearest five, but as he did so, I slipped in
under an uplifted arm and was included in his embrace with four Germans.
He looked at me in surprise, but he did not have the nerve to reject me; and
that is how I obtained my first job in Chicago. Trucking dressed hogs and
pounding ice at $1.75 a day, my earnings that winter amounted to less than
fifty dollars.

WORK IN A PLANING MILL

After a week's daily round of inquiry for any kind of work, I was taken on at
the Palmer and Fuller planing mill and assigned to the task of keeping a man
operating a planing machine supplied with rough lumber. A few days later a
fellow laborer inquired what wages I expected to get. One dollar and a half
a day I suggested. "You will like hell," he sneered. "That's all the machine
men get; you'll get a dollar or maybe a dollar ten." Then I noticed that I was
the only man of my race on the job, so when Mr. Shepard, the foreman,
came around, I asked him. Looking me over approvingly, he remarked,
"You're a pretty good man at lumber, I'll pay one dollar and a quarter a day."
This proposition, while complimentary, was by no means satisfactory, so I
took my time that evening and resumed the quest for more remunerative
employment next morning.

CHICAGO AND ALTON RAILWAY SERVICE

This was obtained in the Chicago and Alton Railway freight house in May
1871. I was advanced from trucker to checker after six weeks, later to entry
clerk at the door scales, and finally entrusted with the right to sign the agent's
name to receipts for carload lots of cured meat which I tallied at various
packinghouses, consigned to New Orleans, Louisiana, and other southern
cities. Subsequent to the Chicago Fire, when cars were much in demand,
I was placed in charge of demurrage on coal cars and still later on lumber
shipments from yards between Randolph and Halsted streets on the south
branch of the Chicago River. This was all very flattering, but unfortunately it

brought no increase in wages because only a limited number of clerks were allowed by the higher officials.

The man who looked after the lumber shipments from Halsted to May streets, where the lumberyards terminated, was paid sixty-five dollars a month, but he was related by marriage to Superintendent McMullin. During his absence on a two-month vacation, I looked after his route in addition to my own but got nothing more than exercise out of it.

Once when I was sent by agent Reid to the pilot office where railway systems diverged, to fill a vacancy resulting from death, I found a man there ahead of me appointed by the superintendent. Desirable positions and even sinecures were invariably given to relatives of the railroad officials, and it should be added that men whose positions I coveted or aspired to never advanced further in the service.

My meager wages of $1.50 a day were supplemented by what I could earn by night work with a gang selected by head checker, Mike Ryan, to transfer carloads of shingles, pig iron, or staves and heading from foreign cars on adjoining tracks to Chicago and Alton cars at so much a car according to class. It was by favor of Ryan that I got this chance to earn about twelve dollars a month as a night laborer when opportunity offered.

TRIED COMMERCIAL EMPLOYMENT

Obviously, there was no future for me in this service. Through an acquaintance made in tracing misdirected freight with Mr. Gates of the shipping department of the John V. Farwell and Company wholesale dry goods house, I obtained a job at two dollars a day. In that branch of the service you can make fifteen dollars a week after four years, if you are lucky enough to remain that long.

One day a problem in arithmetic which had been going the rounds reached me and was easily solved. Always aiming to return a compliment, I proposed a mathematical puzzle. The chief examiner asked me for the solution, which ran into quadratics. Confidentially he suggested a society of which he was a member that could advance my interests. I was out of the ordinary run of wage earners.

My optimism in regard to commercial business faded, for soon I discovered that membership in favored organizations, as well as the backing of friends or relatives in the retail dry goods trade who patronized the wholesale house, exercised a controlling influence in all departments. To ignore the

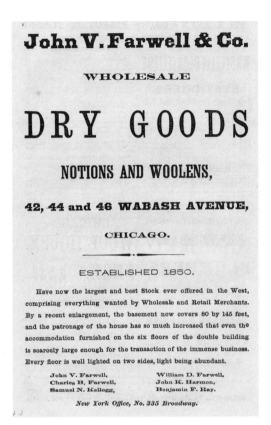

Despite his classical education in Ireland, O'Neill discovered that he had few opportunities for advancement at the John V. Farwell Wholesale Dry Goods Company. The firm was burned out by the Great Fire of 1871 and rebuilt at Franklin and Monroe streets. (Elias Colbert, Chicago: Historical and Statistical Sketch of the Garden City [Chicago: P. T. Sherlock, 1868])

requests of those who buy their stocks from the house would be poor business, and that view held in other commercial lines.

BUILDING OUR FIRST HOUSE

Hard on the heels of the Great Fire of October 8–9, 1871, came the housing problem and the inevitable increase in rents. The law of supply and demand, of which we became the victim, stimulated the desire to be sheltered by a roof of our own. Happening on a handbill advertising lots for sale on Halsted and Thirty-first streets, I investigated but found to my dismay that the prices were beyond our reach. A real estate boom was on, so I bought a lot on a side street for $550, paying $50 down and assuming a mortgage for the balance at

The Berlin journal Illustrirte Zeitung *captured the terror Chicagoans experienced during the Great Fire of October 8–9, 1871, which destroyed the city's business district. Fully one-third of Chicago's population of 100,000 had been born in Germany, and the catastrophe received widespread international coverage.* (Illustrirte Zeitung, November 18, 1871)

8 percent interest. On the remainder of our capital, exactly $100, the erection of a home was undertaken. The lumber firm of Gardner and Spry, in whose ships I had sailed the previous year, furnished the material, accepting $50 cash and giving credit as required to be paid in installments of $10 every two weeks. The lumber, I regret to relate, being left unguarded at night, came in handy to those living in the vicinity needing an occasional board or scantling, so that when the two carpenters had used up all that was left and got their $50 according to agreement, I had a wooden box, twenty by sixteen feet, resting on cedar posts four feet from the ground. There were no partitions or material from which to make them, and in the absence of front or back steps, a packing box served the purpose for a time, but we made a home of it and got away from exorbitant rents for the rest of our lives.

All building mechanics were busy during those times rebuilding the burned area, so it was as a special favor that a bricklayer acquaintance was induced to build a chimney for me on Sunday. But how? I got a wagonload of bricks gratis from the ruins of the Chicago, Alton, and St. Louis Railroad freight house, being an employee; bought a barrel of mortar mixed and ready for use; and carried the hod myself. The chimney had just reached the opening for it in the roof when the mortar ran short. Not far away in a neighbor's backyard was a pile of mortar left over by plasterers, but the human dog-in-the-manger who owned the premises would neither give, sell, or let me take it away. I saw him bury it in the lot later. What a contrast in Christianity there was in his behavior and that of the Swede who cut out the stringers of the front steps to oblige me after working hours. This gigantic young man was an expert in his trade. When I asked him his price after finishing, he replied; "Oh, nothing! You are a poor man like myself trying to get along."

This and similar gracious acts by men of other races have never been forgotten, and it affords me pleasure to say that they have been paid with interest in later days when opportunities never anticipated came my way.

The chimney being built, my friend the bricklayer announced in a spirit of liberality, "I'm not going to charge you anything for my work, but I want you to buy my wife, Maggie, a shawl."

It is with no sense of egotism that I record that the empty wooden box, occupied as our first home, was partitioned, lathed, trimmed, and equipped

All Saints, the O'Neills' family parish in Bridgeport, was founded in 1875 to serve Irish families living east of Saint Bridget's and north of Nativity. The Gothic church, designed by Gregory A. Vigeant, stood at the corner of Twenty-fifth Place and Wallace Street from its dedication on August 21, 1881, until it was closed in 1973 and razed. (H. L. Schroeder and C. W. Forbrich, Men Who Have Made the Fifth Ward *[Chicago: Schroeder, Forbrich & Co., 1895])*

This was the rear view of 2702 South Wallace Street. Looking carefully enough, one might recognize the "box" that O'Neill first built for his wife and growing family. (Photograph by Mary Lesch)

The street view of 2702 South Wallace Street shows the addition of the second floor. The O'Neills' Bridgeport home was demolished in March 2006. (Photograph by Mary Lesch)

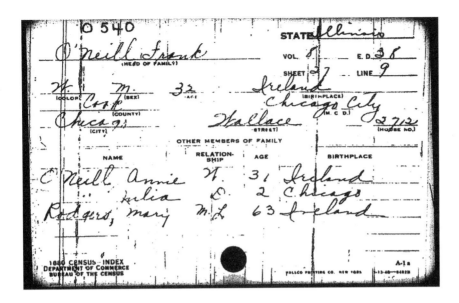

At the time of the 1880 federal census, the O'Neill household in Bridgeport included Francis, age thirty-two; his wife, Anna, age thirty-one; and her mother, Mary Rogers, age sixty-three. Four of the O'Neill children had died between 1871 and 1880—the only surviving child was Julia Ann, born on December 6, 1879. (1880 Census Index, Department of Commerce, Bureau of the Census)

The O'Neill neighbors on Wallace Street included many Irish families with young children and fathers who were skilled laborers. Unlike rural Ireland, the Bridgeport Irish lived in close proximity to one another in a densely populated neighborhood. (The Tenth U.S. Federal Census, 1880)

This rare bird's-eye view of Bridgeport captures the crucial role the railroads played in Chicago's urban development. The O'Neill family home on Wallace Street was located just a few blocks east of the Chicago and Western Indiana railroad embankment. (H. L. Schroeder and C. W. Forbrich, Men Who Have Made the Fifth Ward [Chicago: Schroeder, Forbrich & Co., 1895])

with doors and blinds by me before and after working hours and often by lamplight at night. Eventually that wooden box became a nice five-room cottage with porches, and later a two-flat building by which we emerged into the landlord class on an initial capital of $150.

APPOINTMENT ON THE CHICAGO POLICE FORCE, JULY 12, 1873

Considering the experience above noted, a position on the police force with its salary of one thousand dollars per year appealed to me. But how to obtain it was a problem. A formal application signed by five citizens and testimonials from a member of Congress, the superintendent of the Chicago and Alton Railroad, and others equally prominent were ignored by the Board of Police and Fire Commissioners notwithstanding the favorable recommendation of Chief Elmer Washburn. All appointments in those days were charged to the political account of aldermen and others in high favor with the existing administration. I did not have such influence. Discouraged by failure, I was leaning against a lamppost, out on a street corner, not knowing what to do, when along came Alderman Tracey, master mechanic for the Union Stock Yards and Transit Company. "What are you doing here?" he inquired. After listening to my tale of woe, he continued, "Come on in with me." It appears that the alderman was entitled to name two of the one hundred new men provided for the annual appropriation. Addressing the secretary of the board, he demanded my appointment. "Why, Alderman, you got your man already," reminded the official. "So I did," came the prompt reply, "but I'm entitled to two, and this is the other man." The memory of that kindly act, which was a momentous event in my life, rebounded to the advantage of many others, since the beneficiary of it attained rank and authority in later years.

SHOT BY A BURGLAR

Everyone is aware that a policeman's life is both eventful and hazardous. No less obvious is that fact that no one afflicted with timidity or indecision of character has any business on the police force, especially in a large city. Of

Just weeks before he joined the Chicago Police Department, Francis O'Neill became a naturalized citizen. Standing before Judge Lambert Tree on May 23, 1873, he swore to support the U.S. Constitution and "renounce forever all allegiance and fidelity to every Foreign Prince, Potentate, State or Sovereignty . . . particularly . . . the Queen of Great Britain and Ireland." (Clerk of the Circuit Court of Cook County, Illinois, Daley Center, Room 1113, Chicago, Illinois 60602) this axiom I had personal experience in the morning of August [17, about] one month after my appointment, July 12, 1873. Hearing a shot, I turned the corner of Clark and Monroe streets and faced a young man with gun in hand pursued by a Pinkerton watchman. A quick side jump spoiled his aim for my body, but the bullet plugged me in the left breast. I had no time to pull my revolver but used the club to knock the weapon from his hand before he could fire again. By this time my left arm hung limp and powerless, but I contrived to prevent the Pinkerton man from blowing out the burglar's brains. Next day I was a hero and a cripple and promoted for conspicuous bravery by the Board of Police and Fire Commissioners from probationer to regular patrolman. The bullet, it appears, glanced from my shoulder blade downward, and as the X-ray was then unknown, I am carrying that bullet with me to the grave. The disabled left arm gradually regained power, a rigid finger being left me permanently as a memento of my first, but by no means last, experience as a target for criminals.

Clark and Monroe was a busy area when O'Neill was shot by John Bridges on August 17, 1873. Despite the wound to his left breast, he captured the robber and saved him from being killed by a Pinkerton detective. O'Neill's heroism ensured him a permanent position on the police force. (Chicago Public Library, Special Collections and Preservation Division)

"Archey Road," immortalized by Finley Peter Dunne in his "Mr. Dooley" newspaper column in the 1890s, was Bridgeport's main thoroughfare. Newly arrived immigrants found this stretch of Archer Avenue, with its unpaved streets and small shops, reminiscent of the villages they left behind in Ireland. (Chicago History Museum, ICHi-09283)

APPOINTED STATION KEEPER

After traveling beat, as it was then called, in Bridgeport and Hamburg, the roughest districts in the city, with the usual encounters with disorderly elements for five years, I was appointed station keeper, now desk sergeant, but not without complications. On the transfer of George Washington Hubbard to a more desirable assignment, I was called in to fill the vacancy. The suggestion of Lieutenant Beadell, one month or so later, that I see my friends, if I had any, was disconcerting. I realized at once that I had been betrayed by this suave hypocrite who had repeatedly assured me of my safety, while deliberately preventing me from visiting police headquarters by keeping me on day duty continuously.

Cherishing but little hope of disrupting a prearranged program, I proceeded to city hall and appealed to Alderman Gilbert, then acting mayor, who promised to see what could be done about it.

Fortunately, Police Magistrate Summerfield happened along and inquired, "What brings you down here?" and added, "Come with me," when he heard my story.

When we entered the private office of Valorus A. Seavey, then general superintendent of police, Judge Summerfield boldly demanded my appointment to fill the vacancy I had been occupying for months. Chief Seavey, who had been my patrol sergeant in years gone by, was kindly disposed, but as another candidate had been selected for the position, he would see what he could do for me some other time. Conscious of his political strength in the administration, the judge would brook no refusal and insisted on my instant promotion. I returned to the Deering Street Police Station a regularly appointed desk sergeant, to the utter discomfort of the plotters.

It can be assumed that the official career of a member of the Chicago Police Department is replete with episodes and problems associated with the nature of his diversified duties. Only those of notable consequence can be mentioned in this condensed review.

In 1872, when this photograph was taken, the Deering Street Police Station in Bridgeport was a simple frame structure at the corner of what is now Twenty-ninth and Loomis streets. At the time O'Neill joined the force in 1873 and was assigned to Bridgeport, the Board of Police and Fire Commissioners amended the department uniform code to authorize lighter fabric for the "pantaloons worn in summer." (Chicago History Museum, ICHi-25743)

TRANSFERRED TO THE OFFICE OF THE GENERAL SUPERINTENDENT

An order from police headquarters early in the year 1883 called me to the office of Austin J. Doyle, general superintendent, who informed me that owing to the excellence of my reports, I had been selected for service as assistant chief clerk. A combination of qualifications was so essential to meet the requirements of that responsible assignment that seldom was anyone able to weather a change of administration.

In the production of multiple copies of general orders, special orders, and other documents by means of the hectograph and mimeograph appliances of that day, my style of writing proved most suitable. Moreover, at no time was any script of mine marred by erasers or correction allowed to pass. Were any changes necessary, a new page was invariably supplied.

COMPLIMENTED BY THE MAYOR

One day the draft of a proclamation by Mayor Carter H. Harrison, the elder, written as usual with pencil on soft paper, was given to me with the request that eight copies be written and distributed to the newspapers. Typewriters were unknown then. Next morning I was personally complimented by the mayor; that was the first time his proclamation had been correctly printed.

On another occasion the exact language of his Fourth of July proclamation became a matter of vital importance. While watching the pyrotechnics set off by Mayor Harrison on his front lawn at his home on Ashland Boulevard one Fourth of July, a young man was hit in the face by a fragment of an exploded skyrocket. When his suit for damages came to trial a few years later, the decision hinged on the question: Was Carter H. Harrison as a citizen complying with the provisions of the Fourth of July proclamation issued by Carter H. Harrison, the mayor of Chicago? The complainant's attorney objected to the copy of the proclamation presented. Nothing but the original document would be accepted in evidence, and there seemed little prospect of producing that.

It had been my practice to preserve communications from the mayor and heads of departments in labeled pigeonholes entirely apart from ordinary correspondence in the vault. At the end of each year the contents of those special receptacles were tied in parcels, dated, and flung high up on the top shelf. Procuring a ladder, I dug out of the dusty mess the proper parcel and in it found the precious penciled original proclamation. When

I handed it to Levy Mayer, attorney for the defendant, in the courtroom, he exclaimed, "You're the savior of our case!"

And by the way, that was the only document stored in parcels on the almost inaccessible top shelf ever called for during my stay of nine years in that office.

POLITICAL INTERFERENCE

The ideas of the chief of police, as he is called colloquially in that organization, or management of the department which he is supposed to control, seldom coincide with those which the mayor and his party leaders desire. Political obligations and considerations not infrequently disrupt his plans, and promotions and changes of his choice have to be postponed or abandoned to satisfy the demands of those who have to be reckoned with. More than once, and in different administrations, the author of this review was the victim of such complications.

In the reorganization of the police department following the election of Mayor George B. Swift in 1888, it had been the intention of Chief Frederick

John D. Shea joined the Chicago Police Department just a few weeks after O'Neill, in August 1873, and he quickly rose through the ranks, becoming one of the city's most celebrated detectives. (Chicago Chronicle, *March 20, 1898*)

Ebersold to appoint me lieutenant in charge of the Deering Street District, from which I had been transferred to police headquarters. Powerful influences succeeded in having the contemplated discharge of Inspector John D. Shea, chief of detectives, commuted to reduction in rank to lieutenant and transferred to the station the chief had intended for me.

Among a batch of candidates for the police force examined by me in 1890 was one well qualified for the service, except that he failed to come up to the standard height. This defect was not conspicuous in his appearance, yet I could not personally overlook it. Shortly afterward Aldermen McAbee, his backer, came in and informed Mr. Brennan, chief clerk, that he had just come from the mayor's office and wanted his candidate, whom I had rejected, sworn in. It was explained to him repeatedly that I who had conducted the examination reported that the man was not tall enough. This the alderman admitted and had no complaint to make on that score. Knowing from experience, as did Mr. Brennan, that under pressure mayors occasionally desire certain concessions be made, yet rarely express these desires in writing, I interposed, "Do I understand you to say, Mr. Brennan, that you will be satisfied with my decision?" Glad of an escape from an awkward position, he promptly answered, "Yes." Without hesitation I announced, "That man is 5 feet 8 inches tall." "Good for you," exclaimed the delighted alderman, grasping my hand in appreciation.

HOW I GAINED PROMOTION

One morning, a month or so later, after a long list of promotions and changes had been published, Alderman McAbee came to my desk and asked, "Why haven't you been promoted?" "Because I have no friends," was the laconic reply. With the cheering announcement, "By God, you have," out he went, but came back soon with a delegation of aldermen to demand my promotion. The chief, Frederick H. Marsh, explained to them that he was as anxious to promote me as they were, but such was the pressure and insistence in behalf of others that he had been unable to do it. "Now that you are engaged in preparing the appropriation bill," he suggested, "if you provide for one more lieutenant than the present number, your friend and mine will get that place." This was done, and when the appropriation ordinance was signed by the mayor, the order for my promotion was issued without delay, lest other complications arise. My promotion was dated January 1 of the current year [1890].

Since the transfer to Police Headquarters in 1883, my assignment remained undisturbed during the incumbency of Chiefs Doyle, Ebersold, Hubbard, and Marsh, but Chief Clerk Brennan was not so fortunate. He was transferred to East Chicago Avenue Station with the rank of lieutenant by General Superintendent Hubbard in Mayor John A. Roche's administration, thereby suffering a loss of five hundred dollars a year in salary.

OFFICIAL LIFE OF POLICE CHIEF

With every change of administration comes a change in the mayor's cabinet, and being subject to more criticism than others of it, the new general superintendent, or chief of police, of whom much is expected, soon falls into disfavor, and to such extent that prior to the reappointment of Chief Joseph Kipley by Mayor Carter H. Harrison the younger, in 1899, not one chief in the history of the Chicago Police Department had been so favored. In fact, up to that time the average term of service in that office was one year and eight months.

Born in Clare County, Ireland, in 1834, Simon O'Donnell came to Chicago as a teenager and joined the police force in 1862. He served as superintendent of police from 1879 to 1880 and returned to the Twelfth Street District, where he was regarded as a "bluff and tireless commander." (Chicago Inter Ocean, January 26, 1890)

Experienced police commanders, businessmen, and military men alike have failed to surmount the difficulties of conflicting political and diversified selfish interests. Ever recurrent is the demand for a change. Away back in 1880, Chief Simon O'Donnell, a compromise appointee, begged to be relieved of his responsibility and restored to his former captaincy of the West Twelfth Street Police District after an experience of less than one year. In much more recent times, Colonel Leroy T. Stewart resigned after six months' attempt to run the police department on military lines.

Chief Frederick Ebersold, who rose to rank in the Civil War and came up through the police department, was invited to resign because of an unwillingness to approve the list for promotion and assignment selected by the party leaders. Being a holdover officeholder from the previous administration and a Republican, his claim was insecure.

POLICE HANDICAPS

Inspector Lyman Lewis, a Vermont Yankee, was his most talked-about successor. To digress: Lewis, a patrolman, found his assignment to Captain Gund's command on the North Side, or "beyond the Rhine," rather unpleasant. To Captain Gund there were but two classes of men—Dutch and Irish. Those unable to speak Dutch or German were classified as Irish. Lewis and John P. Nelson, a Norwegian who came under the latter heading, contrived to be transferred to the South Side where no discrimination prevailed. Lewis chanced to become acquainted with Mr. Keith, also a Vermonter and a big cog in the political machine. Through Keith's influence, Lewis gained steady advancement.

Mayor John A. Roche, who succeeded the elder Harrison, was no politician. His two sponsors, George R. Davis, county treasurer, and George B. Swift, commissioner of public works, attended to that. In sizing up the rival candidates, Mr. Swift, after conversing with Inspector Lewis for an hour or more at the Desplaines Street Police Station, decided against Lewis, and the prize fell to Inspector George Washington Hubbard, who though also a native of New England was more of a pagan than a puritan.

A seasoned bachelor unhampered with relatives, Chief Hubbard found little difficulty in carrying out the policy of the party leaders. So submissive was he that he declined to name his own secretary or chief clerk, a position I had filled for months since the transfer of Chief Clerk Brennan, who suggested that there was no hurry, as a very competent man, Frank O'Neill, filled the post.

A NEW CLERK

A bank clerk, Warden S. Minkler, who was a deacon in the church attended by Commissioner Swift, received the appointment, but such was his ignorance of the complex duties of his position that Chief Hubbard diplomatically relieved him of all responsibility except to stand around and talk to people of interest to the party. All official matters, correspondence, and details were attended to as before, while Mr. Minkler was treated with all due respect and consideration.

About this time it was decreed that all city employees should reside within the city limits. In writing this general order, I was figuratively sawing off the branch on which I sat because by living in Hyde Park I was obliged to return to the city every evening and remain overnight until after the election.

A NEW ORGANIZATION

With one year and eight months' incumbency to his credit, Chief Hubbard was succeeded by Frederick H. Marsh. Mr. Minkler resigned and Mr. Brennan came back to his former assignment as chief clerk. After a short vacation, Chief Hubbard was assigned as lieutenant at the South Englewood Station, so that he could complete twenty years of service to be eligible for a pension.

As a matter of party policy a neutral or "dark horse" obtains a coveted position, when rivalries are too intense. Many considerations, of which the general public is ignorant, influence the selection of appointees for important positions.

Such was the popularity of Frederick H. Marsh in Ogle County, Illinois, that he had been elected twice as the Democratic candidate for sheriff in that Republican county. This led to his appointment as United States marshal in the city of Chicago and ultimately, favored by these circumstances, to the position of general superintendent of police on January 1, 1890.

TRANSFERRED ON REQUEST

Another turn of the political wheel landed the Republicans in power again. As there was a demand for a disciplinarian this time, Robert W. McClaughry, former warden of the Joliet Penitentiary, was installed as Chief Marsh's successor in May 1891. Having served continuously at police headquarters for eight years and being deprived of sunshine and fresh air, I was anxious to

The Illinois State Building at the 1893 World's Fair in Chicago, designed by well-known Chicago architect, W. W. Boyington, was controversial because of its large size and huge dome. Critics charged that the Illinois Building and the adjacent United States Government Building overpowered the Art Palace. The O'Neills would have been able to walk to the fair from their home in Hyde Park. ("World's Columbian Exposition of 1893, the Illinois building," Paul V. Galvin Library Digital History Collection— Illinois Institute of Technology, August 26, 1998, http://columbus.iit.edu/; Mary Lesch collection)

enjoy some daylight. The new chief, being a kindly man, transferred me as lieutenant to the Hyde Park District where I lived.

As preparations for the World's Fair were then in progress, I was assigned to steady day duty by the inspector. Another lieutenant was also assigned to night duty, while a lieutenant and sergeant in the confidence of the combine took charge of the activities in the vicinity of the World's Fair grounds. I was well aware that this arrangement was prompted by sinister motives.

Mayor Hampstead Washburn's administration came to an end on the election of Carter H. Harrison the elder—his fifth term—in 1893; Chief [Robert Wilson] McClaughry was supplanted by Chief Michael Brennan, my former associate. As the choice of the latter, and the mayor, for captain to command the World's Fair District, my name led the list for weeks and until political policy broke the "slate."

A native of County Mayo, Michael Brennan served as chief of police from 1893 to 1895 and was responsible for promoting Francis O'Neill to chief clerk. (Chicago Inter Ocean, January 26, 1890)

CROWDED OFF THE SLATE FOR CAPTAINCY

A few days before a comprehensive general order was issued, John P. Hopkins, the leader of a Democratic Party faction unfriendly to Mayor Harrison, called on him at the city hall, remarking, "I understand there is no politics in the police force now." "No, John, no politics now," responded the mayor. "Then, as a citizen," added Hopkins, "I've come to recommend Lieutenant Thomas P. Kane for captain of police. He was my boyhood friend in Buffalo, New York, and as a good Democrat he is entitled to promotion." On the theory that this was a good opportunity to placate a rival and repair his political fences, the slate was changed in Lieutenant Kane's favor. Not wishing to deprive me of promotion, Mr. Hopkins advocated my appointment to the command of the South Chicago District. Lieutenant Patrick Powers's delegations from that town descended on city hall in his behalf and so impressed the mayor that I was sidetracked again. So there was politics in the police force after all.

The conditions which developed during the progress of the fair convinced me that in losing the appointment, I was favored by the Fates. Many things besides a knowledge of police business had their values in the mael-strom of selfish human interests. Powerful influences paralyzed the arm of the law, and even Chief Brennan himself, though issuing drastic orders, was obliged to yield to expediency.

APPOINTED CHIEF CLERK OF THE POLICE DEPARTMENT

His plans upset and ill at ease, Chief Brennan called me to his office and offered me the position of chief clerk, saying in his old familiar way, "Frank, if you will take the outer desk you will save me four-fifths of my trouble." As the tenure of office in that position was as uncertain as that of chief of detec-tives, I hesitated, although it was a promotion. Rather than disappoint him, I accepted the proffered place.

Although Chicago's downtown was destroyed in the Great Fire of 1871, by the 1890s a new city had emerged with such notable landmarks as the First National Bank (1882), at the northwest corner of Dearborn and Madison streets, designed by Burling and Whitehouse. (Chicago Public Library, Special Collections and Preservation Division)

In 1883, O'Neill was promoted from the Deering Street Station in Bridgeport to Central Station police headquarters in city hall. The Cook County/City Hall Building, designed by architect James J. Egan, a native of Cork City, Ireland, and built between 1873 and 1885, occupied the entire block bounded by Randolph, Washington, Clark, and LaSalle streets. (Chicago Public Library, Special Collections and Preservation Division)

In those days, in fact at all times, party leaders intent on patronage, getting even with opponents, or pretense of retrenchment led to much confusion after every change of administration. Even now, a generation later, I enjoy the recollection of having saved not a few worthy men from the "ax." The command to make out an order to retire Inspector Lyman Lewis from the service was so unexpected that I ventured to call Chief Brennan's attention to the consequences of this act. He explained that as the city council had purposely failed to provide for only five inspectors in the police appropriation, he was obliged to do it. I warned him that he could not afford to let Lewis go and subject himself to the accusation of bigotry and prejudice. Economically it may be all right, but diplomatically it was indefensible. Inspector Lewis was the only native American of any prominence in the police department. He was also a Protestant and a Mason, while the mayor, chief of police, and three inspectors were Catholics and of Irish ancestry. The other remaining inspector was a Luxembourger of Catholic antecedents. All that the public will consider, I cautioned him, is that the only Protestant

American of high rank in the police department was forced out without apparent justification. The chief, who had been impressed by my protest, said he would take it up with the mayor. The result was that an Irish inspector, ripe for retirement, was substituted for Inspector Lewis.

APPOINTED CAPTAIN OF POLICE

When another "shake up" in the police department brought the opportunity for my deferred promotion on April 17, 1894, Chief Brennan inquired, "Who is the best man to fill your place?"

"Morgan Collins," I replied.

"Yes, he is a good man, but who can take his place in the secretary's office?"

"Daniel Lynch of the same office," was the answer.

This sketch of O'Neill as a captain appeared in the Chicago Chronicle, *February 20, 1898.*

STOCK YARDS POLITICIAN RESENTFUL

Prior to annexation to the City of Chicago, the Town of Lake, a great industrial center, was controlled politically by a limited coterie whose influence may be considered dictatorial.

The intrusion of a captain of police in command of the Stock Yards District from the old Chicago force, while not welcomed, aroused no open hostility because after nine years' assignment at police headquarters, under five administrations, I needed no introduction in any part of the city.

CONGRESSIONAL INVESTIGATING COMMITTEE CALLS FOR REPORT

Less than one week had passed of a much-needed rest I was enjoying on a Michigan farm, when I was notified that a congressional investigating committee had called for an official police report on the railway strike. Not caring to entrust the writing of such an important report to other hands, I hastened back to Chicago. Imagine my surprise to find that all pages of the report book covering the stormy first week of the strike had been cut out with a sharp knife during my absence. No one knew anything about it, yet someone certainly did. Nothing but the desire to embarrass me could have prompted such a malicious act of vandalism. Having participated in all of the activities of the police in the riotous days, a good memory enabled me to forward to the police headquarters a report, which was complimented by the committee as being the only one worthy of the name produced by the Police Department of Chicago. Following is a copy of that report.

REVIEW OF THE GREAT RAILWAY AND SYMPATHETIC STRIKE OF JUNE, JULY, AND AUGUST 1894, IN THE 8TH POLICE DISTRICT

Sir:

The great strike of 1894, which will be historic in the annals of American labor disturbances, although begun in other parts of the city on June 29th, did not call for police interference in the Stock Yards district until July 2nd. No stock or other trains had come in for several days and the business of the greatest live stock and provision emporium of the world was fast becoming paralyzed.

At four o'clock in the morning of the above date Lieutenant Keleher, with a detail of twenty men, succeeded in breaking the blockade and in getting into the yards via Brighton Park with several Chicago, Burlington and Quincy cattle trains. He was relieved at 7 A.M. by Lieutenant Fitzpatrick who continued to escort the cattle trains until noon, when a total of 467 cars had entered the yards. In the early morning strikers showed determined opposition, but the officers put them to rout. A striker attempted to throw a brakeman off of a train west of Ashland Avenue. Lieutenant Keleher, at the risk of his life, slipped aboard and drawing his revolver made the desperate striker and his companion jump for their lives.

Another brakeman was thrown from a train by strikers and slightly injured about this same time.

Prior to this and from the inception of the strike I had details made to guard night and day all tracks and crossings, particularly at outlying points, such as the signal tower at the crossing of the Grand Trunk and Panhandle system of tracks. As this tower controlled all switches of the Grand Trunk, Panhandle, and Baltimore and Ohio, and Northern Pacific Railways in that vicinity and cost upwards of $40,000.00, the desire to blow it up and blockade those roads was no secret. In the day time Lieutenant Fitzpatrick had charge of the 40th Street tracks over which all trains arriving at and departing from the Stock Yards daily passed. Sergeant Curtin was in charge of the details on Stewart Avenue between 39th and 47th Streets, while acting Sergeant Crotty had charge of the men guarding the Monon roundhouse and the different railway interests in the vicinity. A small detail was retained at the station when possible under the charge of acting Sergeant John Duffy to respond to emergency calls which were almost constant. Lieutenant Keleher with Sergeants Begley and Moran took charge of affairs during the night, the details being about the same as in the day. Under no circumstances could an officer leave his post until actually relieved by his successor. All pretense of doing regular patrol duty was abandoned now and our energies directed toward the preservation of peace and the protection of property along the different railway lines.

Considerable tendency to upset and derail isolated cars and disable switches was manifest during the afternoon of July 2nd. Lieutenant Fitzpatrick with his men was kept busy in dispersing crowds and preventing violence along the 40th Street tracks.

Toward evening an effort was made to take a Swift and Company train of dressed beef intended for the eastern markets out of the Michigan Central yards west of Halsted Street. Coupling pins were repeatedly pulled and the engineer and trainmen were mercilessly jeered and stoned. The police were well nigh powerless in such a mob and even while Lieutenant Fitzpatrick was on the steps of the cab to protect Fogarty, the engineer, stones crashed through the windows. I arrived on the ground about this time with reinforcements of stationed policemen along both sides of the train and together we succeeded in clearing the tracks after driving the mob out into the plank road. I then called to the engineer saying, "There is a clear track for you now, come on." He appeared to be quite careless about it and leisurely stepped

John E. Fitzpatrick, inspector of police in charge of the First Division during the Pullman Strike of 1894, provided compelling testimony to the United States Strike Commission. (Chicago Inter Ocean, January 26, 1890)

out of the cab and stood beside his engine. He refused to pull his train out and neither request nor entreaty from Mr. Louis Swift or the railway officials could induce him to change his mind. The engine was then detached and Mr. Fogarty climbed aboard and started away amid the exultant shouts from the multitude.

A detail of police constantly guarded this and similar trains which were iced daily until they were finally pulled out of the yards.

That the tendency to quit work is contagious even when no grievance exists became unpleasantly evident at this time. Thousands, who had thoughtlessly given up their positions held by them for years in the great packing houses and other corporations, thronged the street crossings of the different railway lines and by their presence intimidated those who were inclined to work. In order to have the necessary switching, Swift and Company purchased one of the Union Stock Yard and Transit Company's locomotives and with a crew of their own men protected by a detail of ten policemen under the command of Sergeant Quinlan, contrived to carry on their business successfully. Their example was followed soon after by Armour and Company, Nelson Morris and Company, and the International Packing and Provision Company. A sufficient detail of police was furnished to each company. Commencing on this date and at various times during the continuance of the strike the working force of ninety men at this station was augmented by reinforcements from the 1st, 4th, 5th, 10th, and 12th districts, but at no time did I have more than 190 patrolmen available for post duty. An additional patrol wagon with crew from the 4th division was temporarily assigned to this district also.

The forenoon of July 3rd was uneventful, but in the afternoon I learned of the intention of general manager Newell of the Lake Shore and Michigan Southern Rail Road to take out a train of Nelson, Morris and Company's dressed beef. I made an earnest effort to ascertain the hour when he was to be expected. No one, not even Mr. Ashby, superintendent of Union Stock Yards and Transit Company, could tell me, as Mr. Newell seemed determined to keep the secret to himself. While making a flying call with Lieutenant Keleher in the patrol wagon to Lake

According to O'Neill's account of the bitter 1894 Pullman Strike, police officers effectively dispersed crowds while U.S. marshals "discreetly kept themselves out of sight." (Harper's Weekly, July 21, 1894)

Shore and Michigan Shore roundhouse in search of information, Mr. Newell with his son and a few United States Marshals steamed up the tracks on a locomotive to the Yards, into which they dashed at such speed that Lieutenant Fitzpatrick, and his men who were purposely awaiting his arrival, could not get on. The police started in pursuit on foot. I entered the Stock Yards gate with the patrol wagon intent on protecting a railway official who evidently scorned protection. I saw the Lieutenant and his men hustling along the tracks and chasing some strikers who were about to overturn some cars and thereby prevent the locomotive's return by that route. When Mr. Newell's crew began to couple up the beef train, which stood at 47th Street and Centre [Racine] Avenue (one and one half miles from where he passed the police) a curious crowd commenced to assemble about the engine and taunt the engineer. Being provided with an injunction issued by a judge of the United States Court, Mr. Newell ordered his son to read aloud the document, which the latter pompously drew from his pocket. When the import of the injunction became known a

few of the boldest ridiculed and insulted Mr. Newell grossly, telling him to stick the paper in his _____ pipe, for all they cared. As
the injunction would not enjoin a Stock Yards mob or command
the least respect under the present circumstances, the project to
take out the train had to be abandoned and Mr. Newell, disgusted
with his failure, ordered a return homeward. While the injunction was being read some cunning hand placed a coupling pin
in such a position that the first revolution of the driving wheels
drove it through the cylinder head and disabled one side of the
locomotive. Mr. Newell complained of the lack of police protection, but when the facts in the case are understood it is plain
there was no one to blame but himself.

    At three o'clock A.M. July 4th, the United States Regulars ar-
rived in the Yards and camped at Dexter Park. Some difficulty was
experienced in taking the coaches out of the yards. Lieutenant
Fitzpatrick was struck with a stone on the cheek while protecting
the engineer. About five o'clock A.M. a detail of twenty-five men
under the command of Inspector Hunt, me, and Lieutenants
Keleher and Fitzpatrick escorted out of the Michigan Central

*On the evening of July 6, 1894, sympathetic strikers overturned railway cars, but O'Neill believed
that deputy United States marshals also engaged in violence and may have set at least one of the fires
"so that their services would be viewed as necessary."* (Harper's Weekly, July 21, 1894)

Harper's Weekly *depicted the arrival of federal troops in a positive light, but in O'Neill's experience during the Pullman Strike, they "were unequal to the task of taking a train of cattle more than half a mile from the [stock] yards."* (Harper's Weekly, July 21, 1894)

yards the beef train which engineer Fogarty had refused to pull out on the evening of July 2nd. Very little difficulty or opposition was experienced so early in the morning, as the disaffected element was yet at home and had not expected such a move. As the train moved out along the 40th Street tracks east of Halsted Street, the United States Regulars came out of camp and marched beside it as far as Clark Street. There being no necessity for their escort they returned and Lieutenant Fitzpatrick with a detail of police accompanied the train as far as Woodlawn. This is the train for which the Regulars received so much undeserved praise. No appreciable opposition was encountered and the danger, if any, had passed before they appeared on the ground.

Rumors of exciting times at the Stock Yards caused great crowds from all over the city to assemble there and to literally fill the streets and railway lines in the vicinity of 40th and Halsted Streets. The crowds were looking for entertainment in this way instead of celebrating the "glorious fourth" in the customary manner. No particular damage was done to railway property during the day, but it was evident that taking out the beef train in the morning was not regarded with favor, and gave rise to many expressions of disappointment by the mob.

Late in the afternoon a train of coaches, flat cars and stock cars carrying United States Cavalry, artillery, and equipment came in on the 40th Street tracks. Notwithstanding that soldiers with drawn revolvers guarded the couplings; the train was cut three times between Wallace and Halsted Street. John Burke, the famous Indian fighter, was perched on the brake of the last car confronting a howling mob which followed behind. Finding his car slowing up almost to a standstill, he looked around to ascertain the cause and saw the remainder of the train from which he had been cut off, about 50 yards distant. He climbed down with alacrity and amid the howls of the mob sprinted for the receding train, upon which he ascended with an evident sense of relief. An attempt to derail the train by throwing a switch beneath it resulted in the arrest of the perpetrator. In accordance with orders from Inspector Hunt on the previous evening, with a detail of ten picked men, I met a Michigan Central locomotive manned by railway officials at Clark Street at 6:00 A.M. July 5th, and escorted it safely to the Baltimore and Ohio chutes, where a train of cattle was speedily loaded. A strong force of United States Regulars commanded by Captain Herts took charge of this train. The soldiers with fixed bayonets marched on either side of the train and guarded every coupling, while a company of cavalry cleared the way ahead. Crowds of hundreds of people, attracted mainly by curiosity to see real live United States Soldiers equipped for action, poured in from all directions over the viaducts and along the tracks; they perched on the roofs of sheds, freight cars and even houses. Howls and jeers rent the air but little violence was attempted. As the train pulled out of the yards and passed east on Halsted Street multitudes filled the tracks and adjacent streets and grounds so thickly that the soldiers were crowded against the cars. While Mr. Wright, a Michigan Central official was throwing a switch in advance of the train and behind the cavalry escort, he was struck on the head and knocked senseless by a stone thrown by an unknown person. His place was promptly taken by Agent D. T. Cotter who, under the protection of Lieutenant Fitzpatrick, performed all of the required switching. Police officers were strung along the roofs of the cars to watch the movement of the mob. I stood on the roof of the caboose guarding the superintendent of signals of the Michigan Central Railway. The Herculean soldier who marched behind had a very uncomfortable assignment, being crowded almost off his feet by the howling mob. Beneath me in the caboose were a score of deputy United States Marshals, who discreetly kept themselves out of sight. When the train reached Stewart Avenue, it was found that the mob had overturned cars in every conceivable direction along the tracks for blocks in advance and effectively barred further progress. About this time an incoming suburban passenger train on the Pennsylvania Railway slacked up about 50 or 60 yards south of where the cavalry halted. In an instant the engineer and fireman were dragged out of the cab and the passengers in great alarm fled precipitously from the coaches. The cavalry, seeing the commotion, dashed towards the engine, but too late. The harm was done and the guilty parties were indistinguishable in the crowd. There being no possibility of clearing the tracks in less than half a day there was nothing to be done but submit to a humiliating return to the Yards at high noon.

The United States Regulars, Infantry and Cavalry were unequal to the task of taking a train of cattle more than half a mile from the yards. The train was backed up to the chutes and the cattle unloaded, and with the morning escort I rode the engine out of the Yards and downtown via Brighton Park. When passing through Brighton Park I saw portions of a Panhandle train derailed. At about two miles further on we found the remainder of the train. With permission from the Michigan Central officials, I returned to Brighton Park with a detail of men and the Panhandle train crew and held a vicious mob of at least two thousand who were just about to set the derailed cars on fire. While the dismembered train was being made up, a passing passenger train was vigorously stoned a short distance away from us. Officer Pat Murphy seized one young rioter and brought him to me, but he was followed by a howling mob. Here was a dilemma. Nothing short of my entire force could successfully get that prisoner to the station, over half a mile distant, and I knew there was no patrol wagon to respond to my call. Should I take him to the

Although Illinois governor John P. Altgeld's pardoning of three Haymarket defendants in 1893 effectively ended his political career, he continued to speak out against injustice. At Cooper's Union in New York City in 1896, Altgeld criticized President Grover Cleveland's decision to send federal troops to Chicago during the Pullman Strike, claiming that "instead of overawing the mob or exerting an influence for good, their presence added to the excitement and served as an irritant." (Harper's Weekly, July 14, 1894)

On the evening of July 6, 1894, Assistant Fire Marshal John Fitzgerald and his men were surrounded by a crowd of thousands who set fire to cars on the Panhandle railroad. O'Neill recalled that "with a force of eighteen men," he "hastened to his relief . . . and experienced little difficulty in dispersing the mob, which was composed largely of minors of both sexes." (Harper's Weekly, July 21, 1894)

station? My object in coming back to Brighton Park would have been defeated and the train and the crew would be at the mercy of the mob. I decided to let the prisoner go gracefully if possible. I questioned Officer Murphy as to the nature of the young man's offense, and finding that while he had thrown the stone; it did not strike the coaches or do any damage. I set him at liberty and gained the good will of the mob, which quietly withdrew and offered us no further opposition. On returning to the station word reached me that a thieving mob was looting the freight cars in the Wabash Yards between 45th and 47th Streets; the watchman and the deputy United States Marshals were powerless in the face of the mob. Because the patrol wagons and the ambulance were out on runs, I put together a detail of five men and walked three quarters of a mile to the yards where we arrested seven men whom we caught carrying away sacks and barrels of flour. With our prisoners grasped by the wrists and carrying sacks of flour on our shoulders as evidence, we were reluctantly compelled to foot it back to the station, weary in limb and angry in spirit. What a sight we were, daubed with flour which formed a paste with the copious perspiration which oozed through our clothing. I, though still on foot, immediately returned to the railway yards with an increased force and clubbed all the intruders off of the premises. Nothing but provisions had been taken, and the mob by their words and looks regarded our sudden advent as an unwarranted interference. Several other arrests were made before they realized that we would stand neither crime nor impudence. A sufficient police detail was left in charge of the yard and continued there until the end of the strike. Special agent E. J. Gregory of the Chicago and Western Illinois Railway fired on a mob from the platform of a blocked passenger train at the 40th Street crossing during the afternoon and wounded two young men named Toney Happ and Ed O'Neill. A mob numbering in the hundreds attacked the Chicago and Western Illinois signal tower at 49th Street with a view of taking the signal man, but Acting Sergeant Crotty, with a small police detail, prevented the success of their design. A few blocks further on the same mob upset a Grand Trunk box car, but were immediately dispersed by the police. In the early part of the night a wave of incendiaries passed over the Grand Trunk tracks between Centre [Racine] and Ashland Avenues. Scarcely a flag shanty or depot escaped the vandals. Although once detected and foiled by the police, the incendiaries succeeded in firing and destroying the two story frame hay warehouse at Loomis Street. The police were absolutely swallowed up in the throng and were constantly running from place to place putting out incipient blazes and assisting the fire department. With the ticket agent they contrived to save all of the papers and documents when the depot at Ashland Avenue was burned down. This was an eventful and memorable day in this district.

Comparative quiet reigned the next morning, July 6th. Wrecking crews ventured to operate along the Stewart Avenue and 40th Street system of tracks early in the forenoon. Some opposition was encountered at the intersection of the lines mentioned, where a large crowd congregated. The mob was repeatedly driven away and finally clubbed away. Three incendiary fires which were stealthily started among the cars in secluded places and in the old Grand Trunk round house, were kicked out by the officers without having to sound the fire alarm. An attack was made on an incoming Pennsylvania Railway suburban train as it passed the crossing and two men who were caught stoning it were arrested. Six men whom I saw seated in the shade of a fence at the crossing and who remained undisturbed during the excitement I ordered driven away. When the officer went to execute the command the six men with one accord proudly displayed their deputy United States Marshal badges and resumed their pose of ease and indifference. As the train passed out of this district and into Captain Madden's territory a vicious mob suddenly appeared north of 39th Street and bombarded it with stones, shattering all of the windows. On seeing this our men ran in that direction and we fired at them at long range. The mob scattered at once and disappeared through the stone yards. I notified Captain Madden by phone of the occurrence and a squad of his men arrived promptly on the ground. While making this charge on the mob, Lieutenant Fitzpatrick who was running by my side, slipped on a rail and sprained his ankle. This mishap, while it disabled him for a few days, did not prevent him from doing good police service at the time. In the afternoon a small gang upset a flag shanty at Morris and Wright Streets and L. R. Ritchie, a deputy United States Marshal was injured by the shanty falling on him. Early in the afternoon a constantly increasing mob obstructed the intersection of Halsted and 40th Streets and by their taunts and howls, intimidated the teamsters going in and out of the yards on the plank road. The detail of police being insufficient at that point I took with me from Stewart Avenue what men I could spare and partially dispersed the crowd. After clearing the way and opening the crossing some teamsters, through cowardice, refused to proceed, although no violence had been offered them. A few who had supplies for Armor and Company and other packers were furnished police escorts. At five o'clock the arrest of John Sherley, who was acting suspiciously among the cars in the Michigan Central yards by Officer Orlikrewsky resulted in a desperate struggle. The prisoner resisted violently and aided and encouraged by the mob, had broken away and escaped into the crowd, when Officer Nye came up and assisted in his recapture. The officers fought their way through to the patrol box at Root Street. When the patrol wagon arrived an excited mob surrounded them and seized the horses. The officers pulling their revolvers cleared a space and drove off with the prisoner amid a shower of stones. About four o'clock, I was notified from the station that Fire Marshal Fitzgerald urgently needed police protection and assistance at a conflagration on the Panhandle tracks between 45th and 47th Streets, where a mob of thousands hampered his men and even set cars on fire in his presence. With a force of eighteen men I hastened to his relief on the electric cars, the patrol wagon and the ambulance being out, and experienced little difficulty in dispersing the mob, which was composed largely of minors of both sexes.

Lieutenant Healy, with a wagon load of officers from the 11th precinct, arrived shortly later and swiftly put to rout the mob further south. In their panic to escape the onslaught of the police, the mob swarmed over the prairie and tramped down a ten acre field of oats as level as if a steam roller had passed over it.

From the roofs of the cars I directed the movements of the police, who drove all trespassers from the extensive Panhandle freight yard, extending from 39th to 44th Streets, which the fire had not reached. When the fire was under control, I stationed men at different points on the roofs of cars with orders to protect the property at all hazards, even to the extent of shooting those caught in the act of incendiarism, and remain at their posts until relieved. A detail of nine men in charge of Sergeant Moran patrolled the Panhandle yards and tracks at night and no further fires or damage to railway property occurred in that vicinity. In the day time Lieutenant R. Walsh, who came with a squad of nineteen men from Inspector Bonaack's command, was placed in charge of the police details on the Panhandle system of tracks and as the strike troubles subsided his jurisdiction was extended to include the Grand Trunk lines as far east as Halsted Street. The strikers and their sympathizers became extremely active in their hostility and destructive acts on the night of July 6th. Railway cars were set on fire wherever the incendiaries could escape the vigilance of the police. Railway watchmen were powerless and the vandals, under cover of darkness, easily escaped detection. It was openly claimed that many of the fires were set by deputy United States Marshals so that their services would be viewed as necessary. In one case at least the claim appeared to be well founded. Four alarms and a still came in from the vicinity of 45th Street and Stewart Avenue late in the afternoon and early evening. My suspicions were aroused and I detailed Officers Hohne and Reidy in plain dress to enter the yards secretly, hide among the cars and discover the incendiaries if possible. Shortly after midnight, noticing a moving light in an empty box car a short distance away, they ran to the car and found two men within, while a third stood outside. On seeing the officers the three men stepped upon a wad of blazing waste and extinguished it. The officers showed their stars and demanded an explanation. The trio displayed deputy United States Marshal's stars and stated that a passer by had thrown the blazing waste into the car. No claim was advanced that any effort was made to discover and arrest the alleged incendiary. As no more fire alarms were received from that neighborhood the inference is obvious.

During the forenoon of July 7th, a Grand Trunk wrecking train with a coach attached to it, guarded by Company C, 2nd Regiment, Illinois National Guard, stationed at Englewood,

numbering 42 men commanded by Captain Mair, six deputy
United States Marshals and Police Sergeant Finley started out to
clear the tracks. I was notified that they expected to work through
as far as Elston before night. When they passed westward across
Halsted Street, I instructed Officers Dunlea, Phelps, O'Brien,
Brennan and Ptacek to follow them and report if any attempts
were made by strikers or others to injure or in any way interfere with railway property. At 3:15 P.M. Officer Charles R. Phelps
called up and informed me that a terrible riot was in progress
at 49th and Loomis Streets between the soldiers and the mob;
several members of the mob had been killed and a score or so
wounded. Police reinforcements were urgently needed. A patrol
wagon of police in command of Lieutenant Keleher was rushed
to the battle while Lieutenant Fitzpatrick with a few men started
for the scene on foot. Fitzpatrick and his men had reached 49th
and Halsted Streets when the wrecking train, soldiers and all,
passed eastward on their way back to town, having abandoned
ground. They shouted to Fitzpatrick to return to the station
for more help or he and his men would be annihilated. In the
meantime I had gotten my reserves out of bed and another patrol
wagon and, picking up Lieutenant Fitzpatrick and his squad,
galloped to the scene of the riot. Inspector Hunt, who had just
arrived at the station, remained to summon help from other pre-
cincts. In passing Camp Wheeler I notified Colonel Moulton
to follow up as quickly as possible with all of his available force.
Both patrol wagons dashed into the mob almost simultaneously
and, cutting it in two, charged furiously with revolver and club
and routed them utterly. The firearms were sparingly used and
then only to cause a stampede, but the clubs played a lively tat-
too on the anatomies of those not too young or too old to bear
such heroic treatment. It was raining rocks on us for a short time,
while the snap and bark of the revolvers of both contending parties sounded like a small boy's celebration of the 4th of July. The
desire to seek safety in flight subordinated all other passions and
the mob which sullenly withstood the murderous fire of the militia fled in panic before an equal number of Chicago policemen.
After the tracks were cleared and while chasing the rioters on
the cross streets, I noticed that a saloon run by an anarchist at

Instead of waiting for police reinforcements, Captain Thomas I. Mair ordered Illinois national guardsmen to fire into a crowd at Forty-ninth and Loomis streets, an action that O'Neill criticized as making the strikers "more desperate." (Harper's Weekly, July 21, 1894)

the corner of 49th and Bishop Streets was full of men who were shouting defiance and denunciation of us. Acting on a sudden impulse I decided to clear out the saloon. We rushed in impetuously and administered a salutary drubbing to all found within except the proprietor, who stood behind the bar in mute terror. When Colonel Moulton arrived with two companies of his soldiers the battle was over. Five officers and their men remained on the ground after the departure of the wrecking train and busied themselves in caring for the wounded and in doing other police duty. The mob had set two cars on fire and was tearing up the rails when Lieutenant Keleher and his men rushed in and attacked them. Captain Mair's soldiers, when closely surrounded and stoned beyond endurance by the mob, fired a volley over their heads. Many of the bullets passed through the frame buildings and entered adjoining structures. As this did not have the desired effect, a second volley was fired into the mob. A great many were wounded, and while the rioters fell back the shooting only rendered a portion of them still more desperate. Officer Dunlea stated that he requested Captain Mair to hold out five minutes longer for the police reinforcements which he was confident would arrive. The Captain replied that he did not think he had enough ammunition to battle the mob, which numbered from eight to ten thousand. John Jackman, said to be an inoffensive citizen, and John alias "Engine" Burke were fatally shot by the soldiers and died the next day. Only those who were seriously wounded required police assistance. All of the others were quietly taken away by their friends. Of the number wounded all recovered except Jackman and Burke.

A few hours after the events above narrated, the police stationed where the battle took place notified me that a threatening mob was congregating at the Ashland Avenue crossing. I immediately called on Colonel Moulton of the Illinois National Guard at Camp Wheeler and represented to him that a demonstration of his entire force, Infantry, Cavalry and Artillery, in the disturbed district, would have a repressing effect on the foreign elements, which constitutes a majority of the population in that in portion of the district, and give them an opportunity to realize the strength of the forces opposed to them. The urbane Colonel readily acquiesced to the idea and promptly mobilized his forces as suggested.

The sight of this formidable array had the desired result and the mob peacefully melted away without further trouble. The crisis had been reached and the fight was won in the interest of constituted authority. The backbone of the strike was broken and no open defiance of the law was attempted thereafter. Gradually crime and disorder diminished as the strike came to an end.

On the previous evening, July 6th, five companies of the second regiment of the Illinois National Guard under the command of Colonel Moulton reported for assignment. Quarters were secured at the ball grounds corner of 48th and Halsted Streets and named Camp Wheeler. One company of Cavalry and D Battery commanded by Captain Russell joined the company the next day. Additional forces of the Illinois National Guard under the command of Major McFadden arrived on July 7th and made Camp Dexter, at 43rd Street Union Stock Yards, their headquarters. The soldiers at Camp Wheeler were assigned as occasion required on the Grand Trunk tracks from the Panhandle crossing to Centre [Racine] Avenue, at the Wabash yards at 47th Street and Stewart Avenue, and at the Chicago and Eastern Illinois yards at 51st and Wallace Streets. These details were gradually withdrawn as peace and order were restored. The soldiers of Major McFadden's command at Camp Dexter were picketed throughout the Union Stock Yards exclusively by Lieutenant Keleher on July 7th, 8th, and 9th where he was succeeded by Lieutenant Healy of the 10th precinct, who was temporarily assigned to this district. Dynamite scares commenced to be circulated at this time and timid persons were considerably alarmed. It finally dawned upon their unsuspecting minds that they were being "played" and they no longer retired at night in momentary expectation of being "blown up."

The officers and soldiers of the 2nd regiment of the Illinois National Guard willingly and faithfully cooperated with the police, promptly responded to all calls and rendered very efficient service wherever they were assigned. In their zeal to repress disorder and crime, considerable promiscuous shooting was done by the militia. Several indiscreet persons can bear testimony to the accuracy of the soldiers' aim. A few who failed to respect the challenges of the soldiers on picket suffered some trifling bayonet wounds, but fortunately no fatalities resulted in any of those cases.

When the strike was under control cases of individual assault or "slugging" were not infrequent occurrences; the victims invariably being those who had refused to go out on strike or those who returned to work. A number of arrests were made for this offense, but few of the victims appeared in court to prosecute their assailants. Fifty Detective Sergeants from the Central Station, expressly assigned to this district during this period to catch the sluggers, did not make a single arrest.

It was now found necessary to make special detail of officers at various points from the Stock Yards gate to Wabash Avenue to prevent the slugging of teamsters in the employ of Swift and Company, Armor and Company and Nelson Morris and Company.

The teamsters delivered daily supplies to butchers all over Chicago; they commenced coming out of the Yards shortly after midnight and continued until just before noon. While returning from work on the evening of July 17th, Oscar E. Vardaman, an engineer in the employ of the Union Stock Yard and Transit Company, was met on 48th Street near Union Avenue by four striking fellow employees. They reproached him for his lack of spirit and he fatally shot one of the men, named Albert Miles, in the back. The bullet entered near the spine and lodged in the stomach. Vardaman was arrested by Sergeant Clancy and is now under indictment for murder.

Shortly before 11 o'clock on the night of July 18th, flames were seen creeping up from the platform of Nelson Morris and Company's retail meat market at 4122 South Halsted Street. Business men in that vicinity turned in an alarm. The building which was a large two story frame store was soon all ablaze with its fatty contents. The illumination quickly attracted a large crowd. Major McFadden's soldiers aided the police in keeping the streets clear and the fire department succeeded in preventing the spread of the fire beyond the building and a few shops and barns belonging to the Union Stock Yard and Transit Company, which stood in the rear. Although the crowd was large, it was quite orderly and no disposition to interfere with the work of the fire department was manifested, as stated in some newspaper reports. The fire was communicated to the building from a box car in the rear, which was probably set on fire by an incendiary.

In the afternoon of July 24th half a dozen hoodlums diverted themselves by stoning the trainmen on the Grand Trunk tracks near Centre [Racine] Avenue. Officer Lingren, one of Lieutenant Walsh's men, attempted to arrest them, and while seizing one was hit on the crown of the head with a stone by another, and severely wounded. The officer was partially stunned by the blow, but contrived to shoot at and wound two of them as they ran away. They escaped at the time, but were arrested and punished afterwards.

There being no further need for the services of Lieutenant Healy in this district, he was ordered back to his own station at noon July 26th, when Lieutenant Keleher resumed command of the details at the Union Stock Yards and continued in command thereafter until the end of the strike.

And now comes the saddest tale of all to record, the death of Officer William Feeley, who on the night of July 31st was run over and instantly killed on the Grand Trunk tracks near Robey Street [Damen Avenue]. He was detailed with another officer to patrol the tracks from Ashland Avenue to the Panhandle crossing and rode on the trains when the opportunity was offered. It appears that he jumped off while the train was in motion, stumbled and fell across the adjoining tracks stunned. A few minutes later an east bound switch engine ran over and horribly mangled him. He was alive but unconscious when found and died soon after.

From the commencement of the strike, exaggerated reports of intimidation, pin pulling, switch throwing, and assaults made by timid railway employees and officials poured into the office with such frequency the two Desk Sergeants were kept busy attending to them. Complaints were frequently duplicated, the same case being reported by different persons from different locations.

New employees who succeeded the strikers charged every mishap resulting from their own inexperience to the strikers from the pulling out of a draw head, to the opening of a switch or the breaking of an imperfect coupling; these incidents of common occurrence in times of peace were invariably attributed to the malign work of strikers. Altogether 92 arrests were made for offenses connected with the strike, including riot, arson and malicious mischief. Great credit is due to the officers for their patience and endurance. From the necessity of keeping up the details day and night and of remaining on post until relieved, regardless of the length of time on duty; they worked from 13 to 18 hours each day according to the exigencies of the occasion. Men, who ordinarily lost time monthly by reason of sickness or other disability, animated by a worthy spirit, braced themselves up and performed their duties uncomplainingly to the end.

Respectfully submitted,

Francis O'Neill

Captain, Commanding 8th District

Complimentary and appreciative letters coming from the corporations interested, and various other sources, were most gratifying. More than that, special writers blazoned our deeds on the front pages of the press with pictures of the commanding officers and several heroic patrolmen. Considering the forceful methods which the police were obliged to use in dispersing the crowds and suppressing violence, it was remarkable as an evidence of their self-control and moderation that no one was seriously injured in those conflicts.

CIVIL SERVICE EXAMINATION

The civil service law [Civil Service Act of 1883] being then in effect, an examination was held for an eligible list for captains. As a holdover captain I was not required to take an examination, but as an appointment or promotion under that law afforded protection against arbitrary reduction or dismissal, I took it. Imagine my delight on seeing my name at the top of the list of eligible candidates with an average of 99.80 to my credit, a record never since equaled at a promotional examination.

The spring election of 1895 landed the Republican candidate, George B. Swift, in the mayor's chair. He was known as the man who "did politics with an ax." Holdovers were apprehensive, for only those strongly identified with the party could hope to escape the carnage.

Alderman John J. Badenoch, prominent party leader, headed a delegation recommending Inspector Ross for general superintendent of police. Ross was a fine physical specimen of manhood. Mayor Swift was what is often referred to as a sawed-off. After listening to the litany of the candidate's perfections, the mayor with palm extended under his chin replied, "Yes, Ross is all right—from that down!" The upshot of it was that Alderman Badenoch himself was tendered and accepted the office. The slate makers got busy, and as usual, the victors claimed the spoils. No new offices being created, vacancies had to be, and biennial struggle for retention and promotion in the police department was renewed.

With neither political nor social support, the outlook for me was by no means encouraging. On their own initiative, corporations upheld my record, and it developed that Warden S. Minkler, onetime chief clerk of the police department, but now Mayor Swift's private secretary, was a loyal friend. He had not forgotten the kindly consideration shown him in the days gone by.

In Chief Badenoch's general order reorganizing the police department, seven of the fourteen captains then in the service were forced out. Fortunately, I was not one of them.

ARRESTED TWO ALDERMEN

That the unexpected happens was well exemplified in my experience a few months later. After seeing an out-of-town visitor on a train, I stood waiting for a streetcar at the corner of Madison and Wabash when I was shouldered off my feet by a large man coming up behind me. I was in full police uniform and facing the giant exclaimed, "What do you mean?" Instead of explaining,

STRIKE AN OFFICER

Aldermen Lammers and Haas Mix with Captain O'Neill.

BOTH ARE ARRESTED

Assault Committed at Madison Street and Wabash Avenue.

Policeman Waiting for a Car Gets in the Way of the Fifteenth Ward Representatives.

O'Neill's arrest of Republican aldermen Joseph A. Lammers and Joseph F. Haas in 1896 received widespread coverage in the Chicago press. Mary Lesch's grandmother, Julia O'Neill [Mooney], was with her father when the aldermen shoved O'Neill out of their way. Julia O'Neill, a pretty young lady, was just sixteen years old. (Chicago Inter Ocean, February 13, 1896) he swore at me and landed three blows before I disabled him with a strangle-hold. His companion, a much smaller man, announced that they were both aldermen. By this time a crowd had assembled, and I proposed to accompany them to city hall, but as my assailant continued to struggle and swear, the patrol wagon was called. When it arrived he was willing to walk. "You have had your chance to walk," I proclaimed, "you'll ride now!" With both aldermen I rode to the Harrison Street Police Station, where they were duly booked like ordinary prisoners. I must add that I called on the smaller man to assist me instead of interfering by pulling his companion away from me.

This was one of the momentous incidents of my police career. Here were two Republican aldermen, both prominent leaders, arrested and taken in a patrol wagon to a police station by a Democratic captain of police. Nothing short of decapitation could atone for such indignity. It was the sensation of the hour; the press featured it, and the popular verdict was much in my favor.

APPLAUSE FOR CAPTAIN O'NEILL.

Receives Letters Approving His Action in Arresting Aldermen.

Captain O'Neill of the stock yards police station, whose fight on Madison street with Aldermen Lammers and Haas caused a sensation at the time for the reason that the aldermen were taken to the Harrison street station, is the recipient these days of many compliments because of his action. The compliments are in the form of letters, and they come from nearly every place.

Professors of the Chicago University, Judges of the courts, bankers and packers have written him commending him for his action, and wishing him good luck at the trial, which will come up in a few days.

Chicagoans praised O'Neill's booking of Alderman Lammers and Alderman Haas as "ordinary criminals" and voted Lammers out of office in April 1896. (Chicago Inter Ocean, February 19, 1896)

The irate aldermen, out on bail, reached Chief Badenoch at a banquet and demanded my head. Instead of complying, he explained that as alderman he had known me for years as an intelligent, coolheaded man, adding to their discomfiture by saying, "Captain O'Neill has good fighting blood in him." Of course that didn't end it. Calling me to his office a few days later, Chief Badenoch informed me that as strong pressure was being brought to bear on His Honor, Mayor Swift, it would be advisable to drop the case. That politically it would be, I well knew, but it would also brand me as a moral coward. Putting the problem before the chief in another light, I said, "Pardon me for reminding you that I am not the lone complainant in this case, I am also the officer who made the arrest, and according to the Book of Rules, I am obliged to be present in court when the case is called. Otherwise my failure to appear will bring disgrace on the police department." Bristling, he exclaimed, "By God, I don't want you to do that." "This I can do," I ventured to suggest. "I will not press the case, and will abide by any disposition the judge at the Harrison Street Court may make of it." This was accepted as the best way out of the dilemma. After several continuances the belligerent alderman pleaded guilty and was assessed a fine of ten dollars and cost. Be it remembered that the police magistrate, holding an appointive office, was enmeshed in a predicament no less serious than mine. Had not the press and public supported my action, there would have been another vacancy for ravenous politicians to scramble over.

A MISUNDERSTANDING WITH ASSISTANT CHIEF ALEXANDER ROSS

A rather absurd complication arose on another occasion owing to the regular appointment of a poundkeeper for the Stock Yards territory. The appointee reported to me with credentials in which there was no mention of the man whose place he was to take. Twice I failed to connect with the chief at his office. Next day monthly time rolls were due. The new poundkeeper was properly accredited thereon, and so was his predecessor as patrolman, the latter having previously been one. Notations to that effect were appended in red ink. All of this was explained to the inspector who took the rolls with the others to Assistant Chief Ross for auditing. Not relying on the inspector's assurance that he would explain everything, I headed for city hall and met the assistant chief at the entrance. He was in a towering rage and ordered me into his office. I told him I had come purposely to see him. He accused me of attempting to steal a Democrat into the department and that I was too intelligent a man to make such a blunder. I retaliated by telling him he was too intelligent to overlook my notations in red ink written for his information. His repeated question, "What did the inspector say about this?" convinced me that the inspector was at the bottom of the trouble. "Why didn't you call me up?" he shouted over and over again. "What am I here for?" The answer nearly choked him: "You are here to fulfill the duties of your office as prescribed in the Book of Rules. The power to appoint or dismiss abides in the General Superintendent only. In his absence from the city or his inability to act, that power is conferred on you, not otherwise." "Come with me to the chief's office," he commanded.

This order was very welcome, so up we went. Chief Badenoch, it appeared, was prepared for us. He dismissed the subject lightly with the advice to me to keep calling up until answered, as he finished up everything daily before leaving his office. It turned out later that the complication or informality had its origin in the desire of the chief to oblige his friend, Alderman Tom Carey, by retaining the old poundkeeper in the service, but the blundering protest of Ross aborted the scheme. In fact, Tom Carey came out of Chief Badenoch's office as Ross and I entered.

DEFIANT SALOONKEEPERS

In the Stock Yards District, peopled by thousands hailing from all European countries, and who cherish and practice the customs and even prejudices of their ancestry, some turbulence with occasional bloodletting was inevitable. The police, however, proved competent to handle such matters; the only difficulty being to regulate or control a few saloons whose proprietors, fortified by political and high police influence, disregarded all restraint. In spite of the combined influence, the chief offenders were obliged to move out of the district.

One saloon adjoining our neighbors, the fire department, enjoyed the patronage of the police court assemblage, and a rear exit from the patrol barn led directly to the back door of the saloon, obligingly innocent of bar or locks at all hours. All law and restraint being openly flouted, I addressed a written report of the conditions to the general superintendent with a recommendation that saloon license be revoked. This, with other documents, was sent according to routine by messenger to the police inspector at Hyde Park for transmission to police headquarters. Nothing happened, but a week later a liquor agent confided to our license officer that my orders meant nothing to

them. Everything could be fixed at Hyde Park, where any adverse report of mine was pigeonholed.

A challenge such as that could not be ignored, and as there was another road to city hall besides the Hyde Park route, I made out another similar report and sent it by special messenger direct to the office of the general superintendent. The saloon license was promptly revoked, and prestige of long-continued immunity from police interference was shattered at last.

The brewery which supplied the beer it seemed had been a liberal contributor to the administration campaign fund. Through that and other influences the license was restored in a week, but the proprietor was required to apologize to me publicly in the squad room for his offensive remarks before he could open the doors for business.

PICKPOCKETS LANDED AT THE BRIDEWELL

One Sunday evening a gang of veteran pickpockets invaded the streetcars which stopped to take on passengers opposite the entrance to Oswald's Gardens on South Halsted near Fifty-second Street. A police detail ordered to the scene captured four of them busily crushing through the crowds. An arrest to them was but an incidental annoyance. When brought to the police station, the leader sneeringly told me they would be free within twenty-four hours, in spite of anything I could do to punish them. Why not be sensible and fix it up, as was done at other places? "It may be so that I can't send you to the House of Correction," I remarked, "but, I'll try."

When the case was called in court the next morning, the fines of one hundred dollars and costs, each, did not disconcert them at all. Requesting that mittimuses be made out at once, I ordered the officers on the patrol wagon to take the pickpockets to the House of Correction or Bridewell direct, instead of to the Maxwell Street Station as was customary. Anticipating a call from city hall, I relieved the desk sergeant from duty and took his place at the phone myself. Within minutes the call came announcing "This is the city attorney speaking." "I can't get you," I replied, "speak a little louder," and so on with variations. From experience I knew what he wanted to tell was the suspension of the fines of the pickpockets, and although I was aware of the fact that the city attorney had no legal right to suspend fines, I did not care to antagonize him. Had the pickpockets been left at Maxwell Street to be picked up later by the Bridewell bus from the Harrison Street Station, the city attorney could have liberated them there. Once in the Bridewell, they were beyond his assumed jurisdiction and the arrangement hitherto found reliable failed in this case.

Without multiplying instances of this nature, it may be stated that law-breakers cannot successfully defy the police. The officer in command of a police district, if determined to exercise power with which he is invested, can overcome obstacles, but in doing so he is sure to incur hostility and invite transfers, which were abundantly mine for seven adventurous years.

THE GREAT RAILWAY OR DEBS'S STRIKE

As captain in command of the Stock Yards District, I was soon saddled with responsibility. The great railway or Debs's strike, of which this district was the vortex, broke on the second day of July [1894]. Realizing the serious-ness of the situation, I took personal command day and night for six weeks, sleeping on a mattress in the attic of the station for a time, so that police reserves could be housed. As the small reinforcement sent from Hyde Park was promptly withdrawn twice, it became evident that no dependable co-operation could be expected from that source. A personal interview with Chief Brennan solved the problem. Reinforcements from the Central, East Chicago Avenue, and Desplaines Street stations were sent to me to remain as long as necessary.

Regardless of what I endured at that time, I ordered an escort of police for the Ross funeral long after he had left the service and when I held a higher rank than he ever attained; all of which goes to show that Mayor Swift was a good judge of human nature.

The election of Carter H. Harrison II to the mayoralty in 1897 placed the Democratic Party again in the saddle, and after a reign of two years, Chief Badenoch was succeeded by Joseph Kipley, an experienced officer. Embit-tered by his forced retirement before his years of service entitled him to a pension in the Swift administration, Chief Kipley paid his enemies back in their own coin.

A NEW DEPARTURE IN POLICE PROMOTION

In his reorganization of the police force, new departure was made in the appointing of two lieutenants and one sergeant as inspectors in the three principal police divisions, on the claim that they were heads of departments and not subject to civil service jurisdiction. Only captains would have been eligible if a promotional examination had been held.

This scheme no doubt originated in the fertile brain of Robert E. Burke, president of the Cook County Democracy, then the dispenser of patronage in the new administration. The legality of those appointments was questioned in the courts, so a new way of circumventing the spirit of the civil service law was devised. An original examination open to all applicants was announced. As the motives for this unusual proceeding, though legal, were well understood, very few registered. When asked why I hadn't done so, I explained that the examination was evidently "framed" for the benefit of those recently appointed, and moreover I didn't like to be humiliated by having my name appear below theirs on the eligible list. "You take the examination," advised my questioner, the respected Father Ed Kelly. "The farther down your name is, the more it will emphasize the farcical nature of the examination." My anticipations were realized; I was fifth on the list. The test questions were but two: "What languages do you speak besides English?" And "What experience have you had for the position to which you aspire?" One of the elect spoke German and had two years' experience; another spoke German, Polish, and Bohemian and had one year experience; the other favorite spoke only English but had three years' experience. A fourth spoke German but had no experience. With an allowance of five points for each extra language and five points for each year of experience, the scheme as planned was obviously successful. My name followed those of the linguists on the posted eligible list. It may be pertinent to add here that eventually the Illinois Supreme Court decided against their claim to office.

Soon after Joseph Kipley's reappointment as general superintendent of police in 1899, the first chief to be so honored, I found myself unexpectedly transferred from the Stock Yard to the Second or Harrison Street Police District. Political influence had so undermined police discipline that the authority of the chief was openly flouted by commanders strongly entrenched in political backing. This district, in which I found myself ostracized, was a maelstrom of iniquity. Crime was organized, syndicated, and protected. Panel houses, hopjoints, and confidence games flourished, and the price according to schedule. All local sources of information were closed against me. In this conspiracy of silence, all beneficiaries of the system, politicians, police courts, and police, were equally involved, and it was confidently believed that my stay would be brief. The practice of personally scouting around at all hours, picking up a little information on the way, and persistent action, brought increasingly good results.

OFFERED A SHARE IN THE RING

One night a well-known politician unable to effect my transfer quietly slipped into my office to remonstrate with me. He proposed that if I wouldn't be so rough, I would be taken care of like the others.

"You know that I was brought down here and given my orders," I remarked. "Do you think I can dawdle around this station and allow panel-house women and confidence men to carry on their operations unmolested?"

"Why, Captain, that's all right," came the soothing reply. "You can make all the pinches you want to. We will take care of them in police court, but for God's sake don't send them over to that son of a b____ on the North Side."

This expression had reference to my practice of sending a personal letter with the arresting officer, accompanied by the complaint, to the state's attorney's office in the criminal court building beyond the Chicago River, when I found there was no chance of obtaining justice in the police courts.

Continuances and changes of venue could be had by the defendant or criminal ad libitum. The victim robbed of all or most of his money could not remain in town long enough to prosecute. Both courts were held in the police station, and as both justices were in the combine, a change of venue was a mere delusion. In routine arrests of lewd women a much simpler arrangement was quite effective. All that was necessary was to casually meet the magistrate on his way to the police station from the street car and salute him with a handshake and leave a nicely folded five, ten, or twenty-dollar bill in his receptive palm.

A detailed volume of my experience in the Harrison Street Police District in those days might well be named "Hell with the Lid Off."

There came a day when political expediency necessitated my transfer. In Mayor Harrison's fight against the so-called Yerkes' Franchise, the support of a majority of the city council was indispensable. My transfer was the price of two essential votes, but it took eleven months of unremitting effort to accomplish it.

A PANEL-HOUSE ROBBERY

Another whirl of the wheel brought me back for four months at a later day, when an arrest of consequence brought me into sudden prominence again.

A mule buyer for the British government, while spending a few hours between trains on State Street, was inveigled into a panel house and robbed
of a wallet containing five thousand-dollar bills, twenty hundred-dollar bills,
and some change. This was a big "trick" and the customary detail from the
inspector's office went to work on it. A telephone call from a friendly sergeant
located over seven miles away led to our meeting at midnight in a secluded
place. It appeared the woman accomplice who sneaked the wallet through a
secret panel of the room in which the victim was being entertained rushed
into the madam or keeper's room and throwing the money on the table exclaimed, "Gee, see what I got off of a farmer." A dressmaker who happened
to be present was so excited by the sight of the money that she hastened to
tell her boyfriend, who in turn conveyed his information to the sergeant.

Next morning, I quietly instructed two plainclothesmen to bring me
the madam. Anticipating interference, when I heard pounding on the office
door for admittance, I stood the madam in a corner, fully hidden, when I
swung the door wide open to admit my impatient callers, the inspector and a
police court attorney. Surprised at finding me alone, as they supposed, they
made some irrelevant remarks and withdrew, but their motives were well
understood. To cut the story short, after an hour's interview I accompanied
the woman to her room to get her keys—keeping in actual touch with her
all the time—and from thence on foot to the Masonic Temple Safety Vaults
to get the money. With the madam and the money I proceeded to Chief
Kipley's office. The chief and Mayor Harrison had been keenly interested
in the solution of this sensational crime. Both the madam and keeper of the
panel house and the woman lure were promptly indicted but never punished. The complainant came four times to Chicago from Syracuse, New
York, to testify. The keeper's case was called, postponed, and forgotten. The
actual thief, after a little wordy fencing among the attorneys, pleaded guilty
but was never sentenced. The oft-repeated question "Why don't the police
drive the thieves out of town?" could not be answered on a page, much less
in a paragraph.

FREQUENTLY TRANSFERRED

Many transfers to and from police districts far apart followed. In fact, I had
been transferred seven times in the two years preceding my unexpected appointment as general superintendent. Some of these transfers were made for
the betterment of the services; others were sacrifices to political expediency.

At no time were they an indication of the mayor's or chief's displeasure as far as I was concerned.

No office in the administration of Mayor Harrison on his reelection to a third term in 1901 was more discussed or sought than that of general superintendent of police to succeed Joseph Kipley, who had resigned.

UNEXPECTED APPOINTMENT AS GENERAL SUPERINTENDENT

Imagine my surprise, on returning from a Sunday trip to Palos Park, to find a sealed letter—delivered by messenger—from His Honor the mayor instructing me to be at his office at 5:00 P.M. Monday, April 30, 1901, with bonds for office of general superintendent of police. This indeed was an instance of the dark horse winning, for I was not even a candidate.

CHANCE FOR A RUMMAGE SALE.

CHIEF OF POLICE O'NEILL FINDS THAT THE LAST TENANT LEFT THE USUAL AMOUNT OF RUBBISH.

Chicago Daily News *cartoonist Luther Daniels Bradley (1853–1917) depicted the newly appointed Superintendent of Police O'Neill rolling up his shirtsleeves to attack Chicago corruption, especially its gambling resorts and illegal saloons known as "blind pigs."* (Chicago Daily News, May 1, 1901)

experience as a desirable asset in my office. His impatience led him to call on me one day a month or so later to remind me of my promise, and he left in high glee when told that his transfer, among others, would be issued in a few days.

That evening the head of a detective agency—a former inspector of police —invited me by phone to call on him at his home, which was within walking distance of mine. After some casual conversation he inquired if I intended to transfer this inherited so-called secretary to police headquarters. When told that such was my intention, he blurted out, "Don't you do it, he will burn you up. When he left your office today, he made the rounds of the clubs in the downtown district to notify them of his position in the chief's office."

This efficient "confidential man" of the former administration didn't even wait for the transfer to take effect before commencing the customary

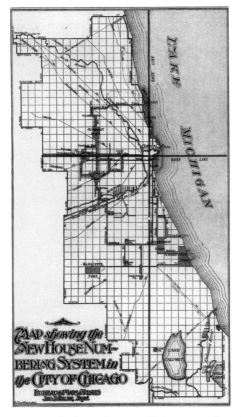

This 1910 map of Chicago, created for the new house numbering system, shows the scope of the city as it was in O'Neill's era. (Chicago Public Library, Municipal Reference Collection)

proceedings. He was transferred all right, according to expectation, but not to police headquarters, to which he aspired. Had I not been forewarned, this experienced whilom secretary would have involved my reputation, and but few would believe that I wasn't aware of his activities.

A CALL FROM A TAX FIXER

The financial tangle arising from the reassessment of all real estate in Chicago and Cook County in the years 1929–30 by the Illinois State Tax Commission brings to mind an incident which goes to show that the gentle art of "tax fixing" is by no means a modern enterprise.

An efficient young ward politician in high favor with the state's attorney and then employed in the assessor's office came to my office shortly after I became chief of police and asked for my tax books, so that he could fix my taxes for me. When told that my assessment was satisfactory and required no readjustment, he left abruptly. He exploded to an acquaintance in the outer office, "What do you think of that blankety-blank imbecile in there? By hell, he won't even let me fix his taxes for him!"

Soon, news came of a gambling house started across the street from Buffalo Bill's Wild West Show at Comiskey's Baseball Park. My wrecking crew promptly attended to that. Disregarding the protests and remonstrances of my tax-fixing friend, the police demolished the gambling furniture on the sidewalk. One eyewitness ruefully remarked, "I guess we gave our money to the wrong man."

AN AMBITIOUS VISITOR

Of all the persistent processions of people to police headquarters who desire to see the chief personally, none was so well remembered as the visit of an old man who, with an ingratiating smile, congratulated me like an old acquaintance. He announced that he had worked for my father on the farm in my childhood days. His name was Michael Muhir but admitted that it had been changed to Moore in this country. After telling me of his success and prosperity, owning two dairy farms near Elgin some forty miles from Chicago, he confidentially explained the object of his call. He had been a citizen and a voter for many long years and never held nor sought an office. Neither did he want one then, but he had a son-in-law who had ambition, and now that the son of his old employer was in power, was this the time to gratify it? When I inquired what he expected me to do for him, he calmly replied that the position which most appealed to him and his ambitious son-in-law was commissioner of public works!

The son-in-law was a Republican, but liberal. He would, of course, vote for and support Mayor Harrison if appointed. A word from a man of my influence, so close to the mayor, would no doubt secure the coveted position. Vain hope.

After all, Mike Muhir or Moore was but an extreme type of the many whom on every change of administration clamor for favors and positions. To paraphrase the Gospel, many are called, but few are chosen, and it is but a brief step from congratulations to denunciations, as everyone in authority will testify.

POLICE REORGANIZATION

The customary reorganization of the police force at every change of administration, which was in many ways a demoralization, was dispensed with. Weeks of uncertainty awaiting the framing of a slate and the issuance of the "Big Order" cannot be otherwise than detrimental to police efficiency. From long service and association I knew the rank and file as few knew them. Transfer from one command to another was no cure for incompetence. In my experience from the bottom to the top of the service, the Chicago police force could be relied upon to carry out all orders and instructions, earnestly issued, if upheld and supported by the general superintendent.

For once there was no politics in the police department, but there was discipline. The customary reorganization was omitted, but I was confronted with the unpleasant duty of filing charges against the chief of detectives, based on sensational accusations published in the *Chicago Tribune*. The panel houses had been practically suppressed, but gangs of confidence men and safe blowers were still operating. Their suppression was easily accomplished. Calling into the private office two men of the Detective Bureau, whom I knew had been detailed on confidence men, I inquired how many they had sent to the penitentiary in the last year. "Not any" was the answer. They were told that I had ideas of my own on this subject, but as they were already on that detail they would get two weeks to show what they could do. The senior lieutenant in the Detective Bureau was next summoned to an interview. His attention being called to the prevalence of safe blowing, he assured me that he would have the safe blowers under arrest shortly. "I am pleased to hear you say that," I remarked, "because that will belie those who told me you were in league with them." No arrests followed, but the safe blowers sought safer quarters in which to operate. The confidence men were warned that "the new chief won't stand for anything," so they too left town, there being no reliable protection available in this new order of things.

HABEAS CORPUS WRITS

A Kansas sheriff, in pursuit of a fugitive from justice, arrived in the city one morning, fully equipped with documents and requisition papers. The fugitive, picked up in a barroom, was no sooner brought into the Detective Bureau than an attorney appeared and informed officers that he would apply for a writ of habeas corpus. When brought to my attention, I ordered the prisoner turned over to the sheriff, with the advice that he drive around the outskirts of the city until such time as he could take the train at the first station beyond the city limits.

The writ was issued, and the officers were ordered by the court to produce their prisoner in court the next morning or be jailed themselves. On explaining their predicament to me, I replied, "All right, go to jail, you'll be taken care of. I'll fight this case out in the public press, and abide the consequences." Next morning the sheriff with his fugitive was already in Kansas, and the court, or judge, declined to accept the challenge.

In another case of earlier date, a fugitive from justice was taken into custody on the strength of a telegram from the chief of police of Portland, Oregon. When the case came up in court, on a writ of habeas corpus, the judge, disregarding the statement of the police that a messenger with the requisition papers was on his way from Oregon, not only freed the fugitive but made out bench warrants for the officers on the charge of false arrest. I personally signed their bonds. When the case was called in court next day, the messenger was on hand, but the fugitive and complainant against the police were not. From the police point of view, the high-handed action of Judge Altgeld was a clear case of obstructing justice.

EMMA GOLDMAN'S ARREST

The [attack that led to the] assassination of President McKinley on [September 6, 1901,] at Buffalo, New York, stampeded scores of leading anarchists from that city at once. Among the seven taken into custody by the Chicago

Police was a Russian doctor, an intimate friend of Emma Goldman, on his way back to San Francisco, California. Miss Goldman made her way to St. Louis, Missouri, and back to Belleville, Illinois. From a member of an anarchist group on my Secret Service roll, it was learned that she was corresponding with friends in Chicago. This information was turned over to Colonel Stuart, chief of the federal Secret Service in this district.

On the date and hour of her arrival in the city, obtained from the same source, two men of the Detective Bureau, armed with her picture and description, were stationed at the railway station to take her into custody. So well was she disguised as a little old farm woman with a shawl on her head and a basket of vegetables on her arm that she passed out of the Polk Street

Emma Goldman (1869–1940) was arrested in Chicago on September 11, 1901. Because Goldman was an anarchist, she was held for questioning before she fulfilled her plans to travel to Canada. There had been a rumor of a conspiracy being planned in Chicago to assassinate President McKinley. O'Neill questioned Goldman, determined she was not part of a conspiracy, and subsequently released her. (Chicago Public Library, Special Collections and Preservation Division)

Depot unrecognized and into a buggy which awaited her around the corner on Clark Street.

A week later my Secret Service man rushed into the office shortly after noon, when all but a clerk were out to lunch, with the information that the elusive Emma Goldman was then in an apartment on the North Side all ready for travel and awaiting the return of an English friend who had gone out to purchase railway tickets to Canada. Assistant Superintendent Herman Schuettler and Detective Charles Herts, the first officers to come in, hastened over to the address, which by the way was but a few doors from the home of the chief of detectives. As the doorbell brought no response, they gained admittance to the adjoining house from which they could see Miss Goldman through windows on the same level, all dressed up and ready to leave. Imagine the slim Herts, supported by the Herculean Schuettler, bridging the space between the buildings, lifting a sash, and paying an un-welcome visit to the "Lady in Waiting" within.

Quite consistently Emma Goldman denounced the police and volu-bly expressed her contempt for both law and officials yet entertained some respect for intelligence and courteous treatment at police headquarters. There being no evidence of their complicity in the assassination, all seven in custody were liberated.

PRESIDENT ROOSEVELT'S VISIT TO CHICAGO

When President Roosevelt visited Chicago the next year [on April 2, 1903], no precaution for his safety was overlooked. Independent of the uniformed guards, a detail of detectives specially selected for their fine physical appearance, and garbed in high hats and appropriate dress, accompanied him everywhere. At the Auditorium banquet, the chief federal official of the president's entourage objected to the presence of the detectives in the banquet hall as he and his staff would be all that was necessary. To this, I replied that notwithstanding his assurance, no one could relieve me of my responsibility as general superintendent of police of the city, in view of the assassination of President McKinley at Buffalo. The detail would be main-tained while the president remained in our jurisdiction.

On his way back to Washington from a trip to the Pacific coast, President Roosevelt transferred to an eastern train at Aurora, Illinois, and of course was greeted by enthusiastic crowds. Complying with the request of the chief of police of the city for aid in the emergency, a company of Chicago police

Upper left: Badges with ribbons were a familiar note of honor for dignitaries of all orders when they were celebrating an event. O'Neill wore this badge when President Theodore Roosevelt visited Chicago on April 2, 1903. (Photograph by Jennifer Riforgiate; Mary Lesch collection)

Upper right: Chicago celebrated its centennial on September 26 through October 1, 1903, and O'Neill wore this badge to honor the event. (Photograph by Jennifer Riforgiate; Mary Lesch collection)

Lower left: O'Neill served on the Ways and Means Committee for the Autumn Festival in Chicago in 1899. The badge may have served as a ticket for admission to the festivities. (Photograph by Jennifer Riforgiate; Mary Lesch collection.)

Chicago's Irish Nationalists sponsored two competing events on August 15, 1902, giving new meaning to Finley Peter Dunne's sarcastic observation that "if Ireland cud be freed be a picnic, it'd . . . be an impire." Chief O'Neill joined the crowd at Sunnyside Park on the North Side in support of John Redmond's fight for Ireland "in the halls of Parliament" as well as the movement to "revive Ireland's ancient language and literature." On the South Side, 3,000 Irish gathered at Oswald's Grove to advocate physical force in the campaign to free Ireland from British rule. (Photograph by Jennifer Riforgiate; Mary Lesch collection)

from the traffic squad led by a lieutenant and sergeant were sent. All of them six feet tall or more and weighing not less than two hundred pounds, their appearance in the parade vied with the president in public acclaim.

PRINCE HENRY'S VISIT

Police efficiency was strained to the utmost while Prince Henry of Prussia, the kaiser's brother, was in Chicago March 1902. Besides guarding the Auditorium and vicinity, the entire route from the hotel to Lincoln Park, where the prince laid a wreath on Lincoln's monument, was policed, as well as the route from Germania Hall to the Union Station, where his party entrained for departure from the city.

TAKING THE POLICE OUT OF POLITICS

Not long after this I lunched at the City Club on the invitation of attorney Walter L. Fisher, later secretary of the interior, and, of course, was subjected to many inquiries concerning police affairs. To the suggestion that I talk to the audience first in my own way, they readily agreed. The following is the substance of my address:

> In every mayoral campaign no assurance of reform is so empha-
> sized as the promise to take the police force out of politics, and
> this they invariably do, to the extent of taking the other fellows
> out and putting in their own. A new administration, like a new
> manager in a commercial house, loses no time before taking
> stock. The appointment of a new chief of police or general super-
> intendent is inevitable. Then all ranks from the chief down to
> and including sergeants are classified and listed. After each name
> in appropriate columns are remarks: rank—when promoted—
> by whom—attitude last election—advancement—retains rank—

The official portrait of O'Neill as superintendent of police appeared in many of his books on Irish music. While this photo was not dated, he was appointed superintendent four months before his fifty-third birthday, so he was probably fifty-three years old. (Mary Lesch collection)

reduction—discharge. Occasionally a few slated for discharge or reductions in rank are saved by powerful influences, thereby reducing the vacancies to be filled by friends of the elect. I remember an occasion when the slate was ready for a general order; some lieutenant had to be sacrificed to create a vacancy for the friend of an insistent politician. The method of selecting a victim is similar to that of a steer seeking a weak spot in a fence between him and a clover field. When found, power will force an opening. In this instance, Lieutenant Anson S. Backus, a well-educated American with clear record and no pronounced politics, was the victim. Ineligible for pension on account of age and length of service, Lieutenant Backus peddled cigars for a living until he was reinstated in the next administration.

"What asses we have been," remarked Victor F. Lawson, publisher of the *Chicago Daily News*, who had been an attentive listener to the process by which the Chicago police force is "taken out of politics." The relatively few so-called native Americans connected with the Chicago police force is due not to prejudice or discrimination but to the fact that the strenuous, hazardous life of a policeman, in this or any other city, has no attraction for an American with brains or business capacity, and it is only when he is unsuccessful in other walks of life that his friends plant him on the police rolls. Men of that caliber, though seldom conspicuous for ability in the police department, are favored with more than ordinary consideration. About 65 percent of police membership in Chicago is of Irish ancestry, and the majority of those are natives of Illinois and contiguous states.

It so happened that I fell heir to the Kellogg Switchboard strike, in progress for some time before my appointment as chief of police, and the responsibilities inseparable from that and others during my incumbency.

CHICAGO CITY RAILWAY STRIKE

The tie-up of the Chicago city railway lines in the south division of the city was broken in eleven days, but not before half a dozen members of the police detail had been suspended from duty. Influenced no doubt by friendship for organized labor, a few exercised no vigilance in preventing obstruction being placed on the car tracks. After one line had resumed its runs, protected by police stationed at intervals along the route, another line was started, and

This plain star is an example of the type of stars the police used in the nineteenth century. Its simplicity prompted O'Neill to design a new star that would be more difficult to counterfeit or alter. (Photograph by Jennifer Riforgiate; Mary Lesch collection)

O'Neill carried a dress baton on formal occasions and when he marched in a parade. (Photograph by Jennifer Riforgiate; Mary Lesch collection)

so on to the end. A siege of the company's shops and offices was relieved, in spite of determined opposition by strikers and sympathizers. The details of how the strike or blockade was overcome on different routes, one at a time, would be too much of an infliction on a reader or listener at this late day— twenty-eight years after their occurrences. There followed a strike of three months' duration in the packinghouse district of the Union Stock Yards. Minor labor troubles, as well as prolonged strikes, required so many men for special details that but few were available for patrol duty.

COMMITTEE OF CITY COUNCIL INVESTIGATING CITY HALL

Rumors of brewing trouble and impending disclosures brought on the appointment of a committee of eleven aldermen to investigate all departments of the city's service. Inevitably the police department became the main target, although the fire department came in for a share of it this time. Only that in which the present writer figured will be discussed here. Several days of each week and occasionally twice in one day, for two months, I was called before the committee to answer offhand questions propounded by Brode Davis, a fifty-dollar-a-day attorney representing the Citizens Association. Reading from his notes, Attorney Davis badgered me about the number of burglaries and few arrests reported from a certain police district in the northwestern part of the city, specifying a month in the previous year. I admitted it was a poor record for the police department. Worrying over this accusation at night, it occurred to me to examine the patrol sheets next morning. My relief could be imagined on finding that all patrolmen but two—one for day and one for night duty—were detailed at strikes during the entire month in question. I was permitted to testify again, and on evidence of the patrol sheets, which I presented for inspection, the bottom fell out of the attorney's trap.

*O'Neill's attention to detail enabled him to challenge Brode Bradford Davis, "a fifty-dollar-a-day attorney" who investigated alleged police graft during a city council probe sparked by the Citizens Association. The chief discovered that far from being delinquent in their duty, patrolmen reassigned to strike duty accounted for the decrease in neighborhood arrests in 1903. (*The Book of Chicago *[Chicago: Chicago Evening Post, 1911])*

The following letter was a copy of the most specific of several confidential communications received at this time. What language can adequately characterize such villainy?

Chicago, December 18, 1903
Honorable Francis O'Neill
Chief of Police—Chicago

Dear Sir:
As an act of simple justice I deem it an obligation I owe myself and you to say that I was approached some time ago by a man whom I have know for years as H___t K___g for the purpose of prevailing upon me to give him a clue to some one who had a grievance against you and who had no conscientious scruples about blackening your character to such an extent as to force your resignation. I told him though I knew you by reputation for years though not personally acquainted with you; still I never heard anything to your disparagement. He offered me money if I would help him to put up some job on you. He told me if I would set him on the track of some one of your former enemies who would have no hesitation in swearing your life away he would give me one hundred dollars. He told me if I would get one of those gamblers with whom I sometimes associate to do the job of forcing you from your position under a cloud he would give me five hundred dollars. And he said furthermore if I would make him acquainted with a very clever man whom I know and who would be able to stand a rigid examination before the graft committee and who would testify to facts against you which he would give him in writing, that he (H__t K__g) would give him two thousand dollars that would take him out of misery and enable him to go to some country, preferably to Europe. I refused to enter into Mr. H__t K__g's conspiracy against you and told him if he persisted in his crusade of moral assassination against you I would go to you and give the whole thing away and I would have done so but I was afraid I would have to appear before the Graft Committee. I don't want notoriety of any kind so I abandoned the idea of telling you about this foul conspiracy lest my testimony would be published in the papers and it would give

mortal offense to my wife and family who have no love for noto-riety. K__g placed me under injunctions of the strictest secrecy and threatened me with violence if I made disclosures. Of course I took the hint considering the fact that H__t K__g could hire men like the car barn bandits to assassinate both you and myself. And permit me to advise you in conclusion to be careful for I judge from his pent-up animosity towards you that he would not hesitate to have you assassinated if he could down you by no other means.

George Thorndyke

A friendly alderman, unrelated by race or creed, privately sent word that no evidence reflecting on my integrity had come before the committee. This relieved the tension, yet the malice betrayed by Attorney Davis was, to say the least, disquieting. I requested the messenger to ask the alderman why I was being subjected to such persecution. "Tell the chief," came the reply, "I know of no reason except that his name is O'Neill."

PICKETING A HOTEL

A hotel of rather shady reputation, patronized almost exclusively by transients, had existed for years in the business district in the heart of the city. Court proceedings instituted by attorneys representing Montgomery Ward and Company failed to accomplish their object; for although damaging evidence had been presented by the prosecution, the defense proved that reputable patrons including clergymen were also enrolled on the hotel register.

The managing editor of the *Chicago Daily News* inquired of me one day if nothing could be done by the police to close up that obnoxious hotel. "Evidently not by legal means," I replied, referring to the lawsuit mentioned previously, "but I have in mind another resource that may have some effect."

With the approval of the mayor, I instructed the captain in command of the First District to assign a discreet officer in uniform in front of this hotel. When questionable couples approached to enter, he was to glance at them and pretend to make a notation in his memorandum book. This detail was to cover from noon until four o'clock next morning and to continue until further orders.

The day preceding the mayor's departure from the city for his summer vacation in northern Michigan I consulted him in regard to the continuance of this detail.

"Why do you ask me?" he inquired.

"Because any change of that nature I make during your absence," I replied, "will subject me to criticism."

"I hadn't thought of that, but what has been the result of your plan so far?"

"The patronage has fallen off one-half and relatively increased that of others," I told him.

"They have been taught a lesson at least," concluded the mayor. "You may discontinue the police detail." The captain was instructed accordingly.

An alert subordinate grasping the possibilities of this sudden decision lost no time in conveying the information to the party boss, a minor official whose intercession had so far proved unavailing. The party boss promptly sent for the hotel proprietor and suggested that before the mayor started on his vacation he may induce him to call off that crippling police detail. So together they went to city hall and, leaving the anxious hotel man in the lobby, the cabinet member (party boss) let himself in to the mayor's sanctum by a private door. Conventional greetings befitting the occasion were exchanged and, coming out smiling, the influential party boss assured the harassed hotel man that he had succeeded in his efforts and that the police detail would be discontinued at once. For this pretended service he received one thousand dollars, and the keen lieutenant did not go unrewarded either.

ADDRESSING CHIEFS OF POLICE CONVENTION

Conditions in Chicago, owing to strikes before and after my appointment as head of the police department, prevented my attendance at the annual convention of the [International Association of] Chiefs of Police in 1901. A letter from Chief Major Sylvester of Washington, D.C., president of the international organization, requested that I prepare an address on anarchy and anarchists for the next meeting, to be held May 1902 at Louisville, Kentucky. It would appear that the name and fame of the city of Chicago has been linked with that subject since the days of the Haymarket Riot, sixteen years before.

The address which follows was so well received that I was booked for another at the next meeting, the theme to be one of my own selection.

ADDRESS AT THE ANNUAL CONVENTION OF THE INTERNATIONAL ASSOCIATION
OF CHIEFS OF POLICE AT LOUISVILLE, KENTUCKY, MAY 1902, BY FRANCIS
O'NEILL, GENERAL SUPERINTENDENT OF POLICE OF CHICAGO: "ANARCHY
AND ANARCHISTS"

Mr. President and Gentlemen, Chiefs of Police in Convention:

When I received the letter from Major Sylvester, one of our members, a few weeks ago, asking me to prepare a paper on the history of anarchy in this country and abroad, I felt like forwarding my regrets and "taking to the tall timber" to avoid undertaking to write on such a formidable subject. However, being unwilling to shirk my duty, I endeavored to produce something which I venture to hope may be of interest to the honorable members of this convention.

Anarchy is a subject that has attracted the attention of deep thinkers for the past century. It has had able, although illogical advocates, whose teachings have led their deluded and impulsive disciples to assassinate not a few rulers and other persons in high station; yet, so far as I can see, the world is now no nearer an anarchistic state than it was in the days of Bakunin, Proudhon, and Marx, who were its greatest apostles. Hundreds of volumes have been written on the subject, and it would be presumptuous on my part to attempt to write a history of anarchy; and for that reason I wish to say that this is not a history but a brief synopsis of the movement. The members of this convention, I believe, do not care to listen to historical details, concerning the origin of anarchistic doctrines and I will, therefore, try to be as brief as the scope of the subject will permit.

What is anarchy? The *Century* dictionary defines it as "lack of a ruler or of government; a state of society in which there is no capable supreme power and in which the civil functions of the state are performed badly or not at all."

An anarchist is defined by the same work as "one who advocates anarchy, or the absence of government as a political ideal; a believer in anarchic theory of society; an adherent of the social theory of Proudhon; one who seeks to overturn by violence all constituted forms and institutions of society and government, of

law and order and rights of property, with no purpose of establishing any other system of order in the place of that destroyed."

Parsons, the American anarchist, who was convicted and
hanged for his connection with the bomb throwing at Criminal
Court, defined anarchy this way: "Anarchy is a free society where
there is no concentrated or centralized power; no state, no king,
no emperor, no ruler, no president, no magistrate, no potentate
of any character whatever. Law is the enslaving power of man.
Anarchy is the natural law instead of the man-made statute, and
gives men leaders in the place of drivers and bosses."

In the last century men of great talent and profound learning
espoused the cause of anarchy. Among them were Pierre-Joseph
Proudhon, a Frenchman; Karl Marx, a German; and Nicholas
Bakunin [Mikhail Bakunin], a Russian, who is recognized as
the father of Nihilism in Russia. Had these men devoted their
extraordinary talents to other lines of literary work and effort, they
would undoubtedly have accomplished great good for the world.
And yet it cannot be denied that there were causes in some of the
European countries that created a feeling of discontent with the
then existing conditions, for which the government was held to
be responsible by the poorer classes, or proletarians, as they were
referred to by revolutionary writers. The peasantry and laboring
classes had been oppressed for centuries and when they began to
learn their power from the reading of tracts and books written by
men of undoubted genius, they became fired with hatred toward
the rich and the form of government under which they lived. In
Germany, France, and Russia there were a great many leaders
who were prolific in writing inflammatory articles for the rabble,
and, as a natural consequence, the time came when anarchy
under the name of communism showed itself in a most terrible
form. I refer to the Commune of Paris in 1871, when the street ran
red with blood.

For some years prior to the Commune, Germany, realizing
the danger that was impending from the communistic propagan-
dists, who were liable to sap the very foundation of their government, made it so hot for the leaders of anarchy that many of them
fled to London and there found asylum. They continued to write

revolutionary articles that found their way to Germany through the medium of anarchistic newspapers, and although the leaders were banished from the country, they did practically as much harm as before. In 1878, after two attempts had been made upon the life of Germany's ruler, Emperor William, severe repressive measures against anarchists were instituted by that government.

England is really responsible for much of the strength shown in the conspiracy of anarchists against all governments, for London was the harbor of refuge in which the German anarchists thought out that speculative anarchy which finds its followers in almost every civilized country at the present time.

Robert Owen, an Englishman, wrote volumes and lectured on the subject of anarchy, calling it socialism in 1835, the name which was later adopted both in Germany and France. Owen, however, was not rabid in his utterances and was opposed to violent measures to attain the Utopia of which he dreamed. Being a man of broad views and moderate in his language, he accomplished some practical good in his lifetime.

The conditions which led up to the French Revolution, which drew a broad red line across the world's history, cannot very well be discussed in an article of this nature. It was an object lesson, showing the practical workings and result of anarchy.

Nicholas Bakunin [Mikhail Bakunin], the founder and most practical advocate of Nihilism, the name by which Russian anarchy is known, was the son of a noble Russian family. The origin of Nihilism was a social movement in Russia in opposition to the tyranny of custom, but later on the movement became an organized and secret effort on the part of a large number of malcontents to destroy the existing order of things. This movement originated about 1840.

Bakunin, who had received a military education, was piqued because he had been given an ordinary commission which sent him to a remote village district. After two years of disappointment and dreaming, he resigned and went to Moscow, where he joined a band of young men who made a study of German philosophy, which at that time was only another name for anarchy. Bakunin, who was more vigorous and radical than any of the others, assumed leadership of the circle which included some prominent men, among whom were Turgenieff [Turgenev], the great novelist, and Belinsky, the critic. Bakunin went to Berlin in 1841 to revel in his new philosophy among a circle of friends, who, like himself, were of strong revolutionary spirit. Later he visited several European cities, creating a disturbance wherever he went. After an exciting career he was banished to Siberia for life. Powerful influence assisted him to escape, and he secured the means of access to a vessel bound for London.

That an idea may be formed of what kind of a man Bakunin was, I will quote from one of his last speeches delivered in 1868. "Our first work," he said, "must be the destruction and annihilation of everything as it now exists. You must accustom yourselves to destroy everything, the good and the bad, for if but one atom of this old world remains, the new will never be created. According to the priests' fables in olden days a deluge destroyed all mankind, but God specially saved Noah that their seeds of tyranny and falsehood might be perpetuated in the new world. When you once begin your work of destruction and when the floods of enslaved masses of people arise and engulf the temples and palaces, then take care that no ark be allowed to rescue any atom of this world, which we now doom to destruction."

Proudhon, the French anarchist, made almost as startling a declaration when he exclaimed: "Government of man by man in every form is oppressive. The highest perfection of society is found in the union and order of anarchy." Born in 1809, he was really the father of French anarchy. In his great work, "What Is Property?" published in 1840, he declared that property was theft and property holders thieves. It is to this work that the whole school of anarchy in any of its forms can be traced. He was an ardent hater of the rich and unsparingly denounced property owners on all occasions. The importance of his work is shown by the effect which it has had upon even conventional political economy, and it is claimed that it was from this work that Karl Marx derived his inspiration.

The revolt of the Commune of Paris after the Franco-German War was not exactly an anarchist uprising, although the anarchists impressed their ideas upon much of the work done. At the present day there is no practical distinction between socialism and anarchy in France. All socialists are practically anarchists, although all anarchists are not precisely socialists.

The International Society, organized in 1864 by Karl Marx, who then lived in Germany, was responsible to a great extent for the seeds of anarchy which were planted in the United States. Anarchy as we know it in the United States is more nearly akin to Nihilism than to the doctrines extant in France. It is founded upon the teachings of Karl Marx and his disciples, and aims directly at the complete destruction of all forms of government and religion. The central council of the society was established in New York City by Marx in 1873, although he lived at that time in London. It was about this time, the year of the great panic, as you will remember, that anarchy began to rear its head in America. Owing to the depression of business all over the country, troubles followed as a natural consequence, and it was then that the apostles of Marx began to sow the seed of dissatisfaction and insurrection, which culminated in the Haymarket massacre in Chicago.

In the railroad strikes or riots in Pittsburgh in 1877 many deeds of violence, riot, and bloodshed were inspired by members of the International Society. A good-sized council of the society existed in Chicago at that time, and the members seized upon the opportunity to widen the breach between capital and labor. Men of foreign birth, employed in shops and factories, who had theretofore been content with their wage and hours were induced to join the society under the pretext that it was a labor organization. In some cases intimidation was resorted to. Leaders of the society made inflammatory speeches at meetings that were held nightly, seeking to excite the minds of the weaker ones to an open defiance of the law. These leaders were willing to furnish the ammunition, but they were looking for some poor weak-minded tool to take the initiative in deeds of violence.

At first the authorities of Chicago paid little or no attention to the vaporings of these fellows and things ran smoothly until what was known as the "Black Road Riots" occurred in 1886. A strike was on at the McCormick Reaper Works, and matters soon came to a crisis in the vicinity. Here the arm of the law was compelled to strike a blow at the anarchistic movement, which had assumed larger proportions—much larger, in fact, than the authorities had supposed. There were several days of rioting in which the strikers, incited by the leader of anarchy, were clubbed and shot down by the police.

I cannot undertake to recite in detail the events of that terrible night of May 4, 1886, when the bomb was thrown in the midst of the police at Haymarket Square, as the story is doubtless well known to all of you. A mass meeting, which was addressed by the most rabid anarchists in the city, was in progress when the incendiary language indulged in by several of the leaders passed the bounds of patience and tolerance and the police decided to put a stop to such gatherings once and for all. It was ten o'clock at night when several hundred blue-coated men, prepared for any emergency, marched to Haymarket Square confronting the motley crowd, which yelled in approval of the utterances of the speakers. A captain of police commanded the crowd to disperse "in the name of the law." The speaker, Samuel Fielden, jumping off the wagon from which he had been addressing the crowd, replied in a clear, loud tone of voice, "We are peaceable." Instantly a dynamite bomb came hissing through the air and exploded in the midst of the officers. The explosion created frightful havoc and dismay, and was immediately followed by a volley of shots from the mob on the sidewalk and in the street in front of the police, all directed at the police. One police officer was instantly killed and thirty-seven others were wounded, of whom ten died within the year as a result of their wounds. Everybody in the vicinity of the explosion was thrown to the ground, and in the confusion that followed, the Chicago Police showed of what stuff they were made. Every man who was able to draw his revolver did so and used it, standing, kneeling or lying down. The number of killed and wounded anarchists as a result of this fusillade was never known. It is probable, however, that their fatalities were in excess of the police. The leading instigators of the massacre were soon tried and convicted, four of them expatiating their crime on the gallows; one of them committed suicide in his cell; while three others were sent to the penitentiary, two for life sentences. Those confined in the penitentiary were later pardoned, since which time they have shown no disposition to identify themselves with anarchy and anarchists. One of them is at the present time conducting a saloon in Chicago in a manner unobjectionable to the authorities. There are still in Chicago a large number of anarchists, but they are no longer defiant. They have been made to feel the effectiveness of the law when the community is aroused, and to all outward appearances, fear the law, if they do not respect it. They no longer indulge in incendiary talk calculated to incite acts of violence. Close surveillance is kept on the leaders by the police in Chicago, and they cannot make a move of any importance that is not known to the authorities in a short time. By way of illustration, I will cite the arrest of Emma Goldman, the high priestess of anarchy, who was arrested in Chicago three days after the assassination of President McKinley. She contrived to leave Buffalo a few hours after the assassination unobserved by the police in that city. After a few stops on the way she reached St. Louis, Missouri. Her arrival there was immediately known to the police department in Chicago through certain lines of information always maintained. So was her departure from the "Bridge City" with Chicago as her objective point. So perfect was her disguise that she actually passed out of the railway station in Chicago unsuspected by the officers who were specially detailed to apprehend her and who were armed with a photograph and perfect description of her. She contrived to reach trustworthy friends far remote from the heart of the city, and was engaged in making arrangements to depart for Canada when arrested by officers connected with the General Superintendent's office. Dr. Saylin, a Russian Nihilist, her disciple and admirer, who left Buffalo in haste a few hours after the assassination, was promptly taken into custody in Chicago while on his way to Colorado. Altogether seven leading anarchists were held in Chicago with a view of establishing some connection between them and [Leon] Czolgosz, the assassin. This was the story of Chicago's ability to "keep a line" on persons of this class.

In this connection, I will say that I regard Emma Goldman as one of the most dangerous apostles of anarchy in America. She is a persuasive, almost magnetic talker, and Czolgosz, who admitted having heard her speak, was no doubt influenced and inspired to do something out of the ordinary in order to be regarded as a hero by his fellow anarchists. Seeking the opportunity, he found it, and shocked the world by the assassination of President McKinley.

The arrival of a prince or potentate from any part of Europe to this country is a matter of the gravest concern and anxiety to the chiefs of police into whose jurisdiction such visitor may decide to come. On the occasion of the most recent visit of Prince Henry to the country great precautions for his safety were taken, mainly because of the avowed hostility of several "men of action" among the anarchists in Chicago and vicinity. In one case an Italian anarchist was reported to be shooting at a target in his basement two days before Prince Henry's arrival. As a result he was kept under surveillance, as well as a number of others who were suspected of sanguinary intentions. Fortunately everything passed off quietly, and whatever alarm had been excited was allayed only by his departure, uninjured and unmolested.

In Chicago we have not above a half dozen of the rabid type of anarchists known as "men of action." Members of this advanced class are far more numerous in Eastern cities, particularly in Toledo, Cleveland, Buffalo, Patterson, and New York City and also in St. Louis. The group at Patterson, New Jersey, is looked upon by anarchists as the most daring of any. Bresci, the Italian, who went from that city in 1900 and assassinated King Humbert of Italy, was a person of more intelligence than Czolgosz. The report that he was drawn by lot to commit the deed seems to be well founded.

The popular belief that an anarchist is a man of unkempt appearance, wearing long hair and shaggy beard, and who guzzles beer in a dimly lighted basement with his comrades, is not justified by the knowledge which the police of Chicago have of this class of people. Most of the anarchists with whom I have talked are men of considerable mental power and educational attainments. They are, as a rule, well read in history and matters of general information. They bear no resemblance to the unkempt fellow we see cartooned in the press. They no longer call themselves anarchists; they are philosophers or advanced thinkers. They have studied the works of all the great revolutionary writers of the past and have the theories and doctrines of each writer at their fingers or rather their tongue's ends, but these glib talkers are not the men who assassinate rulers. They are given to denunciations and oratorical outbursts, and incite and inspire others with less sense and more courage and recklessness to give their teachings practical effect.

In Europe there is greater danger from socialism in its various phases than in this country. America, with its free institutions and free government, is not a fertile field for the propagation of the seeds of anarchy, which with its emblem — the red flag — was throttled in Chicago more than fifteen years ago. And from present indication there is very little likelihood of its again gaining dangerous strength in this city. The red flag is no longer defiantly flaunted in the breeze, and its followers have not forgotten, and probably never will forget, the 4th of May 1886 when they were put to rout by the Chicago Police, and the 11th of November 1887 when their leaders were hanged. However, precautionary measures should always be taken by every police department in the country, and they should keep constant watch on the leaders or "men of action," who, should the opportunity present itself, might attempt to inflame their followers to renewed deeds of violence. The European countries in which anarchy has made the most headway in the past four years are Russia, Italy, France, and Spain. The propaganda of the anarchists in Germany has, to a large extent, subsided. Russia thought she had crushed Nihilism more than twenty years ago, when several leaders were executed for the assassination of Czar Alexander II. The execution took place in the open and was witnessed by over one hundred thousand people, of whom hundreds were crushed to death in the crowd. This public execution was intended to serve as an object lesson to any in the throng who in the future might imbibe the theories of Bakunin and attempt to put them into practice. But this did not put an end to Nihilism, it has thrived there ever since. The most recent evidence of this fact being the assassination of the Russian Minister of Interior less than one month ago. If I am not mistaken Russia is now on the eve of serious internal troubles bordering closely on anarchy. Other assassinations of European rulers by anarchists in recent years were those of Empress Elizabeth of Austria in 1898, of President Carnet of France in 1894, and in 1897 the Prime Minister of Spain was shot to death by an Italian anarchist. Less than two years ago an attempt was made upon the life of Prince Albert Edward, now King of England. The attempt was made while the Prince was on a visit to Germany by an anarchist fanatic only sixteen years old.

Quoting in part from the work of a modern writer, I wish to add that neither Nihilism nor anarchy affords any solution of the problem which will arise should society, as we understand it, disappear. Advocates of destruction content themselves with declaring that the duty at hand is tearing down—the work of building up may come later. There are several reasons why the revolutionary program stops short at the work of anarchy, among which is the fact that there are as many panaceas for the future as there are revolutionists. The anarchists are all agreed that the present system must go and so far they can work together. Their dream of the future is, accordingly, as many colored as Joseph's coat. Each man has his own ideal and each man seeks his own path into utopia.

It is not my purpose in this paper to suggest or outline a means of suppressing or exterminating anarchy in America. It would be well, however, in my opinion, for the members of this convention to discuss the question with the view of familiarizing themselves with the subject, in order that mutual aid may more successfully be rendered in the future in the suppression and control of anarchy and anarchists.

REAPPOINTED GENERAL SUPERINTENDENT FOR SECOND TERM

After the reelection of Carter H. Harrison II in 1903 for a fourth term as mayor, he suggested that I prepare new bonds for reappointment, "if you want the job," before I left to attend the annual convention of the International Association of Chiefs of Police held at New Orleans, Louisiana.

The occasion may be opportune to refer to our harmonious official relations. All matters worthy of his attention were submitted daily to His Honor the mayor for his consideration. No action involving policies or police changes were undertaken without his approval, and there was never a question of his support when orders had been executed.

Having been elected to the Board of Governors at the Louisville Convention in 1902 and booked for another address of my own selection at this

O'Neill was reappointed to be superintendent of police two times, serving three terms under two mayors, Carter H. Harrison II and Edward F. Dunne. This document was signed by Carter H. Harrison II and dated June 22, 1903. (Mary Lesch collection)

meeting, I decided to break away from conventional platitudes and introduce something new and on a subject of universal interest to those present.

The theme was so pertinent and applicable to their individual problems that its delivery was punctuated by applause at every pointed paragraph. As I left the platform to resume my seat far down the hall, hands were extended on either side in friendly greeting and appreciation. All wanted copies of the address for their mayors and other supervising officials, but as there were but two copies available, it was printed in the *Detective*, a police periodical, for distribution.

ADDRESS AT THE ANNUAL CONVENTION OF THE INTERNATIONAL ASSOCIATION OF CHIEFS OF POLICE AT NEW ORLEANS, MAY 1903, BY FRANCIS O'NEILL, GENERAL SUPERINTENDENT OF POLICE OF CHICAGO: "THE CHIEF OF POLICE, HIS DUTIES AND HIS DIFFICULTIES"

The official life of a Chief of Police of a large city is mainly an unremitting effort to say "NO," and to say it with the least possible offense to those whose requests and demands are denied. If the Chief is an experienced and forceful man, who enters his office with a determination to give a good and efficient police administration, he must be prepared to resist the powerful pressure of political and other influences the moment he assumes the duties of his office.

Not only must he maintain his resistance against pressure without an instant of relaxation, but this must be steadily increased until the repression of adverse influences reaches the point which will win the approval of sensible people and convince the public that every consideration must be subordinated to the good of the service. It will not do to resist part of the time, and then relax into easy-going methods occasionally. The instant the resistance is relaxed the spring flies back with a force proportioned to the pressure which has been exerted upon it. The successful Chief of Police must continue on his course evenly and steadily during every moment of his official existence.

The badge for the International Association of Chiefs of Police second annual convention held in New Orleans on May 12 to 15, 1903, was made of cast metal. Conventioneers today wear badges for entry to their meetings but rarely are they cast in metal. (Photograph by Jennifer Riforgiate; Mary Lesch collection)

That alert, stubborn resistance to "pull"—which forms the spring against which the executive of the police department must keep his shoulder sternly set—comprises various forces, but mainly they are evident in efforts to get at the public crib to obtain "soft snap" assignments, to secure special exemptions or privileges and to prevent or minimize the punishment of criminals and transgressors of the law.

Other elements enter the problem, but these are the principal ones which may profitably be taken into account and carefully analyzed.

Political, social and ethnological influences must be reckoned with. No layman who is not brought into daily contact with the routine of business at police headquarters in a large city can form any idea of the demands made upon the time of the Chief of Police in the multiplicity of matters which are daily obtruded on him for consideration.

When the police force is not under strict civil service laws the woes of the chief are considerable. If the policemen's clubs were made out of gold instead of locust or hickory, competition for them could scarcely be more strenuous. Citing an incident in the experience of one of my predecessors, Chief Michael Brennan, will serve to illustrate.

Early one morning Alderman Stuckart entered Brennan's office with a big muscular fellow in tow. They were pleasantly welcomed by the Chief, who informed them in as few words as possible that no vacancies existed and that there was no likelihood of one occurring in the near future. Half an hour later the same alderman returned with another man bent on securing a similar appointment. Again the Chief patiently made the same explanation. Four times the program was repeated by the alderman. When he brought in the fifth man, however, the patience of Chief Brennan was exhausted and he exclaimed:

"Can't you understand, Alderman, that I must do some police work, and that I must be permitted some time in which to do it? This is the fifth call you have made to this office this morning for the purpose of getting a constituent appointed on the police force. In every instance I have told you plainly that there are no vacancies, and that no appointments are possible.

Still, here you come with another man! This is carrying things altogether too far. I hope you will not annoy me further."

Placing his hand on the Chief's shoulder, the alderman regretfully replied: "I know that as well as you do, Chief, but can't you see that I must square myself with my people and particularly with those who run the ward and who give me my seat in the Council? I dislike to come here and take up your time on a mission which I know is hopeless, but there is no other way out of it; my men will not be satisfied with my explanations and nothing but a statement from your own lips in their hearing will square me, and I may as well tell you right now that I have two more such calls to make today, and that you will materially injure my interests if you do not give me a hearing."

On another occasion, while I was acting as Chief Brennan's private secretary, this tireless and typical alderman came to me with a troubled face and worried manner. Dropping dejectedly into a chair he made known his mission.

"I am slowly but surely being driven to insanity," he said. "There is a certain patrolman out my way who is determined that I shall secure his promotion to the position of sergeant. He never sleeps! It is impossible to shake him. No matter how early I rise in the morning, or how late I return at night, he or one of his emissaries is camped on my front doorsteps, and he has a faithful lookout posted at the rear of the house so that I cannot make my escape by way of the alley. The unfortunate widow of Scriptural celebrity was a shy, shrinking and purposeless creature compared with this patrolman. Time and again I have discussed his case with the Chief, and I understand that there is not the slightest chance in the world for his promotion under present conditions. If I had a dozen interviews with the Superintendent I couldn't grasp the hopelessness of this man's case any better than I do now; and I have explained every circumstance to him over and over again, but without making the slightest impression upon his hopes or determination. He will not listen to reason, and now I am ready to resort to other methods. Is there not some ordinance or rule of the department which says that officers who annoy the Department Chief with delegations in their behalf shall be subject to discipline?"

"Yes," I replied, "there is such a rule, and your best plan is to bring your man in for an interview. Meantime I will acquaint the Chief with your circumstances and call his attention to the ruling which covers the case."

This scheme was carried out and the next morning the alderman and the patrolman appeared, the latter smiling with satisfaction over the prospect that the Chief had weakened, and that a short interview with him would "fix things" all right and secure his promotion to the pay and dignity of a sergeant.

After the alderman had defined the object of their case, the Chief put on his severest expression and turning suddenly to the policeman he said: "Do you know officer, that you are violating one of the rules of the department by coming here in order to secure promotion by political influence? Well you are! And the penalty for it is suspension or dismissal from the service, according to my discretion. I guess suspension will answer while I take your case under advisement."

This turn of affairs was a terrible shock to the patrolman, and threw him into a spasm of fear. His irrepressible ambition to wear the uniform of a sergeant suddenly left him, and all his thoughts became centered on saving himself from disgrace and in retaining his position.

Then the Alderman made an earnest plea that the man be spared the penalty on condition that the offense should never be repeated. After seeming carefully to weigh his argument of intercession, the General Superintendent finally acceded to the Alderman's request. When they came out of the Chief's private office the patrolman grasped the alderman's hand and wrung it with a grip which told of the gratitude he could not put into words. That patrolman never asked for promotion after this experience; he was content to let new honors seek him instead of seeking them, and he is still a patrolman.

Thus far I have written only as to how the time, the energy and the hopes of the head of the police department are consumed by place hunters. When there is no civil service such things are inevitable, but under civil service law rigidly enforced, as it is in Chicago under the present administration, those drawbacks are reduced to a minimum. Ever since the passage of civil service law there has been a constant tightening of the lines and those who now come to exert their "pull" or influence are but a corporal's guard as compared with the legions which stormed police headquarters in the older days.

If the Chief of Police obtained his position through politics and wire-pulling he will be encumbered with obligations which will be pressed upon him unremittingly with merciless importunity and under the most embarrassing circumstances. Even under more favorable conditions he will fall far short of meeting the hopes and expectations of his most ardent friends and despite his best efforts, he will soon have occasion to feel anxious about his waning popularity.

There is a wide difference of opinion as to what constitutes a good police administration. A certain element will not be satisfied with anything short of the absolute ideal in morals. But the reasonable portion of the community realizes that this is an impossibility.

Ideal morality cannot be universally enforced in any community, particularly in a large city, even by a police force made up of men having the moral courage of martyrs and the stern convictions of Puritans.

What, then, is the best that can be expected in the line of approximating the ideal, with human nature as it is constituted? How much can be demanded in the limits of human reason, as to the suppression of vice and crime and the preservation of order in a modern metropolis?

My own definition of a good police administration, as it has been worked out by long years of service in the department is this:

First—the suppression of public gambling to a point where the police force does not know of its existence, and where honest and vigilant effort is constantly put forth to discover its outcropping and to punish its appearance.

Second—the suppression of vice to a point where it cannot affect those who do not, of their own choice, seek its haunts.

Third—the placing of the saloon thoroughly under the control of the law.

Fourth—the reduction of crime and disorder to that minimum which results from knowledge, on the part of the potential lawbreakers, that punishment shall be impartial and exempt from the influence of political "pull" or other form of official corruption, as far as the police are concerned.

These are the main points in my definition of a sound police administration; and if the conditions I have outlined are fairly approximated, the people may well be satisfied and should give that administration their hearty confidence and support, resting assured that they will never know at what cost of vigilance, hard work and perpetual warfare such a result has been attained.

It must be apparent to any thoughtful and well informed man of the world that the materials with which a chief of police has to work are not ideal. The policeman's pay and the nature of his duties are hardly attractive to a man of acute moral sensibilities or highly developed intellectuality—this is not in any sense a reflection upon the mental or moral make-up of the men who constitute the police force. They are human, their wages if comparatively small, and their work of a rough sort and repulsive to the man of refined sensibilities. They are constantly brought into contact with the harsh, the corrupt, the vicious and sordid sides of life, and it is not to be wondered at that many of them yield to the unwholesome influences of such a contact.

This makes it necessary for the conscientious and energetic chief of police to exercise unflagging vigilance to see that his honest efforts are not thwarted by the men under him. He must keep as close a surveillance upon his men as they are supposed to keep upon the public.

"The causes of crime," said Graham Taylor recently, "are as complex as are the conditions of our complicated city life; as it can be traced to no single source, so there is no one specific to cure it. The remedies are as manifold as the conditions which account for our situation. An outbreak of crime is not so sudden as it seems. It is a harvest that was seeded down long ago. It is the outgrowth of conditions tolerated all too long."

It is useless to say that crime and immorality do not exist in any city or town where it is necessary to organize a police force. Such a statement would be foolish upon the face of it, for every city is more or less wicked. Admitting this to be the case, the question arises; can crime and immorality be abolished? In every community robbery, larceny and burglary are the offenses which, when unusually frequent, put the chief on his nettle. He must successfully grapple with what is known as a carnival of crime.

Dishonesty and immorality cannot be completely abolished; if they could be, then we would have reached the golden age of our existence. But crime can be abated, and so can all other violations of law, and the only way to bring it about is properly to enforce the state and city laws. But herein lays a difficulty.

There are but two agencies for the suppression and repression of crime, that is, moral suasion and punishment. The first we can safely leave to the Juvenile Court and the probation officers; the second should receive the serious consideration of all good citizens as well as members of the police force.

It is evident to all thinking people that a spirit of unrest and aggressive discontent and disregard for law manifests itself all over this broad land at the present time, and it is a hopeful sign when citizens become aroused on the subject.

The ease and frequency with which malefactors and transgressors escape punishment for their offenses can be attributed the prevalence of crime to a large extent.

The lack of proper home training and the moral restraints imposed by church influence in early youth are also responsible for the disregard of law.

Unwillingness on the part of complainants and witnesses to appear in court and testify when required; the constant and persistent effort of interested persons to interfere with the operation of the law; the proverbial law's delay; the indeterminate sentence act; and the want of sufficient policemen are the principal causes which multiply the difficulties of the officers.

Repeated and almost inexcusable continuances in court, changes of venue, forfeiture of bond with leave to reinstate are calculated to tire out the average complainant, and the one who has followed his case to a successful termination is soon made to realize that it is a long road from the police station to the penitentiary. The criminal courts not uncommonly usurp the functions of pardon boards and reformatories, and judges permit self-confessed thieves and those who have been adjudged guilty by a jury to go free on their own recognizance, a formality which is simply a waste of stationery. Friendless indeed is the criminal who cannot get a bondsman and thereby regain his liberty so that he may redouble his efforts at plunder in order to engage a criminal lawyer who understands his business.

But politicians, as a rule, do not like to run around interfering with the police officers in the discharge of their duty, but the politician's existence depends largely on his being useful in getting his acquaintances out of trouble, and in keeping his constituents out of jail. Hence he must come to the aid of criminals who fall into the hands of the police.

From the moment an arrest is made the policeman's trouble begins; everybody whom he arrests is the son of someone, a brother-in-law or relative of someone else whose friendship is valuable, or possibly a member of an organization which it will be found desirable to aid or placate.

The first move to interfere with the enforcement of the law is usually made by friends of the prisoner, who endeavor to induce the officer to drop the prosecution or, at least, with hold some of the testimony.

Now as the great majority of policemen will stick to their prosecutions, there is small chance of inducing an officer to quit by direct appeal to him or his commanding officers and, therefore, other means are resorted to. Witnesses upon whom the officer must depend to convict the prisoner are importuned and threatened and not infrequently bought off, so that when the case reaches the police court it fails for lack of prosecution.

Criminals employ lawyers in the police court who are technical, if nothing else, and these attorneys know the ins and outs of police court practice. Numerous continuances for the sole purpose of tiring out the prosecuting witnesses are resorted to in the hope that the anger of the complainant will cool in time, and that by being forced to attend court repeatedly he will at last become weary of the case, despite the efforts of the officer to keep him in line.

When this means fails the next move is to hunt up an unsafe bondsman who will give his services for a cash consideration. This bond secured, the defendant does not appear, and the "straw security" is forfeited with leave to reinstate. The officer must

Above left: Shortly after his appointment as chief of police on April 30, 1901, O'Neill encountered the wrath of First Ward alderman Michael "Hinky Dink" Kenna (1857–1946) when O'Neill began the cleanup of the Levee district in the First Ward, cracking down on after-hours saloons and brothels. (Carter H. Harrison II, Growing up with Chicago [Chicago: Ralph Seymour Fletcher, 1944])

Above right: When O'Neill was appointed chief of police in 1901, he considered himself "under obligations to no one" but Mayor Carter H. Harrison II, pictured here. (Carter H. Harrison II, Stormy Years *[Indianapolis: Bobbs-Merrill Company, 1935])*

follow up the case until the bond is finally forfeited or the defendant appears for trial.

When the criminal is held to the Criminal Court he hopes by some means or other to get the witnesses away from the grand jury. The annoyance incident to following up a criminal case disgusts many people, and they not infrequently drop out at various stages, much to the satisfaction of the criminal and his attorney.

However, if the complainant is still determined to prosecute after the officer has overcome the numerous interferences; an indictment is not a difficult matter. Even after this, the officer must keep a tab on the prosecuting witnesses, for it may be months before the case is called for trial. In the meantime the politicians and friends of the defendant put in their time endeavoring to influence the prosecution.

After the criminal is finally convicted the interference with the enforcement of the law keeps on just the same. The judge is importuned to reduce the sentence or to change it to a short term in the county jail or to grant a new trial; here the politicians and friends get in their best work.

A short time ago in Chicago two men who held up a saloon-keeper were arrested. When their records were looked up it was found that they were charged with seven previous hold-ups, but the judge before whom they were convicted and sentenced to the penitentiary changed the sentence to a short term in the county jail.

Even when the penitentiary doors close behind the criminal, the interference does not stop. The Board of Pardons and the Governor are appealed to by interested persons, and it may be broadly stated that from the time of the arrest of a criminal until his liberation or death, interference with the operations of the law never ceases.

An instance of how habitual criminals from their early youth were finally landed, after repeated failures, in the penitentiary may be of interest. These criminals were socially well connected and had successfully run riot in the southwestern part of Chicago some years ago. They held up and robbed an Englishman of $9.00 on Christmas Eve just before midnight. The Englishman, in a state of great excitement, reported the outrage to me at the station, and his description of his assailants plainly established their identity.

They were positively identified when arrested about an hour later, and when brought into court repeated continuances were taken, as is customary in such cases; but our Englishman was a stubborn individual who was bent upon prosecution, and they were held to the criminal court under heavy bonds. About this time things began to look serious, and there was nothing to be done but to buy off the complainant.

This was finally accomplished by reimbursing him for his loss and promising him $50.00 when the case should be stricken from the docket. He then disappeared from the neighborhood, leaving no address. The bailiff who served the notice of the trial was a brother-in-law of the defendant and by the nonchalant manner in which he left the notice at the police station it was clear that he was aware of the arrangement.

Having failed in so many previous cases the police regretted that our stubborn Englishman had been finally induced to relent, and a scheme was devised which turned out to our entire satisfaction. An officer who knew Mr. Bull at a glance was instructed to look for him in new buildings, as he was a carpenter, and keep widening the circuit until he was found.

On the third day he was discovered on a roof, but nothing was said to him until the morning of the trial, when the officer called on him and read the subpoena from the criminal court, taking him into custody at the same time, and keeping him under cover three blocks from the criminal court building.

Of course, had the Englishman been seen in the court house or vicinity the lawyer for the defense would have made a plea for a continuance on the usual grounds. But when the case was called and our complainant had not shown up, the defendant's lawyer with a flourish announced that he was ready for trial, and asked that the case be stricken from the docket, as there was no one to prosecute, except the police officer who made the arrest, but who had no personal knowledge of the crime.

This was just what we were anxiously waiting for, and the judge was informed by the officer that the complaining witness would be on hand in a few minutes. A third officer, who was to act as messenger, ran to the saloon where the complainant was reluctantly engaged in a game of forty-five with his captor. When brought into court the Englishman testified without hesitation, and the two defendants, to their great surprise, were given a good round term in the penitentiary, a sentence which I am happy to say caused the reform of both, as they are now leading honest lives. This reads like a conspiracy to convict, but it was "straight goods" and accomplished the desired results.

The interference is not only with the policeman in the enforcement of the law, but it extends to interference with higher officials in the enforcement of discipline. A short time ago two clergymen called on the Mayor of Chicago and demanded that a certain policeman be charged instantly. It was explained to the clergymen that under the civil service law they must prefer charges against the officer. With a view to that end I took the names of witnesses. I found that the case against the policeman merited investigation, so I preferred charges against him myself for violation of certain rules of the department. The next day these same clergymen, who had made the complaint and betrayed such indignation because the officer was not discharged without a hearing, came to me and pleaded in vain to have the matter dropped.

It is the misfortune of the Chief of Police to encounter criticism from some direction, no matter what policy he may follow, or which course he may pursue. He is the strong arm of the administration, and whether he is active or passive, does things or leaves things undone, there will inevitably be many whose displeasure or disappointment will be painfully manifest before his term has far advanced. If he is a sensible man, he will have arrived at the conclusion that by following his own mature judgment, guided by an honest and militant conscience, he will come nearer to giving general satisfaction than by attempting to cater to the preference of others.

The official life of a Chief of Police is proverbially short, averaging in Chicago during the past thirty years less than one year and eleven months.

Invariably one plank in every municipal campaign platform by the party out of power is to take the police out of politics. If successful, the pledge is kept to the extent of appointing a new chief of police and taking the other fellows out. What chance is there of taking the police out of politics so long as the head of the department cannot hope to retain his position if his party is defeated? It is the new man who will always work wonders and reform things until he gets enmeshed in the difficulties of his predecessors and the old program of good intentions, intermittent criticism, and eventual disappointment is repeated with variations.

Indiscriminate faultfinding, upon which there is no patent, finds a handy public target in the police, and no matter what other agencies, through the sins of omission or commission, may be responsible for unpleasant conditions, the police alone seem fated to get the blame. The handicaps of defective laws, antiquated justice courts, technical and slothful criminal courts are seldom noticed, and the "fall guy" is invariably the policeman on whom all eyes center.

You may as well charge the ministers of the gospel with inefficiency because they fail to keep their congregations in a perpetual state of grace, or charge physicians with malpractice because their patients relapse into infirmities after undergoing successful treatment at their hands, as to accuse the police of incompetence because crime cannot be eradicated and good order constantly maintained.

The police may suppress crime and law-breaking to the best of their ability, but when malefactors and offenders are released by courts on pleas of leniency, technicalities or other causes, the work has to be done over and over again, and unless in the course of evolution the people develop into a condition of being good and remaining good, the efforts and worries of the police must be expected to continue until the end of time.

EMERGENCIES—SHORTAGE OF FUNDS

The annual appropriation is based to a limited extent on anticipated revenue due from certain corporations. When the latter withhold payment for any reason, payrolls cannot be met, and the reduction in wages or in employees is the usual alternative.

Early in the administration of Mayor Harrison the elder, such an emergency occurred. To meet it, police [department] pay was cut 10 percent. The next year was even worse, and the police suffered a further reduction of 5 percent, paid in scrip, and in most cases, this was subject to discount when cashed.

A similar emergency recurring in September 1903, I was informed by the finance committee of the city council that it would be necessary to lay off three hundred men for the last quarter of the year. Under the provisions of the Civil Service Law, I explained that the latest men appointed would have to be the victims. They were the young, energetic men traveling post. Many of the old men filling comfortable assignments were eligible to pension, and adding that it seemed unworthy of the great city of Chicago to lay off those young men who had given up their former positions and procured uniforms, not yet paid for in many cases.

"But Chief," they inquired, "what can we do about it, when there is no money to pay them?"

"I can carry them," I replied.

"How are you going to do it?"

"All I ask is," I continued, "that you aldermen keep out of my office when I'm auditing time rolls.

"The appropriation calls for full time, although there is much lost time in the service—much of it unnecessary. In an emergency like this, let lost time pay for those who work."

Not without misgivings did they agree to the proposition. Without laying off a man, and not filling vacancies resulting from dismissal or death, all who worked were paid, and there was a small balance left over. The delinquent corporations having paid up at the end of the year, all who had lost wages as a result of the emergency were reimbursed by order of the city council.

PATROLMEN'S PAY INCREASE

For the benefit of all and sundry, I feel justified in recording the fact, now almost forgotten, that the first increase in salary from the standardized one thousand dollars a year for patrolmen was obtained through my appeal to the Finance Committee in the year 1902, as the annual appropriation was under consideration. All other ranks, grades, and employees of the city on the police rolls had their salaries increased at one time or another, except patrolmen, I pointed out in detail. His Honor, the mayor, though not advocating an increase, did not object to the city council's action in voting the patrolmen a raise in wages to eleven hundred dollars a year.

NEW BOOK OF RULES

A comprehensive new Book of Rules and Regulations governing the Department of Police, comprising 163 pages, was compiled and officially recognized by the city council. Many changes and alterations have been made in police regulations in later times.

NEW POLICE BADGES

The old-style star or badge with indented numbers, worn by the Chicago Police as far back as I can remember, had fallen into disfavor. From long use the black enamel had worn entirely, or partially, away from the figures and though such a star had lost none of its significance, it was unreliable in establishing the identity of the wearer. In the administration of Mayor Roche, Chief of Police Hubbard attempted to supplant the star with a shield of his own design, but as the change did not meet the approval of the city council, the old-style star continued in use until the year 1901.

A new star having the city seal in the center and with copper numbers brazed on the nickel surface was introduced by me in that year. Owing to the contrast of colors, the numbers may be read at a glance. That design, having met all requirements, [has been] the official police badge ever since.

BLANK FORMS INTRODUCED

The practice of writing out, in full, reports of accidents, fires, crimes, etc., involved much unnecessary clerical work, besides being in most cases a waste of stationery. To obviate this tiresome routine, a series of blank forms were devised during my incumbency which promoted efficiency, as well as relieving desk sergeants of much of their scrivening.

O'Neill's retired general superintendent star was an example of the new design the chief created in an effort to thwart the making of counterfeit stars to impersonate police officers. (Photograph by Jennifer Riforgiate; Mary Lesch collection)

PECULIAR COINCIDENCE

Eternal vigilance is not more essential to the cause of liberty than to the retention of rank and command in the police department, even under civil service. I ventured to indulge in but one brief vacation while chief of police since the week's rest accorded me following the strenuous Debs's or railway strike of 1894. Unforeseen incidents prevented me from finishing either.

Certain improvements going on in my orchard out in Palos required my personal attention, so with the approval of Mayor Harrison, I left town with the intention of being gone two days. On the second day, one of the Sullivan brothers met a young man on a country road through the woods who offered to sell him a nice rig he was driving for a sum much less than its value. Suspecting that it had been stolen, Sullivan lured him to the farm three miles away, on the pretense of buying it. They arrived just at noon as I had come in for dinner. I invited the young man in to eat with us, but he did not seem to enjoy our hospitality. Without question or explanation, I sat in with the young man after dinner and drove back to the city. His surprise was evident when a policeman came out from the Brighton Park Police Station and addressed me as "Chief."

The rig had been driven away from South State Street, and a fine of seventy-five dollars was imposed in the police court, and I lost half a day of my two-day vacation. But just think of it, a horse thief drives out in the country twenty miles from the courthouse and turns off Archer Avenue into an obscure roadway to avoid arrest and runs into the hands of the chief of police!

RUMORED ASSASSINATION

I certainly made the front page with illustrations on one occasion, by a hoax, the origin of which I never learned definitely, and the story with variations finds mention in the Chicago press from that time to this.

A quiet hour one afternoon at police headquarters—something very unusual—gave me an opportunity to breathe a little fresh air. I told Secretary Markham that I would drive through the West Division and would not return to the office that day. In heading for home in Hyde Park in the evening, I passed into the Brighton Park District, in which my esteemed friend Sergeant James O'Neill lived. He, by the way, is a Belfast man, while I am a Corkonian and kindred only in years of collaboration in the collecting of

Sergeant James O'Neill (right) was Francis O'Neill's friend and collaborator in playing, collecting, and publishing Irish music. Because Francis O'Neill had no formal musical training, he was unable to transcribe his beloved tunes. James O'Neill's friendship and skill in musical notation was invaluable to Francis in publishing his first two books, The Music of Ireland and Dance Music of Ireland. (Mary Lesch collection)

"Mecca" was the name of James O'Neill's house, at 3522 South Washtenaw Avenue in Chicago's Brighton Park neighborhood, where Irish musicians met to play music. When Francis O'Neill paid a surprise visit to his good friend in 1902, Chicago newspapers reported him missing and the possible victim of an assassination attempt. (Photograph by Mary Lesch)

Irish folk music. Time and place being opportune, I decided to indulge in a friendly visit and dismissed my driver for the day.

About eight o'clock, while seated in the parlor contentedly reading afternoon papers, in rushed a patrolman by the kitchen door with the startling news—"The Chief has been assassinated! It is all over town, and they can't locate him." Sergeant O'Neill laughed and, pointing to the front room, remarked, "Why, the chief is in there now, see for yourself." One hasty glance was enough, so out ran the courier as precipitately as he came in. Without delay I started for home on the streetcars. Reporters waylaid me a block from the house, and together we encountered another batch with pencils poised at the front gate, eager for a story. Fortunately the dire news was kept from my wife.

It was surmised that some disgruntled caller from the First Ward "Bad Lands" uttered a wish, which became a rumor and circulated in the vague report of my assassination. The episode, however, proved to be front-page copy for the morning papers, one of which pictured me seated before a music stand, playing a flute, with Sergeant O'Neill standing, accompanying me on the violin, while it may be assumed that the rank and file of the police force was engaged in the search for my mangled remains.

ATTENDED THE ST. LOUIS CONVENTION

The annual convention of the International Associations of Chiefs of Police in 1904 was held at St. Louis, Missouri, when the Louisiana Purchase Exposition was in full swing. As a consequence there was a large attendance of chiefs on this occasion.

When called upon in the routine of proceedings for an address requested at the last meeting at New Orleans, the subject I had chosen follows herewith.

ADDRESS AT THE ANNUAL CONVENTION OF THE INTERNATIONAL ASSOCIATION
OF CHIEFS OF POLICE AT ST. LOUIS, MAY 1904, BY FRANCIS O'NEILL, GENERAL
SUPERINTENDENT OF POLICE OF CHICAGO: "WHAT SCIENCE HAS DONE FOR
THE POLICE: MODERN IMPROVEMENTS IN POLICE METHODS"

The watchman of a century ago with his lantern and staff, who called out the passing hours in stentorian tones during the night, is now but a tradition. He has been succeeded by a uniformed constabulary and police who carry arms and operate under semi-military discipline.

The introduction of electricity as a means of communication between stations was the first notable advance in the improvement of police methods. Not many here present will remember the time when the manipulation of the dial telegraph by the station keeper while sending messages excited the greatest wonder and admiration. The alphabet and numerals in two concentric circles were so arranged that the operator spelled out the words by pressing buttons. The finger or arrow in the center of the dial rattled noisily around and pointed out on both instruments (the sender and receiver) the numbers or letters indicated by the touch of the station keeper.

So little was the means of sending messages by telegraph understood that on one occasion a cabman rushed into a Chicago police station and, handing the station keeper a written description of his rig which had just been stolen, urgently requested that a message be sent immediately to all stations. The latter took the slip of paper and put his instrument into connection with its destination and, after spelling out the message on his dial, hung the piece of paper which the cabman had given him on the spindle. The man lounged around for some time, evidently restless and unsatisfied. At last his patience was exhausted and he belched out, "Ain't you going to send that dispatch?" The station keeper politely informed him that he had sent it. "No, you haint," replied the indignant man. "There it is on the hook."

It may not be out of place to state here that the first suggestion of telegraphy was made about 280 years ago.

Strada, an ingenious and learned Jesuit of Rome, writing on the subject about that time, describes a means of communication by wire and magnetic needle which differs but little from the dial instrument used by the Chicago Police Department up to about twenty-five years ago.

In 1774, about 150 years after Strada wrote, Lesage, a Swiss philosopher, successfully established a real and physical communication between two distant places by means of frictional electricity, the only form in which electricity was at that time known.

The wire rope which formed the medium of communication between the two stations consisted of twenty-four strands, one for each letter of the alphabet, and were attached to a keyboard at either end of the line like that of a piano. The invention of Lesage taken in connection with the idea of Strada, the Jesuit, may be considered as the embryo and prototype of the modern marvel—the telegraph instrument of today.

The adoption of the Morse system of telegraphy by the police was a long step forward and proved of great advantage in the expeditious transaction of official business. The dial was superseded by the ticker in Chicago in the year 1876, and all station keepers, who were by this time called desk sergeants, were required to take up the immediate study of the Morse system of telegraphy.

Scarcely one-fourth of them became proficient before modern science, advancing by leaps and bounds, relegated telegraphy to the realms of antiquity and brought forth that still more modern miracle—the telephone.

Less than one-quarter of a century ago the policeman on post had no aid from science in communicating with his station or in securing assistance in case of need. When required by duty to care for the sick and injured or to remove a dead body, an appeal to the owner of some suitable vehicle was his only resource. In many instances, and especially in the nighttime and in stormy weather, a sick horse was given as an excuse for refusing the officer's request. Peanut carts and even wheelbarrows were occasionally pressed into service when no other means of conveyance were available, and instances are known where an officer of a practical and facetious turn of mind coaxed or dragged a "drunk" surreptitiously to an adjoining post and left him there for some other officer to deal with.

These were desperate times for policemen in a hostile country with unpaved streets and uneven sidewalks, sometimes miles from the police station, with little prospect of assistance in case of need. Scores of instances does the writer remember when prisoners were rescued, officers assaulted, maimed, and even killed before assistance could reach them. It took nerve to be a policeman in those days, but now how it has changed.

The invention of the patrol wagon and signal service had effected a revolution in police methods. It is a milestone in the path of police progress and, like many other epoch-making inventions, was the offspring of necessity.

The roundsman or patrol sergeant who succeeded in meeting his men on the posts once or twice a night did all that could be reasonably expected of him. After seeing the roundsman, the patrolman as a rule relaxed his vigilance and not uncommonly took things easy thereafter. A means of compelling him to travel his post and report regularly was earnestly desired.

At a picnic of the United Irish Societies of Chicago on August 15, 1881, Austin J. Doyle, then general superintendent of police, outlined to Professor John P. Barrett, city electrician, a scheme which, when developed and elaborated by the latter, became the police signal service, originated in Chicago and now in operation all over the civilized world.

An express wagon remodeled with seats within, rails on top, steps in the rear, and drawn by one horse, was the first patrol wagon. At one police precinct in the most turbulent part of Chicago, the police signal service was installed as an experiment. Its success and popularity [were] instantaneous, and the system was extended all over the city as rapidly as the capacity of the police department shops would permit. The covered patrol wagon was a later improvement, resulting from an act of the Illinois Legislature, the open wagon being regarded as entailing too much publicity and humiliation on its patrons.

The employment of drivers, hostlers, and telephone operators still further increased police expenditures, but the improvement in the efficiency of the service was so manifest that the additional outlay was fully justified. A still further utilization of science as an aid in promoting police efficiency was suggested.

It was proposed to place an electric light in a red globe on top of each patrol box. The electric current could be switched on at the pleasure of the operator at the station to notify the officer on post that communication with him was desired. Unfortunately the red signal on the apex of the patrol box would generally be observed by the public before the police and the consequent

An important innovation in the Chicago Police Department was the patrol
box, an octagonal structure eight feet high with a lamp that illuminated
the street and provided the patrol officer with enough light to insert a key in the
alarm box. By pulling on a hook, the patrolman could contact the station
using the signal apparatus. (A. T. Andreas, History of Chicago 3 [Chicago:
A. T. Andreas, 1885], 311)

In reporting a crime
in O'Neill's time, an
officer on patrol in-
dicated one of eleven
alarms. (A. T. Andreas,
History of Chicago 3
[Chicago: A. T. Andreas,
1885], 311)

ALARM-BOX DIAL.

crowd awaiting developments caused the scheme to at last be temporarily abandoned.

Perhaps it may not be out of place to trespass on the patience of the reader by citing a remarkable case in which, had it not been for the prompt and efficient use of the police signal service, a most atrocious murder would have remained a mystery to this day and the perpetrators of it free from police interference instead of having been captured in less than three hours about twelve miles from the scene of the crime.

On the evening of September 2, 1899, two young men called at a boardinghouse at the extreme western portion of the city and inquired for Walter Koeller. They were strangers to the landlady and were told that Koeller was sick abed and could not be seen. They told her that it was very important to Koeller as well as to themselves that he should be seen without delay, and, believing their story, she directed them to his room on the second floor, while she remained in her kitchen, continuing her household duties.

Koeller, who was lying in bed when the two men entered the room, which was dark, arose to strike a light, and as he did so a bowie knife was plunged into his body by one of the men. His companion stood guard at the open door, ready to kill anyone who might come to Koeller's assistance. Again and again the long-bladed weapon was plunged into Koeller's body, until more than a dozen stab wounds pierced his vitals; any one of which it was shown at the coroner's inquest would have caused his death.

The landlady heard the cries of her boarder and ran from her house in search of a policeman. She returned in less than three minutes with an officer, but the murderers had fled. Koeller was dead when found by the officer, who rushed to the patrol box and notified his station of the circumstances. A good description of the assassins was given by the landlady. She stated that one of them carried a satchel.

A message describing the two men and the nature of their crime was transmitted to police headquarters, from whence it was forwarded to every precinct in the city, so that in less than an hour from the time of the murder, it was known in all police stations. This message was transmitted to every police officer on post when he called up to make his hourly report from the patrol box. The murder was committed after eight o'clock, and a few minutes before eleven o'clock Officer Whalen of the Thirteenth Precinct saw two men sneaking along the tracks in the railroad yards at Grand Crossing. One of them carried a satchel. The officer drew his revolver, ordered the suspects to throw up their hands, and marched them to the nearest patrol box under cover of his revolver and summoned the patrol wagon. A blood-stained bowie knife was found on one of them, while the other had a revolver and a dirk and wore blood-stained clothing. A few hours later Inspector Shea had secured a full confession from the murderers. In their confession they stated that they had come to Chicago from a small town in Missouri for the purpose of killing Koeller. Years before that a brother of Honeck, one of the assassins, was killed in a street fight in which an older brother of Walter Koeller was involved. Honeck was less than ten years of age at the time of his brother's death, but he secretly swore to have revenge, which he did by murdering Walter Koeller in Chicago years after the Missouri crime had been forgotten.

Had Koeller's assassins succeeded in boarding a freight train at Grand Crossing without having been seen, they would undoubtedly have escaped the penalty of their crime. Their destination was South America, and but for the signal service system and the police officer's alertness, the murder of Koeller would have gone down in police history as one of the mysteries of Chicago.

It cannot be stated with certainty when the "rogues' gallery," so called, was first instituted as a police adjunct. Desperate criminals had been for a long time photographed in some private establishment under contract until June 1884, when Chicago, again setting the pace by having one of its members instructed in the art, and establishing a police photograph gallery at police headquarters.

According to the *British Journal of Photography*, Chicago was the first city in the world to take this step, as it was the first city in America to adopt the Bertillon system of identification, which was originated in Paris in 1883 and copied by Chicago five years later.

It may not be out of place to state here that it was Captain

Michael P. Evans (then sergeant) who introduced police photography and the Bertillon system in the western metropolis.

It would be superfluous to undertake to do more than mention the Bertillon system of identification to an audience like this in speaking of improvements in police methods.

If anyone had been so bold as to affirm only a few years ago that it would be possible to give such a description of any one individual that he or she could be positively identified among thousands, if not millions, his statement would have been met with ridicule. Today, however, thanks to the research of Quételet, the Belgian scientist, and the subsequent labors of Alphonse Bertillon, the celebrated French anthropologist, we are able to give such a detailed description of any given individual that his identification becomes a matter of absolute certainty.

I fear that in speaking on this subject I would not be justified in omitting to mention the great service rendered the police all over the country by the *Detective*, conducted and printed in the city of Chicago by one of our members, Mr. Philip Holland. Through its means a sheriff away out in Iowa located Barthelin, the matricide who buried his mother in the basement of her residence, as well as murdered his sweetheart and left her to rot among the weeds in the prairie a dozen miles from the heart of the city. The service rendered by a paper like the *Detective*, which circulates among sheriffs and police officials all over this continent, can hardly be estimated.

The forward stride from the night watchman with his lantern announcing the passing hours to the uniformed and disciplined police officer of the present equipped with the telegraph, the telephone, the police signal service, and the Bertillon system of identification is indeed an interesting one to contemplate.

Note: Many advances have been made in police methods since 1904, when the above was written, but it was the limit of police service in its day.

The address was very well received, being informative and appropriate. Of the comments and discussion which ensued, nothing was so keenly enjoyed as the confidential inquiry of my host, the genial Colonel Matt Kiley, chief of police of St. Louis: "Who did you get to write those addresses for you, Frank, or do you write them yourself?"

CAR-BARN BANDITS

As the years roll by, we are occasionally reminded of the "car-barn bandits" of a generation ago, by the death of Captain James Gleason, former chief of police, or some other member of the Chicago police force who is said to have participated in their capture. As there were more than ninety men engaged in the hunt on that day in the Indiana Dunes and marshes, the allusion, while technically true, reflects no special glory on any of them. Those who may chance to read the following outline facts as remembered by the writer, then general superintendent of police, can form their own conclusions.

The robbery of the Street Car Barns at Sixty-first and South State streets and the murder of the cashier, August 30, 1903, the details of which are not essential in this review, was committed by a gang of amateur criminals, influenced by dime novel literature and Wild West exploits, who were born and bred on the North Side, ten miles distant from the scene of their crime. Under the circumstances, despite the intensive efforts of the police, much time had elapsed between the bandits' escape and their dramatic capture November 27, the same year.

The first clue to the identity of those bandits, who had no previous criminal record, was obtained by Lieutenant John D. McCarthy of the Town Hall Station, who informed Inspector Schuettler. Inspector Schuettler took hold of the case himself and cut the lieutenant out of it. When the fugitive bandits were eventually recognized in the Indiana Dunes from a circular broadcast from police headquarters, Schuettler, assistant superintendent of police, without notifying me, sent four policemen at night out into the wilderness to arrest four heavily armed desperadoes ensconced in caves or dugouts. Two of the four policemen were killed and the other two wounded. The latter sheltered behind trunks of trees, except enough to enable them to shoot into the cave, were hit in their exposed parts. The result justified the accuracy of Mrs. Van Dine's warning to Assistant Chief Schuettler and the writer that her son, the leader of the gang, could hit a cent nine times out of ten at a range of forty feet in target practice in the attic of her house.

When I reached city hall the next morning, everything was in an uproar. It did not take long to get fifty policemen armed with rifles on board a special train and on their way to the Indiana Dunes. The bandits had abandoned their den and were lost in the marshy wilderness, but the police spread out and trailed them by their footprints in the light snow. Another company

This collage photographic portrait of the four car-barn bandits must have been as startling to newspaper readers in 1903 as it is today. Peter Niedermeier, Harvey Van Dine, Emil Roeski, and Gustave Marx looked like clean-cut, handsome young men, not the murderers of seven people. (Chicago American, November 28, 1903)

PROFILE STUDY OF BANDITS WHO CONFESS 7 MURDERS.

[From picture formed by photographs taken by Chicago American staff photographer.]

PETER NIEDEMEYER.   HARVEY VAN DINE.   EMIL ROESKI.   GUSTAV MARX.

Herman Schuettler, who joined the Chicago Police Department in 1883, achieved notoriety as the detective who "tracked [Louis] Lingg, the bomb-maker, to his hiding place on the South Side" after the explosion in Haymarket Square on May 4, 1886. Lingg and six other defendants were sentenced to death, but Lingg committed suicide by "exploding a detonating cap in his mouth" before the scheduled hanging on November 11, 1887. (Chicago Inter Ocean, January 26, 1890)

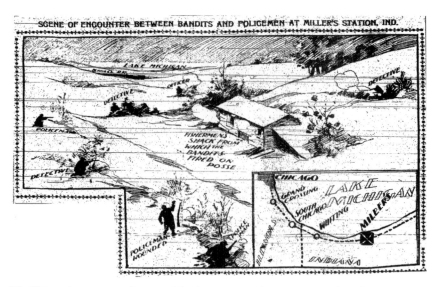

The Chicago American *ran this map of the shoot-out on its front page to provide readers with an overview of the hideout in Miller, Indiana, where the car-barn bandits outgunned Chicago policemen and detectives.* (Chicago American, November 27, 1903)

of forty men similarly equipped under the command of Sergeant James L. Mooney—now deputy commissioner of police—and accompanied by Assistant Chief Schuettler, started on another train to reinforce the first company early in the afternoon. The tragic happenings of the night left Schuettler in a state of indecisive bewilderment, while orders were being carried out.

Hunted by armed police ready to shoot, the desperate fugitives hoped to escape on the locomotive of a gravel train encountered in the flight, but as the switchman refused to uncouple the engine, they killed him. Realizing that the police were in sight, and being utterly exhausted without food or rest, three of them, rather than being shot, gave themselves up to a couple of farmers husking corn in a field. Captain Hugh Melaniphy of South Chicago and James Markham, my secretary, were but a few hundred yards away. The fourth man was found sound asleep stretched out on a bench in a railway switch shanty more than a mile away.

I was in communication with railway officials who cooperated with the police in a very practical way during most of this eventful day. An Indiana sheriff awaited the return train's arrival at a regular stop station to take our bandit prisoners into custody for killing the switchman. On my request, the train went through without stopping, but it did stop further on to pick up Assistant Superintendent Schuettler, who was twenty-five miles distant from where the fugitive bandits were arrested by Captain Melaniphy and Secretary Markham. To evade the crowds at the railway depot, arrangements were made to transfer the prisoners at Archer Avenue to patrol wagons and drive to city hall unobtrusively.

As the patrol wagons pulled up at the curb and unloaded their passengers, Assistant Superintendent Schuettler seized by their coat collars two prisoners and, towering over them, followed by a few patrolmen with the other prisoners, marched into city hall, up one flight of steps, and into my office, where Mayor Harrison and as many aldermen and other officials as could crowd in awaited their coming.

Had my assistant notified me of the receipt of the telegram from the Dunes, as was his duty, a sufficient force of police riflemen under proper command would have been sent to capture that band of armed desperadoes, and no police lives would have been sacrificed. Yet the public innocently believes that Assistant Superintendent of Police Schuettler captured the "car-barn bandits."

Ads proclaiming the spectacular allure of Mr. Blue Beard appeared in the newspapers during the final weeks of the show at the Iroquois Theater on Randolph Street between State and Dearborn. (Chicago Inter Ocean, December 27, 1903)

The new Iroquois Theater, at 24–28 West Randolph, designed by Benjamin Marshall, was supposed to have the latest technical innovations. However a flame from a stage light, a standing-room-only crowd, and inadequate fire prevention systems combined to create an inflammatory disaster. Pandemonium raged within the theater during the fire when patrons were unable to escape. Among the six hundred dead were thirty-eight public school teachers and 103 of their students, who had attended a matinee of Mr. Blue Beard *featuring Eddie Foy.* (Chicago Daily News, December 31, 1903)

REAPPOINTED BY MAYOR DUNNE FOR A THIRD TERM

Mayor Harrison having decided to retire from public life for a time at least, Judge Edward F. Dunne was elected to succeed him. Such a thing as reappointment to a cabinet office in a new administration was never thought of. It neither was sought nor expected by me. There was no lack of candidates, yet my name was sent by Mayor Dunne to the city council for confirmation as general superintendent of police. This third appointment as chief of police of Chicago [on July 11, 1905] and especially by two mayors has no parallel.

THE TEAMSTERS' STRIKE

The teamsters' strike, the greatest and most prolonged in Chicago's turbulent history, broke out suddenly after Mayor Dunne's inauguration. The mayor being avowedly friendly to labor, the labor leaders anticipated an easy victory. The merchants and manufacturers proved obdurate and organized a stubborn defense. As time progressed, the full strength of the police force being insufficient to cope with conditions, the city council authorized the swearing in as special police all capable men who would respond to the call, to serve with the men in uniform in protecting property, even beyond the city limits in occasional contingencies.

ATTORNEYS' SCHEME DEFEATED

The merchants of the Loop delivered to Mayor Dunne a formal demand for police protection for their teamsters and wagon drivers. With the demand was a long classified list of vehicles owned by each firm totaling more than the number of policemen available for that service. Asked by the mayor if we could protect that number, I informed him that we could not. "Then, I suppose," he continued, "I must reply to that effect." Realizing the consequence of that admission, I advised him to assure them that their demand would be

At the conclusion of the prolonged teamsters' strike in 1905, Chief O'Neill tendered his resignation to newly elected Mayor Edward F. Dunne, shown here. (The Book of Chicago *[Chicago: Chicago Evening Post, 1911])*

met. "But you say," protested the mayor, "that we have not enough men." "That is true," I admitted, "but neither have they half enough drivers to man that number of wagons." The merchants' bluff failed of its evident purpose, and nothing more was heard of it.

I was called to the mayor's office on a daily basis, where I had to confront a quintet of strike sympathizers, among them being Commissioner of Public Works Patterson, Clarence Darrow, and Dr. Cornelia De Bey, a mannish woman who was most aggressive. Attorneys for the business interests were equally clamorous in demanding the call of the state militia. The latter proposition I consistently opposed for two reasons. "What would be thought of a great city," I protested, "that was incapable of protecting its business without the intervention of the military?" The other reason I could not publicly divulge. From an anarchist in the German secret service and also on my Secret Service staff, I learned that should the military come to Chicago and spill any blood, the terrorists of Spring Valley, Illinois, intended to drop bombs into the open windows of engine rooms in the heart of the city.

In fancied secrecy and security, the leaders met nightly in a house on Indiana Avenue near Eighteenth Street for conference and conviviality. Plans and schemes were discussed in the hearing of their painted hosts and entertainers, who noted everything of importance that concerned the police department.

Without military aid, so much desired by insistent attorneys, and in spite of all opposition, the police maintained adequate control until the greatest strike in Chicago's history petered out after four months of fruitless struggle.

INCLINED TO RETIRE

1905–1936

Weary in mind and body from the strain of unremitting responsibility, I decided to resign and rest at an opportune time, having less than one week's vacation in a dozen years. There was yet another reason. To yield to the desires of some who came into power with the new administration would endanger a reputation acquired during my long service. So when the strike was declared off officially, I tendered Mayor Dunne my resignation, with a written expression of my appreciation of his kindness and courteous consideration. My last official act was the granting of a year's furlough on July 25, 1905, to my successor, Captain John M. Collins, who lost no time in carrying out the wishes of those whom I had defied.

DIFFICULTIES AND OPPOSITION INEVITABLE

Every head of the police department in a large city, whether known as general superintendent, chief, or commissioner, is certain to encounter difficulties. The general public wants the law enforced. The leaders of the powers that be expect concessions and special favors. Between the two influences he is liable to get forced out before the term of his office expires.

On difficulties not already mentioned, I had more than my share, all of them based on the desire of certain elements to force my resignation. As soon as Mayor Harrison had left the city on his midsummer vacation in 1901, investigators were set to work to dig up something to my discredit in past years. It was surmised that in the mayor's absence discipline would be relaxed and that I might incautiously become involved in questionable associations. As nothing came of this move, a scheme was evolved to indict me on the charge of attempting to violate the civil service law; in back of the scheme was the political leader most interested in my disgrace. It was rehearsed for one week in the home of a police lieutenant. When the time was ripe, the witness was seized on a [subpoena] duces tecum and hurried to the office of the state's

This portrait of O'Neill the civilian is not dated. In a comparison of the pictures of O'Neill as a young married man in his twenties and his official portrait as superintendent with this picture, the distinctive arch of his right eyebrow is still evident. (Mary Lesch collection)

attorney, where he lost his nerve, forgot his lines, and blurted out the truth. Notwithstanding this, he was taken before a grand jury, where he denied knowing anything to my detriment. It appears that the lieutenant had been promised a captaincy in any police district of his selection if he succeeded in smirching me. Instead, he lost his job and his pension.

The publisher of an evening paper, now dead, had been subsidized to harass me daily, but as it did not work, the final effort was to "frame" me. It was very alluring bait indeed if I would only bite, but as I could not be induced to visit the "spot," I escaped all conspiracies unscathed and continued as head of the Chicago Police Department until it suited me to retire from service.

THE END OF A RUGGED ROAD

The anticipation of relief from responsibilities, no less than its realization, begets a feeling of ineffable joy. What buoyancy of spirit was mine when free to follow the prompting of my inclinations, after laying down the official burdens of recent years. No cabinet position is so beset with rivalries, antagonisms, and intrigues as that of general superintendent of police in every successive administration.

A trip to the Atlantic cities from Washington to Boston, where relatives and friends of earlier years were located, enabled me to relax and enjoy the first release from strain in a dozen years. A voyage to Ireland followed in 1906, after an absence of forty-one years, although its verdant shores and bold headlands were glimpsed twice in the four years I sailed "before the mast."

In that year the Gaelic revival was in full blast. The movement, patriotic and nonsectarian, aimed at the regeneration of Irish ideals in music, language, and literature. Although but a tourist, I was recognized in the audience and pressed into service as one of the judges of the musical competition at the Munster Feis held in Cork City that year.

Among the notables met at the Rotunda in Dublin at a later celebration were Eoin MacNeill, Douglas Hyde, and Alfred Perceval Graves, historians, scholars, and poets. From the less renowned in my wanderings, not a little material was gleaned, to be incorporated in publications devoted to Irish folk music and related subjects.

A visit to my old-time friend and school director Tom Broderick, when I taught district school at Edina, capital of Knox County, Missouri, in the years 1869–70, ended my peregrinations after retirement.

LOVE OF NATURE

A love of nature in all its phases, an abiding obsession from youth to old age, inspired a desire to own land on which flowers, fruits, and flocks could be studied and developed to the best advantage. The cherished project was frustrated, sad to relate, by the sudden invasion of the angel of death. An epidemic of contagious diseases swept away our three children, the two oldest passing to eternity in one day. Others followed from similar causes as the years progressed, so that on my retirement from office at the age of fifty-seven, there remained but four daughters of a family of five boys and five girls. With six children interred in Chicago cemeteries, the anticipated pleasures of a country estate had lost their appeal.

The instinctive love of land, however, found expression in the limitation of my investments to lots and lands exclusively, the improvement and supervision of which serve to relieve the monotony of advanced age. The grievous void in my heart has been filled as well as it may be by the affection of four stalwart grandsons, the Mooney brothers, Francis, James, William, and Philip, who have made their mark in the field of collegiate athletics and bid fair to uphold the traditions of worthy ancestry.

Francis and Anna purchased three plots in Calvary Cemetery on August 4, 1879. Five of their children were buried at Calvary: John Francis (1871–71), John Francis (1872–76), Mary Catherine (1873–76), Francis (1875–79), and Philip Anthony (1882–85). (Photograph by Mary Lesch)

O'Neill kept many scrapbooks
of pictures and articles that were
important to him. While several of
the books were devoted to Irish history
and music, one scrapbook contained
magazine and newspaper clippings of
a more personal nature. This image
is one instance which revealed his
deep grief at the deaths of his young
children. *(Mary Lesch collection)*

When his son Rogers O'Neill died on
February 13, 1904, Francis O'Neill
personally designed and had the
O'Neill mausoleum built in Mount
Olivet Cemetery. Rogers was interred
there on June 27, 1905. Anna, Francis,
their daughters, and their deceased
grandchildren are all interred in the
mausoleum. *(Photograph by Mary Lesch)*

ACCUMULATING A PRIVATE LIBRARY

Not until after the foregoing rambling record had been penned did the idea [occur] of extending it to include a brief reference to my library, which in little more than a score of years grew into proportions not contemplated and attracted a publicity never anticipated.

The love of books was an inheritance, and more than a "five-foot shelf" of them was reluctantly left behind when I left the old O'Neill farmstead early in my seventeenth year, to challenge fate. Among them was A *History of the Earth and Animated Nature* by Oliver Goldsmith. The illustrations, being an endless source of pleasure, familiarized me with all forms of animal life and stimulated an interest in a subject which has never grown stale. A supply of back number periodicals and old books constituted a portion of my "tonnage" on every voyage, all of which were eventually begged, borrowed, or stolen, except one entitled *The Atmosphere*. Between the leaves of this volume I preserved the phenomenal fins or wings of flying fish, which in their flight at night from their fierce pursuers, the bonitos and dolphins, sometimes colliding with the sails or rigging, fell on the ship's deck. One of them in flight one dark night struck the boatswain on the side of the head as he was leaning on the rail and keeled him over.

MEETS A FAMOUS BOOKMAN

As far as books are concerned, the intervening years between my settlement in Chicago in 1870 and my transfer from desk sergeant at the Deering Street Police Station to police headquarters in 1882 may be considered devoid of interest. The habit of spending most of the lunch hour prowling among the secondhand book stores daily led me to make the acquaintance of a noted book dealer, Philip Nachten (anglicized Norton), who obtained all of his stock from London, his birthplace. To paraphrase a popular writer, I learned about books from him. His patrons were mainly book collectors intent on finding scarce works and rare editions. His notable patrons were Father Bernard Murray, Dr. Bristol, and William J. Onahan. Mr. Onahan, a brilliant yet modest man, was honored with titles and office beyond most men.

So well recognized was Norton's knowledge of books that to avoid competition which his presence would invite at an auction sale of a shipment of books from London, his bidding had to be done by proxy. In that capacity I often served and learned that next to Americans, or books on early American life and history, Hibernian, or books relating to Ireland, ranked highest in the book trade. In accordance with that trend, my library has nine hundred volumes devoted to Hibernia, one-sixth of which repose in the musical section of my library.

Those consignments of old books from England's overstocked stores, several times a year in the cool months, were discontinued many years ago, owing to the greed and dishonesty of the auctioneers, but during the score of years I had access to them my collection was enriched with many rare and precious tomes on anthropology, ethnology, archaeology, natural history, besides works on travel and exploration, all of them illustrated more or less profusely with woodcuts, lithographs, and copper and steel engravings.

ANCIENT AND RARE VOLUMES

Possibly the most unique and rarest work that fell to my lot is a twelve-volume set of *The Naturalists' Miscellany, or Coloured Figures of Natural Objects, Drawn and Described Immediately from Nature*. It was printed in London in 1790, the text being in both English and Latin. The dedication which follows is characteristic of British loyalty: "To the Most Illustrious Princess Charlotte, Queen of Great Britain, not less Distinguished by Her Virtues than Her Station, the first volume of the Naturalists' Miscellany is with Profound Humility Inscribed by Her Majesty's Most Devoted and Most Obedient Subjects and Servants, George Shaw, Frederick P. Nodder."

Competition for a work wanted by two or more is likely to run the bids beyond the value. At two sales *Marcoy's Travels in South America*, London, 1875, were bid beyond me. Next year at a late sale I got an equally good set for a dollar a volume less. A copy of *Hibernia Anglicana* by Sir Richard Cox, London, 1690, two volumes with frayed covers, was sold for five dollars and a half. A better bound copy, two volumes in one, fell to my bid a year later for ninety cents.

A much more valuable prize than either came my way on another occasion for one dollar and ten cents—a red-letter work entitled *The Antiquities and History of Ireland*, by the Right Honourable Sir James Ware, London, 1705. It was divided into five sections, described on the title page, and beneath which we find "Very useful for all persons who are desirous of being acquainted with the ancient and present state of the Kingdom."

Most publications in the eighteenth and earlier centuries were of large size and bound in leather. There are more books of the previous centuries which deserve mention.

An Answer to a Challenge Made by a Jesuite in Ireland, by James Ussher, Archbishop of Armagh—5 volumes in one, London, 1621—preserves the quaint letter and orthography of those times. What is now regarded as Irish brogue was the current English then. Ussher's "Divell," for instance, has been perpetuated by Pat, and it may not be out of place to remark that it was that celebrated ecclesiastic who determined the age of the world at the birth of Christ.

President Herbert Hoover may be interested in a square quarto entitled *A History of the Rise and Progress of the People Called Quakers in Ireland—from 1653 to 1751,* to which is added a Treatise of the Christian Discipline; it was authored by Thomas Wright and John Rutty, Dublin, 1751.

The Natural History of Ireland is another rare and important work, the full title of which is *A Discourse Concerning the Danish Mounts, Forts, and Towers in Ireland, Never Before Published,* by Thomas Molyneux, M.D., Fellow of the Royal Society of England, Professor of Physick in the University of Dublin, Physician to the State, and Physician General to the Army in Ireland, Dublin, 1725.

AN IRISH BIBLE

Not many are aware of the existence of the Holy Bible translated into Irish by an Englishman and printed at Dublin in 1852. From Canada I obtained a nice plump copy containing 1,572 pages. The translator, William Bedell, was born in Essex County, England, in 1570 and became Protestant Lord Bishop of Kilmore, Ireland, where he won the goodwill of the people by his liberality.

A GENEALOGICAL GEM

The story of one more of my treasures will not I trust trespass unduly on the patience of readers. Among the stock of a New Orleans bookstore, auctioned off in Chicago, was an octavo named *The History of Bandon, and the Principal Towns in the West Riding of Cork,* by George Bennett, Esq., B.L., Cork, 1869. This being a local history, it attracted no attention and was sold to me for thirty cents.

The town of Bandon was located in the territories of the O'Mahonys—my maternal ancestors—confiscated by Queen Elizabeth in 1588 and Castle

One of O'Neill's prized possessions, purchased for $1.10, was Sir James Ware's 1705 The Antiquities and History of Ireland. He donated it to the University of Notre Dame Library in 1931. (Reproduced from the original held by the Department of Special Collections, University Libraries of Notre Dame)

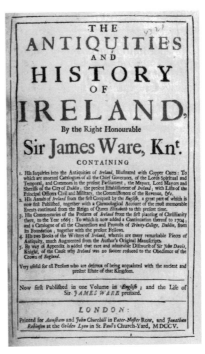

Although he lived longer in America than in Ireland, O'Neill continued to study and collect books relating to the history of his birthplace in County Cork. George Bennett's volume, published in 1869, included luminous color illustrations of Bandon. (Reproduced from the original held by the Department of Special Collections, University Libraries of Notre Dame)

Mahon with fourteen hundred acres conferred on Phane Beecher, son of Alderman Henry Beecher of London. Colonists were recruited in the southwest of England between Wales and Cornwall, and shipped to Kinsale, whence they made their way on foot to Castle Mahon and occupied the confiscated lands early in the year 1620, as did others who followed them in a few years. The first colony arrived in Ireland a few months before the Puritan Pilgrims of the *Mayflower* landed at Plymouth Rock. Many of the names prominent in American life as this is written are among the lists of colonists printed in this book.

Not many years ago a lady who specialized in genealogy and family trees inquired by phone if I ever heard of a book named *The History of Bandon*. The fact that I possessed a copy astounded her. She had been unable to trace a copy in any American library and located but one in Ireland. The clergyman who owned it would answer any question as far as possible but would not let the volume out of his hands for any consideration. Well, I did, and my trust and confidence were justified, for the good lady genealogist, patronized by the Colonial Dames and the Daughters of the Revolution, returned it after two months, during which I have no doubt she copied the contents from cover to cover.

This reminds me by contrast of a volume I lent another lady writer, who utilized the insides of the covers, flyleaves, margins of pages and wherever a blank space was available, to note her memorandums. She explained that she thought that I would find those notes handy should I want to consult the work myself.

MUSICAL COLLECTION

The section of my library devoted to the music of the Gaels—Irish and Scotch—is as comprehensive as an earnest effort could make it. The Bunting, Petrie, and Joyce publications, 1796 to 1909, complete, are in it, and so are dozens of others of less prominence, the oldest being *Orpheus Caledonius*, printed in 1733, and Burk Thumoth's two collections, undated, but actually printed in 1743–45, internal evidence discloses.

Many of the rarities gathered were procured by direct order from catalogs circulated by dealers in old books and through a book agency in London. Although failing to supply any of the books listed in my order at one time, I was notified by the agency that a copy of *O'Farrell's Collection of National Music for the Union Pipes* had come in. It was faded and coverless but otherwise perfect. I ordered it at once, for according to Chevalier Grattan Flood, there was but one copy of this publication, printed in 1797, known to exist in Ireland, and that was in the Library of Trinity College. (The National Library was, in fact, the repository, not Trinity.) I had previously expended six pounds to obtain an exact copy of a sixteen-page treatise on the manipulation of the union pipes which is included in this book and the only one ever printed. Now here comes into my possession at a cost of but six shillings and eight pence another copy preserved in Northumberland in the extreme northeast of England.

PHILIP NORTON, BOOKMAN

My mentor in book lore, Philip Norton, born of Irish parents in London, lived among books from his fourteenth year to the end of his life. With a view to benefit the young men of his parish he opened a reading room, and

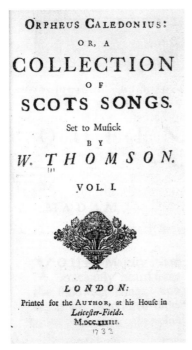

In addition to preserving and transcribing Irish tunes that he heard on the streets of Chicago, O'Neill became an avid collector of Celtic music. Orpheus Caledonius, the 1733 selection of Scottish songs published in London, is one of the oldest volumes in the Francis O'Neill Collection at the University of Notre Dame Library. (Reproduced from the original held by the Department of Special Collections, University Libraries of Notre Dame)

such was the success of the undertaking that the owners of public houses and barrooms and others who should have approved his action denounced him as an enemy to business and a disturber in the neighborhood. Embittered by this hostility, Norton emigrated to Canada and later to Chicago.

A discussion in which Ireland and the Irish were traduced once arose in his bookstore. His Irish blood boiled over, and forgetting the restraint and diplomacy so essential to a salesman, the supposed Englishman's reply in defense of his race alienated a few of his patrons, but his spirit and independence remained unaffected to the day of his death.

UNIVERSITY OF CHICAGO STUDENTS HONORABLE

In concluding this chapter, I take pleasure in stating that students from the University of Chicago on many occasions, when preparing their theses, found information and data in this library of mine which they had failed to obtain elsewhere; and furthermore, that my confidence was not misplaced in the few instances that I allowed those scholarly young men to take out books to study at their homes.

IRISH FOLK MUSIC—A FASCINATING HOBBY FROM YOUTH TO OLD AGE

Musical by instinct and heredity, and born and bred in an Irish traditional atmosphere, it was but natural that I should desire, like so many others similarly endowed, to find some means of giving expression on some musical instrument. The fiddle was my favorite, but the fates were against me, as none of the family sympathized with my aspirations. There being no other instrument available on which to practice but a decrepit flute, I contrived to learn the gamut and a few simple tunes from Timothy Downing, a gentleman farmer of our townland. That comprised the full extent of my musical education, when a sudden impulse to leave home changed my whole outlook on life.

In my sailing days an acquisitive ear picked up not a few foreign airs and dance tunes, and wherever I happened to roam in later years, every opportunity added to my repertory and proficiency.

Few were the chances of meeting and associating with Irish and Scotch musicians before permanent settlement in Chicago in 1871. Membership in the Department of Police in 1873 widened the scope of my acquaintance with that, to me, fascinating class of people. Being a music lover rather than

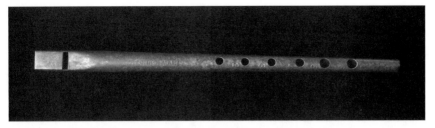

The last tin whistle that O'Neill owned is a cherished family heirloom. He was known to carry his whistle on his person at all times so that he could learn a new tune that he might hear. He was able to amass his large collection of Irish music by learning to play the songs on his whistle. He then would play the new compositions for his friend Sergeant James O'Neill, who wrote down the music. (Photograph by Jennifer Riforgiate; Mary Lesch collection)

a musician, no jealousies or rivalries ever marred our friendly relations. In course of time I became aware of the fact that I was the custodian of a great many airs and dance tunes, unconsciously memorized in boyhood days, not known to any of them.

My grandfather, the head of the O'Mahony clan in his day, kept an "open house" of hospitality in the good old Irish way. Pipers, fiddlers, and dancing masters availed themselves of it, and that is how my mother, of cherished memory, the eldest of his nine daughters, came to learn the scores of dance tunes she lilted, and which I memorized, as she manipulated the spinning wheels or attended to her household duties in later life. Not less musical was my father, God be good to him, who sang the old songs in Irish and English while leaning back in his chair at his own side of the hob.

To preserve for my own family and others who may be interested, this musical heritage initiated a movement that became a hobby and developed into the collection and publication of a series of volumes which have met with generous recognition in many lands.

Playing in concert with others not only added to our repertory but contributed to my proficiency on the flute, while yet no attempt had been made to score the tunes in musical notation. Fortuitously I learned from Joe Cant, a noted Highland piper, that the "best player of strathspeys he ever heard on the fiddle" lived in the rolling mill district. This paragon, James O'Neill, when found shoveling coal, proved to be all that Joe Cant had claimed and much more, for he was an expert at noting down music from the singing, playing, and humming of others. And so two O'Neills from the extremes of Erin, Cork and Belfast, met and, collaborating for years without infringing on their duties, garnered collections of Irish folk music now preserved in print.

IRISH MUSIC CLUB, CHICAGO.

Father W. K. Dollard.   Ed. Cronin.   Rogers F O'Neill.   Francis O'Neill   Timothy Dillon.   John McFadden.   Michael Kissane.   James Kennedy.
John McElligott.   M G Enright.   John Duffy   John Ennis.   Chas. O'Gallagher.   Wm. McCormick   Michael Dunlap.   Thos. Dunphy.   Father J. K. Feilding
John Conners.   Barney Delaney   John K. Beatty.   Tom Ennis   James Early   James Cahill.   Adam Tobin.
Garrett J. Stack.   James Kerwin.

The Irish Music Club of Chicago was a group of Irish musicians who enjoyed playing Irish music together. The group was formed in 1901 and disbanded in 1909. Most notable in this image are Rogers and Francis O'Neill in the top row, third and fourth from the left. (Francis O'Neill, Irish Minstrels and Musicians *[Chicago: Regan Printing House, 1913], 379)*

After James O'Neill had become a member of the police department in which he advanced to the rank of sergeant, his home at Brighton Park became the mecca for Irish music enthusiasts, and it was there that the suggestions of melodies were winnowed and selected for publication.

When *The Music of Ireland*, comprising 1,850 classified numbers, appeared in 1903, it was hailed as the largest and most sumptuous book of music ever published in Chicago. It evidently filled a long-felt want in certain lines of musical study; yet its cost and comprehensiveness led to a desire for a volume of dance music exclusively. To satisfy the disciples of Terpsichore, *The Dance Music of Ireland, 1001 Gems*, came from the press in 1910 [1907]. There was a need for a book of harmonized Irish music; this was also undertaken, although it involved a new problem—finding a capable arranger. Officials of Lyon and Healy, the great music company, found the arranger and named the new book *O'Neill's Irish Music for the Piano, or Violin*. When published in 1915, this collection was greeted with appreciation, and while there was no criticism of the harmonization, it did not inspire any enthusiasm.

The leather cover and gold lettering of O'Neill's first book was very impressive. Yet it was the 1850 melodies inside the book that made this publication so popular with the Irish in Chicago and in Ireland. (Photograph by Malachy McCarthy; Mary Lesch collection)

In his seventh book, published in 1915, O'Neill credited Selena O'Neill with arranging the music. (Photograph courtesy of Francis J. Clarke III)

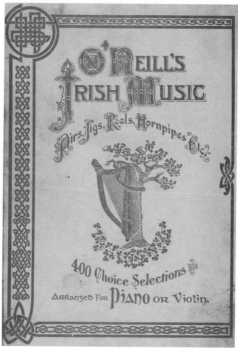

One day I happened to hear Selena O'Neill [no relation to Francis or James O'Neill], a young graduate of the Chicago Musical College, play a few numbers in this collection in excellent style. Replying to my compliments, she said, "I am playing my own harmony, not the way it is printed here." Her performance caught the spirit and rhythm peculiar to Irish music which but few modern musicians acquire.

With a view of definitely deciding their respective merits, both arrangements were submitted to musical experts for comparison. For the sake of impartiality I did not appear in the question at all. They reported in writing that both were musically correct but that the manuscript harmonization was preferred, being more in keeping with the spirit of Irish melody, especially dance music. As a result of that decision, the arrangement of the enlarged

Selena O'Neill, a graduate of the Chicago Musical College, was able to bring O'Neill's collections of Irish music to a larger audience by arranging the music for violin and piano. (Francis O'Neill, Irish Minstrels and Musicians [Chicago, Regan Press, 1913], 405–8)

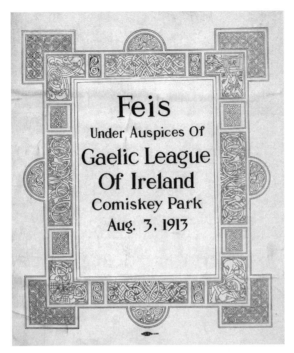

Artist Thomas A. O'Shaughnessy adapted his distinctive Celtic designs at Old Saint Patrick's Church at Adams and Desplaines streets for the program cover of the Gaelic League's Feis in 1913. O'Neill was among the major supporters of the event that brought together Irish musicians, storytellers, and athletes in the new Comiskey Baseball Park at Thirty-fifth Street and Shields Avenue. (Reproduced from the original held by the Department of Special Collections, University Libraries of Notre Dame)

edition of *O'Neill's Irish Music for the Piano, or Violin* contains four hundred classified numbers which are the work of Selena O'Neill. It may be well to state that from association with traditional Irish fiddlers and fluters her execution of *O'Neill's Irish Music for the Piano, or Violin* leaves nothing to be desired, and this fact in itself accounts for her skill in harmonization and consequent increase in popularity of the aforesaid collection.

Irish Folk Music; A Fascinating Hobby, With Some Account of Allied Subjects, published in 1913 [1910], is to a certain extent an autobiography, giving a sketchy account of progress. Quoting from the *Journal of the Iverian Society,* "Irish Folk Music—A Fascinating Hobby is an amazing compilation of biographical and historical details regarding the bards and bardic orders of old Erin, the old harpers as well as the bagpipe and performers upon it. The illustrations are particularly choice and attractive. Annie W. Patterson.

Mus. Doc." Had Chevalier Grattan Flood in his *Story of the Bagpipe* not disappointed the many old-timers who had hoped for a more generous mention of the celebrated pipers of the eighteenth and nineteenth centuries whose names have been preserved for generations, the work named *Irish Minstrels and Musicians; with Numerous Dissertations on Related Subjects* would not have been undertaken. This exhaustive work of nearly five hundred pages, profusely illustrated with halftones involving two years of intensive research, was published in 1913 and was reviewed by press and pen in flattering terms.

It would appear that I had by this time "reached the end of the line." The urge which stimulated my hobby hitherto did not subside, however, as there was much more of an interesting nature available, not dealt with heretofore. After years of inquiry, comparison, and correspondence ending in 1922, my sixth [eighth] contribution to the cause came from the binders. It bears an appropriate name: *Waifs and Strays of Gaelic Melody: Comprising Forgotten Favorites, Worthy Variants, and Tunes Not Previously Printed.*

The numbers in this collection include both Irish and Scotch compositions, those having any known history being accompanied by descriptive text. The usual complimentary reviews on this, no less than former works,

The harp had long been a symbol of Irish music when O'Neill chose this book plate to be a part of the design on the spines of three of his books, Music of Ireland, Irish Folk Music, *and* Irish Minstrels and Musicians. *(Photograph by Jennifer Riforgiate; Mary Lesch collection)*

were so gratifying that only a sense of the proprieties restrains me from quoting a few of them.

The prestige of rank and influence contributed not a little to the success of obtaining cherished tunes from persons disinclined to give circulation, or publicity, for few there are among traditional Irish pipers and fiddlers who do not preserve as personal property certain rare strains that only favored friends may enjoy. As old age approaches and memory declines, it is not unusual for these precious strains to pass away with their custodians.

Such was the incongruity of collecting Irish folk music and superintending the Department of Police of a large city, that the boys of the press favored the enterprise with wide publicity. Kindred spirits from near and far cooperated in many helpful ways, but having been accorded such recognition in the published works as circumstances would justify, any further mention of their names in this limited sketch would be superfluous.

Captain Francis O'Neill
Appointed to the Police Force July 12, 1873
General Superintendent of Police 1901–2–3–4–5
Resigned July 25, 1905

O'NEILL'S HOME LIFE AND LEGACY

FRANCIS O'NEILL'S CHILDREN

John Francis	baptized 11/12/1871	burial 11/22/1871
John Francis	baptized 1872 [?]	burial 8/27/1876
Mary Catherine	baptized 1873 [?]	burial 8/27/1876
Francis	baptized 5/16/1875	burial 8/2/1879
Julia Ann	born 12/6/1879	burial 1/20/1971
Caroline	born 1/9/1881	burial 2/3/1968
Philip Anthony	born 12/17/1882	burial 1/2/1885
Rogers F.	born 2/7/1886	[died 2/13/1904] burial 6/27/1905
Mary	born 5/19/1888	burial 11/13/1990
Anne	born 7/16/1890	burial 1/25/1964

FRANCIS O'NEILL'S RESIDENCES

		OCCUPATION	ADDRESS	PRESENT-DAY LOCATION
1872	Frank O'Neill	packer	461 S. Jefferson	1146 S. Jefferson
1873	Frank O'Neill	packer	Emerald	Emerald between Stearns and Thirty-first
1874	Francis O'Neil	policeman	16 S. Emerald	2516 S. Emerald
1875	Francis O'Neill	policeman	16 S. Emerald	2516 S. Emerald
1876	Frank O'Neill	policeman	16 S. Emerald	2516 S. Emerald
1877	Francis O'Neil	policeman	16 S. Emerald	2516 S. Emerald
1878	Francis O'Neil	policeman	16 S. Emerald	2516 S. Emerald
1879	Francis O'Neil	policeman	236 S. Emerald	2936 S. Emerald
1880	Frank O'Neil	policeman	2702 S. Wallace	
1881	Francis O'Neill	policeman	2702 S. Wallace	

1882	Francis O'Neill	policeman	2702 S. Wallace
1883	Francis O'Neill	policeman	2702 S. Wallace
1884	Frank O'Neill	policeman	2702 S. Wallace
1885	Frank O'Neill	policeman	2702 S. Wallace
1886	Frank O'Neill	policeman	2702 S. Wallace
1887	Frank O'Neill	policeman	2702 S. Wallace
1888	Frank O'Neill	policeman	2702 S. Wallace
1889	Francis O'Neill	sergeant	3723 S. Emerald
1890	Francis O'Neill	sergeant	5448 S. Drexel
1936	Francis O'Neill	retired	5448 S. Drexel

BOOKS BY FRANCIS O'NEILL

1903   *O'Neill's Music of Ireland: Eighteen Hundred and Fifty Melodies: Airs, Jigs, Reels, Hornpipes, Long Dances, Marches, etc., Many of Which Are Now Published for the First Time / Collected from All Available Sources, and Edited by Capt. Francis O'Neill; Arranged by James O'Neill.* Chicago: Lyon & Healy, 1903.

1907   *The Dance Music of Ireland: 1001 Gems: Double Jigs, Single Jigs, Hop or Skip Jigs, Reels, Hornpipes, Long Dances, Set Dances, etc. / Collected and Selected from All Available Sources, and Edited by Capt. Francis O'Neill; Arranged by Sergt. James O'Neill.* Chicago: Lyon & Healy, 1907.

1908   *O'Neill's Irish Music: 250 Choice Selections Arranged for Piano and Violin. Airs, Jigs, Reels, Hornpipes, Long Dances, etc., Many of Them Unpublished / Collected and Edited by Capt. Francis O'Neill, Arranged by James O'Neill. First Series.* Chicago: Lyon & Healy, 1908.

1910   *Irish Folk Music: A Fascinating Hobby, with Some Account of Allied Subjects Incl. O'Farrell's Treatise on the Irish or Union Pipes and Touhey's Hints to Amateur Pipers / by Capt. Francis O'Neill.* Chicago: Regan Printing House, 1910.

1910   *Popular Selections from O'Neill's Dance Music of Ireland: Double Jigs, Single Jigs, Hop or Slip Jigs, Reels, Hornpipes; Arranged by Selena O'Neill.* Chicago: Published by request of the Gaelic Junior Dancing Clubs, 1910, by Capt. Francis O'Neill.

1913   *Irish Minstrels and Musicians: With Numerous Dissertations on Related Subjects / by Capt. Francis O'Neill.* Chicago: Regan Printing House, 1913.

1915   *O'Neill's Irish Music: 400 Choice Selections Arranged for Piano and Violin: Airs, Jigs, Reels, Hornpipes, Long Dances, etc., Most of Them Rare, Many of Them Unpublished / Collected and Edited by Captain Francis O'Neill; Arranged by Selena O'Neill.* Enl. edition Chicago: Lyon & Healy, 1915.

1922   *Waifs and Strays of Gaelic Melody: Comprising Forgotten Favorites, Worthy Variants, and Tunes Not Previously Printed / Collected and Edited by Capt. Francis O'Neill; Arranged by Selena O'Neill.* Chicago: Lyon & Healy, 1922.

1924   *Waifs and Strays of Gaelic Melody: Comprising Forgotten Favorites, Worthy Variants, and Tunes Not Previously Printed / Collected and Edited by Capt. Francis O'Neill; Arranged by Selena O'Neill.* 2nd edition, enl. Chicago: Lyon & Healy, 1924.

THE COMMITTEE

With the initiative of Catherine Mulhall, a fund-raising organization was created in Tralibane, West Cork, Ireland, to preserve and honor the name of (Daniel) Francis O'Neill. The official name of the development group is the Captain Francis O'Neill Memorial Company, Limited. Informally the board of directors of the company is known as the committee. On September 20, 1998, they dedicated a plaque to O'Neill on the Tralibane Bridge to denote the place where O'Neill listened to Irish traditional music at the "pattern." The dedication ceremony was timed to celebrate the 150th anniversary of his birth. A life-size statue of Francis O'Neill, by artist Jeanne Rynhart, was erected near his birthplace in 1999. The committee has remained a strong force in the community, continuing to raise funds in order to create a "Captain Francis O'Neill Summer School." The committee also sponsors annual walks and "patterns." The committee directors are Catherine Mulhall, president; Liam Barrett, chairman; Gordon Shannon, vice chairman; John Collins, treasurer; Mary Kate O'Sullivan, assistant treasurer; Cecelia Wilcox, pro; Timmy McCarthy, organizer for Thursday walks; Nora Cremin, lecturer on Chief O'Neill; and Kathleen Cadogan, rest in peace.

This image of the O'Neill family in their backyard at 5448 South Drexel is undated but was probably taken between 1907 and 1913. Top row, from left to right: Caroline, Anne, May (Mary); front row: Francis and Anna. (Mary Lesch collection)

Before the O'Neill home at 5448 South Drexel was demolished, the Hyde Park Historical Society photographed its interior. The elegant carved doors with etched glass welcomed family, neighbors, and Irish musicians. (University of Chicago Library, Special Collections Research Center, Archival Photofiles, Hyde Park Historical Society, box 6, folder 3, 5448 South Drexel)

Francis and Anna's yard was a favorite gathering place and provided enough illumination for photographs. This photograph was likely taken between 1907 and 1913. (Mary Lesch collection)

A close-up view of the clock and jars on the parlor mantel of the O'Neill home at 5448 South Drexel Boulevard reveals the chief's passion for art and refinement. (Photograph by Jennifer Riforgiate; Mary Lesch collection)

Anna O'Neill reading her paper in a rare photograph of the interior of their home. Above the mantel are an ornate clock and jars that O'Neill collected during their marriage. This photograph was likely taken between 1907 and 1913. (Mary Lesch collection)

The Ronald McDonald House near the University of Chicago Comer Children's Hospital now occupies the site of Francis O'Neill's former Victorian home on Drexel Boulevard. (Artist rendering by Young Ki; courtesy of Pappageorge/Haymes Ltd., architects)

This photograph of Rogers O'Neill (1886–1904) was taken in the last year of his life, when he was seventeen years old. He was a student at Saint Ignatius College when he died of encarditis and meningitis. (Mary Lesch collection)

This tintype of O'Neill (standing) and two pals was labeled "the old rascals." The approximate date of this studio portrait is sometime in the 1890s. (Photograph restoration by Paul Lane, Photo Source of Evanston; Mary Lesch collection)

Mary Lesch (left) and Catherine Mulhall (right) flank the statue of Francis O'Neill in Tralibane. The directors of the Captain Francis O'Neill Memorial Company, Limited ("the committee"), raised funds to commission Jeanne Rynhart, a sculptor, to create a statue of O'Neill that honors his contributions to Ireland and Irish music. (Photograph by John Lesch)

Mary and John Lesch read the plaque at the crossroads. The first phase of the fund-raising effort by the committee was to place a plaque on the Tralibane Bridge "to honor O'Neill on the 150th anniversary of his birth." This was the site where O'Neill enjoyed "dancing at the crossroads." (Photograph by Catherine Mulhall)

The committee (the board of directors of the Captain Francis O'Neill Memorial Company, Limited) has continued to organize programs in Tralibane that pay tribute to Francis O'Neill. Timmy McCarthy leads a group on a walk up to the statue of O'Neill. (Courtesy of Catherine Mulhall)

Members of the committee and their families are pictured here as they complete their walk to the statue of O'Neill. (Courtesy of Catherine Mulhall)

The committee has sponsored dance competitions and demonstrations in Tralibane at the O'Neill statue. In this picture, school-age children are dancing. (Courtesy of Catherine Mulhall)

FRANCIS O'NEILL TIME LINE

1848   August 28: Francis O'Neill born in Tralibane, in West Cork, Ireland.

1865   April: Sailed on the barque *Anne* to Sunderland, England.
        Sailed on the brig *Jane Duncan* to Alexandria, Egypt, then through the
        Dardanelles to Odessa, Russia, on the Black Sea and back to Yorkshire,
        England.

1866   April: Sailed again on the *Jane Duncan* to Kyustendil, Bulgaria, on the Black
        Sea, through the Bosporous, and then to Bowling Green, on the river Clyde,
        close to Glasgow, Scotland.
        Sailed from Liverpool on the packet ship *Emerald Isle* to New York.
        Sailed on the schooner *Louisa Ann* to Brunswick, Georgia, then to St. Croix,
        West Indies, and then back to New York City.
        Late in the year: Sailed on the full-rigged ship *Minnehaha* of Boston to
        Yokohama Harbor, Japan.

1867   Sailed on the *Minnehaha* to Honolulu and on to Baker Island, where the
        ship was wrecked. Eleven days later, the *Minnehaha* crew was rescued from
        Baker Island by the brig *Zoe*. O'Neill sailed on the barque *Comet* from
        Honolulu to San Francisco.

1868   April: Stayed in California and became a shepherd tending eight hundred
        sheep in the Sierra Nevada.
        October: Shipped on the barque *Hannah* from San Francisco to Culiacán,
        Mexico, and then to New York City.

1869   January: Rounded Cape Horn aboard the *Hannah*.
        March: Landed in New York City, having circumnavigated the earth.

Summer: Traveled to Edina, Missouri, in Knox County and became a schoolteacher.

1870   Went to Chicago and worked on ships sailing the Great Lakes.
November 30: Married Anna Rogers in Bloomington, Illinois.

1871   November 12: First child, John Francis, baptized; child died November 22 and was buried at Calvary Cemetery.

1872   Worked as a packer; listed in the *Edwards' New City Directory* as living at 461 South Jefferson.
Second son, also named John Francis, born.

1873   Moved with family to Emerald Avenue between Stearns and Thirty-first, as listed in the *Edwards' New City Directory*.
July 12: Joined the Chicago Police Department.
August 17: Shot by a burglar at Clark and Monroe streets.
August 18: Promoted from probationer to regular policeman.
First daughter, Mary Catherine, born.

1874   Moved with family to 16 South Emerald, as listed in the *Lakeside Annual Directory*. This address was renumbered to become 2516 South Emerald.

1875   May 16: Third son, named Francis, was baptized.

1876   August 27: Both John Francis and Mary Catherine were buried at Calvary Cemetery.

1879   August 2: Son Francis died at age four and was buried at Calvary Cemetery.
December 6: Second daughter, named Julia Ann, born.
Moved with family to 236 South Emerald, which became 2936 South Emerald.

1880   Bought land in Bridgeport and built first home at 2702 South Wallace.

1881   January 9: Third daughter, Caroline, born.

1882   December 17: Fourth son, Philip Anthony, born.

1883   Promoted to assistant chief clerk.

1885   January 2: Son Philip Anthony was buried at Calvary Cemetery.

1886   February 7: Fifth son, Rogers Francis, born.

1888   May 19: Fourth daughter, Mary, born.

1889   Moved with family to 3723 South Emerald.

1890   Moved with family to 5448 South Drexel Boulevard.
        July 16: Fifth daughter, Anne, born.

1891   May: Transferred as lieutenant to Hyde Park District.

1893   Named chief clerk.

1894   April 17: Promoted to captain.
        July and August: Was captain at the great railway and sympathetic strike.
        Received a score of 99.8 on the civil service exam for promotion.

1895   Retained his rank of captain in a Republican administration.
        Arrested two aldermen who shoved him to make him get out of their way.

1900   January 30: Daughter Julia Ann married James Mooney, who later rose
        through the police ranks to become deputy superintendent of police.

1901   April 30: Appointed general superintendent of police by Mayor Carter
        Harrison II.
        September: Arrested anarchist Emma Goldman.

1902   February: Rumors of O'Neill's assassination were greatly exaggerated in front-
        page newspaper reports; the chief was alive and well.
        March: Prince Henry of Prussia visited Chicago.
        May: Addressed the International Association of Chiefs of Police on the
        Haymarket Riot.
        Persuaded the city council to vote the first pay increase for patrolmen, from
        $1,000 to $1,100 a year.

1915   Published *O'Neill's Irish Music: 400 Choice Selections Arranged for Piano and Violin*; arranged by Selena O'Neill.

1922   Published *Waifs and Strays of Gaelic Melody: Comprising Forgotten Favorites, Worthy Variants, and Tunes Not Previously Printed*; arranged by Selena O'Neill.

1924   Published *Waifs and Strays of Gaelic Melody: Comprising Forgotten Favorites, Worthy Variants, and Tunes not Previously Printed*; arranged by Selena O'Neill. Second edition, enlarged.

1931   Donated his library of more than fifteen hundred volumes to the University of Notre Dame.

1934   Wife Anna Rogers O'Neill died and was buried at Mount Olivet Cemetery.

1936   January 28: Francis O'Neill died at his home and was buried at Mount Olivet Cemetery.

BOOKS DONATED BY CAPTAIN FRANCIS O'NEILL TO THE UNIVERSITY OF NOTRE DAME LIBRARY IN 1931

This appendix, arranged chronologically with call numbers and storage size to aid scholars in the O'Neill Collection, was prepared under a grant from the Cushwa Center for the Study of American Catholicism. The authors gratefully acknowledge support from the Cushwa Center and the assistance of the Department of Special Collections, University Libraries of Notre Dame, 102 Hesburgh Library, University of Notre Dame, Notre Dame, IN 46556-5629 (574-631-5636).

Ussher, James. *An answer to a challenge made by a Jesuite in Ireland . . . Whereunto certain other treatises are adjoined.* London: Printed by R. Y[oung] for the partners of the Irish Stocke, 1631.
BX 1775 .I7 U86 Rare Books Medium

Cox, Sir Richard. *Hibernia Anglicana; or, The History of Ireland, from the conquest thereof by the English, to this present time. With an introductory discourse touching the ancient state of the kingdom. By Richard Cox.* London: Printed by H. Clark, for J. Watts, 1692.
DA 910 .C839h 1692 Rare Books Large

Ware, Sir James. *The antiquities and history of Ireland / by the right honourable Sir James Ware.* London: Printed for Awasham and John Churchill and J. Robinson . . . at the Golden Lyon, 1705.
DA 930 .W223 1705 Rare Books XLarge

A *natural history of Ireland, in three parts.* Dublin: Printed for G. Ewing, [1725] 1726.
QH 143 .N219 Rare Books Medium

Orpheus Caledonius=A collection of Scots songs / set to music by W. Thomson. London: "Printed for the author, at his house in Leicester-Fields," 1733.
M 1746 .T5 O7 1733 Rare Books Medium

Rollin, Charles. *The history of the arts and sciences of the antients, under the following heads: agriculture, commerce, architecture and architects, sculpture and sculptures, painting and painters, musick and musicians, the art military.* London: Printed for John and Paul Knapton, at the Crown . . . , 1737.
D 80. R651t En 36 1737 Rare Books Medium

Symson, Matthias. *The present state of Scotland, Enl., corr., and amended from above one thousand errors in the former editions.* London: J. Brotherton [etc.], 1738.
DA 760 .P926 1738 Rare Books Medium

Thumoth, Burk. *Twelve Scotch, and twelve Irish airs with variations; set for the German flute[,] violin or harpsichord / by Mr. Burk Thumoth.* London: Printed for and sold by John Simpson, 1745.
M240 .T48 1745 Rare Books Large

Wight, Thomas. *A history of the rise and progress of the people called Quakers in Ireland: from 1653 to 1700 . . . / by Thomas Wight; to which is added a continuation . . . to . . . 1751. With an introduction . . . and a treatise of the Christian discipline exercised among the said people by J. Rutty.* Dublin: Printed by I. Jackson, 1751.
BX 7681 .W639h Rare Books Medium

Drummond, Alexander. *Travels through different cities of Germany, Italy, Greece, and several parts of Asia, as far as the banks of the Euphrates: in a series of letters.* London: Printed by W. Strahan for the author, 1754.
D 972 .D844t Rare Books XLarge

Dissertations on the history of Ireland. To which is subjoined, a dissertation on the Irish colonies established in Britain. With some remarks on Mr. MacPherson's translation of Fingal and Temora. By C. O'Conor. Dublin: Printed by G. Faulkner, 1766.
DA 930 .Oc5d 1766 Rare Books Medium

Warner, Ferdinando. *The history of the rebellion and civil-war in Ireland / by Ferdo Warner.* Dublin: Printed for J. Williams, 1768.
DA 943 .W243h 1768 Rare Books Medium

Macpherson, James. *An introduction to the history of Great Britain and Ireland / by James Macpherson.* London: Printed for T. Becket and P. A. De Hondt, 1771.
DA 135 .M241i 1771 Rare Books Large

Leland, Thomas. *The history of Ireland from the invasion of Henry II. with a preliminary discourse on the ancient state of that kingdom / by Thomas Leland.* London: Printed for J. Nourse [etc.], 1773.
DA 910 .L539h 1773 Rare Books Large

Vallencey, Charles. *A grammar of the Iberno-Celtic, or Irish Language / by Major Charles Vallancey.* Dublin: Printed by R. Marchbank, for G. Faulkner, T. Ewing, and R. Moncrieffe, 1773.
PB 1223 .V241g Rare Books Medium

Curry, John D. *An historical and critical review of the civil wars in Ireland: from the reign of Queen Elizabeth to the settlement under King William / Extracted from parliamentary records, state acts, and other authentic materials / by J.C.* Dublin: Printed and sold by J. Hoey and T. T. Faulkner, G. Burnet, and J. Morris, 1775.
DA 940 .C97 1775 Rare Books Large

O'Flaherty, Roderic. *The Ogygia vindicated.* Dublin: Printed for G. Faulkner, 1775.
DA 777. Of40 Rare Books Medium

Campbell, Thomas. *A philosophical survey of the south of Ireland, in a series of letters to John Watkinson, M.D.* Dublin: Printed for W. Whitestone [etc.], 1778.
DA 972 .C153p 1778 Rare Books Medium

O'Halloran, Sylvester. *A general history of Ireland, from the earliest accounts to the close of the twelfth century, collected from the most authentic records.* London: Printed by A. Hamilton, 1778.
DA 910 .Oh1g 1778 Rare Books Large

Young, Arthur. *A tour in Ireland: with general observations on the present state of the kingdom: made in the years 1776, 1777, and 1778. And brought down to the end of 1779 / by Arthur Young.* London: Printed for T. Cadell [etc.], 1780.
DA 972 .Y84t 1780 Rare Books Large

A selection of Scotch, English, Irish & foreign airs. Properly adapted for the German flute, violin or fife. [N.p.]: G. Goulding, 1782?–97?
M 5 .S4 Rare Books Small

Collectanea de rebus Hibernicis. 2nd ed. Dublin: Luke White, 1786.
DA 905 .C685 Rare Books Medium

Davies, Sir John. *Historical tracts by Sir John Davies . . . consisting of 1. A discovery of the true cause why Ireland was never brought under obedience of the crown of England. 2. A letter to the Earl of Salisbury on the state of Ireland, in 1607. 3. A letter to the Earl of Salisbury, in 1610; giving an account of the plantation in Ulster. 4. A speech to the Lord-Deputy in 1613, tracing the ancient constitution of Ireland. To which is prefixed a new life of the author, from authentic documents.* London: Printed for John Stockdale, 1786.
DA 941.3 .D287h Rare Books Medium

Historical memoirs of the Irish bards: interspersed with anecdotes of, and occasional observations on the music of Ireland; also, an historical and descriptive account of the musical instruments of the ancient Irish: and an appendix, containing several biographical and other papers, with select Irish melodies. London: T. Payne, 1786.
ML 3654 .W3 1786 Rare Books Large

Murphy, Arthur. *The works of Arthur Murphy, esq. . . .* London: T. Cadell, 1786.
PR 3605 .M 9 1786 Rare Books Medium

The Musical miscellany: a select collection of the most approved Scots, English, and Irish songs, set to music. Perth: Printed by J. Brown, 1786.
M 1738 .M797 Rare Books Small

Vallancey, Charles. *A vindication of the ancient history of Ireland: wherein is shewn. I. The descent of its old inhabitants from the Phaeno-Scythians of the East. II. The early skill of the Phaneo-Scythians in navigation, arts and letters. III. Several accounts of the ancient Irish bards, authenticated from parallel history, sacred and profane, &c . . . The whole illustrated by notes and remarks on each chapter. By Col. Charles Vallancey.* Dublin: for Luke White, no. 86, Dame-Street, 1786.
DA 931 .V241v 1786 Rare Books Medium

Calliope; or, The musical miscellany: a select collection of the most approved English, Scots & Irish songs set to music. London: Elliot, 1788.
M 1738 .C3 Rare Books Medium

The royalty songster; and, convivial companion: a collection of all the most esteemed English, Scotch and Irish songs, &c, sung with the highest applause at the Royalty Theatre, and every other place of public entertainment / by Mr. Bannister . . . [et al.]; collected from the works of R. B. Sheridan . . . [et al.] and other distinguished writers: to which is added a collection of toasts and sentiments, Hippesley's Drunken-Man, and other comic pieces, the whole forming the most general and amusing selection of mirth, wit, and humour ever offered to the public. Ratcliff Highway: A. Cleugh; Ludgate Street: C. Stalker, 1788.
M 1738 .R69 1788 Rare Books Small

Camden, William. *Britannia: or, A chorographical description of the flourishing kingdoms of England, Scotland, and Ireland, and the islands adjacent; from the earliest antiquity / translated from the edition published by the author in MDCVII. Enlarged by the latest discoveries, by Richard Gough. In three volumes. Illustrated with maps and other copper-plates.* London: Printed by John Nicols for T. Payne and son . . . and G. G. J. and J. Robinson, 1789.
DA 620 .C144b 1789 Rare Books Oversize

The musical miscellany: or, songster's companion; being a collection of new humourous songs, duets, catches, glees, &c. / sung at the theatres and public gardens in London with a variety of new songs written on purpose for this work, and adapted to familiar tunes. North-Shields: W. Thompson, 1789.
ML 1741 .18 .M87 1789 Rare Books Small

Grose, Francis. *The antiquities of Ireland.* London: Printed for S. Hooper, 1791–95.
DA 920 .G767 1791 Rare Books Large

The Edinburgh musical miscellany: a collection of the most approved Scotch, English, and Irish songs, set to music / selected by D. Sime. Edinburgh: Printed for W. Gordon, 1792–93.
M 1738 .S5 E3 1792 Rare Books Small

Anthologia hibernica, or, Monthly collections of science, belles-lettres, and history: illustrated with beautiful engravings. Dublin: Printed for R. E. Mercier, 1793–94.
AP 73 .An86 Rare Books Medium

Seward, William Wenman. *Topographia Hibernia: or The topography of Ireland, antient and modern. Giving a complete view of the civil and ecclesiastical state of that kingdom; with its antiquities, natural curiosities, trade, manufactures, extent and population. / The whole alphabetically arranged. By Wm. Wenman Seward esq.* Dublin: A Stewart, 1795.
DA 979 .S49 1795

Bunting, Edward. *New edition of a general Collection of the ancient Irish music: containing a variety of Irish Airs, never before published, and also the compositions of Conolan and Carolan, collected from the harpers, etc., in the different provinces of Ireland, and adapted for the pianoforte / with a prefatory introduction. Vol. 1.* Dublin: Published by I. Willis, [1796].
M1744 .B868 G4 1796 Rare Books XLarge

Macpherson, James. *The poems of Ossian / translated by James Macpherson.* London: Printed for A. Strahan and T. Cadell: and sold by T. Cadel Jun. and W. Davies . . . , 1796.
PR 3544 .A1 1796 Rare Books Medium

The Repository of Scots & Irish airs, strathspeys, reels &c. Part of the slow tunes adapted for 2 violins & a bass, others with variations. The whole with improved basses for the harpsichord on piano-forte . . . Glasgow: McGoun, [1796?].
M 1 .R4 Rare Books Small

Bland and Weller's annual collection of twenty-four country dances for the year 1798: with their proper figures for the violin and German flute: Performed at court, bath, and all public assemblys. London: Bland & Weller, [1799].
M 1738 .B67 1798 Rare Books Small

Musicians' omnibus complete: contains 1500 pieces of music for the violin. Boston: Elias Howe, [18—?].
M 40 .M8 Rare Books Medium

Ballad sheets: [a remarkable collection of twenty-four nineteenth-century ballad sheets.]
[Dublin: v. pub., 1880–99].
M 1745 .I9 B23 1800 Rare Books Medium

Coote, Sir Charles. *Statistical survey of the county of Monaghan: with observations on the means of improvement, drawn up in the year 1801, for the consideration and under the direction of the Dublin Society, / by Sir Charles Coote, . . .* Dublin: Printed by Graisberry & Campbell, 10, Back-lane, 1801.
DA 990 .M741 C789s 1801 Rare Books Medium

Holmes, George. *Sketches of some of the southern counties of Ireland, collected during a tour in the autumn, 1797.* London: Printed by J. D. Dewick, for Longman and Rees [etc.], 1801.
DA 972 .H735 1801 Rare Books Medium

Musgrave, Sir Richard. *Memoirs of the different rebellions in Ireland: from the arrival of the English . . . compiled from original affidavits and other authentic documents; and illustrated with maps and plates / by Sir Richard Musgrave.* Dublin: Printed by Robert Marchbank, for John Milliken and John Stockdale, 1801.
DA 949 .M874 1801 Rare Books Large

M'Parlan, James. *Statistical survey of the country Leitrim: with observations on the means of improvement; drawn up for the consideration, and by order of the Dublin Society, / by James M'Parlan, M.D.* Dublin: Printed by Graisberry & Campbell, 10, Back-lane, 1802.
HA 1147 .L537 M24s 1802 Rare Books Medium

The musical repository: a collection of favourite Scotch, English, and Irish songs, set to music. Edinburgh: C. Stewart, 1802.
M 1738 .M8 1802 Rare Books Small

Hay, Edward. *History of the insurrection of the county of Wexford,* A.D. *1798.* Dublin: Printed for the author, by J. Stockdale, 1803.
DA 949 .H321h 1803 Rare Books Medium

Coote, Sir Charles. *Statistical survey of the county of Armagh: with observations on the means of improvement.* Dublin: Printed by Craisberry and Campbell, 1804.
DA 990 .Ar54 C789s Rare Books Medium

Ledwich, Edward. *The antiquities of Ireland. The 2d ed., with additions and corrections. To which is added a collection of miscellaneous antiquities. By Edward Ledwich* . . . Dublin: Printed by and for J. Jones, 1804.
DA 920 .L499 1804 Rare Books Large

A complete repository of old and new Scotch strathspeys, reels & jigs, adapted for the German flute. Selected from the works of Niel Gow & sons. Edinburgh: Printed for & sold by R. Purdie, [c. 1805].
M 1746 .C738 1805 Rare Books Small

Carr, Sir John. *The stranger in Ireland: or, A tour in the southern and western parts of that country, in the year 1805.* London: Printed for R. Phillips, 1806.
DA 975 .C23 1806 Rare Books Large

Gordon, James. *A history of Ireland from the earliest account, to the accomplishment of the union with Great Britain in 1801.* London: Longman, Hurst, Rees, and Orme, 1806.
DA 910 .G656h 1806 Rare Books Medium

Raymond, James Grant. *The life of Thomas Dermody: interspersed with pieces of original poetry / by James Grant Raymond.* London: W. Miller; [etc., etc.], 1806.
PR 3409 .D4 Z9 1806 Rare Books Medium

Morgan, Lady (Sydney). *Patriotic sketches of Ireland, written in Connaught. By Miss Owenson. In two volumes.* London: Printed for R. Phillips, by T. Gillet, 1807.
DA 990 .C762 M823p Rare Books Small

A Selection of Irish melodies / with symphonies and accompaniments by Sir John Stevenson . . . and characteristic words by Thomas Moore Esqr. London: Printed & sold at J. Power's Music & Instrument Ware House, 34 Strand, and at W. Power's Music Ware House, 4 Westmoreland Str. Dublin, [1808–15].
M 1744 .S54 1808 Rare Books XLarge

Bunting, Edward. *A general collection of the ancient music of Ireland: arranged for the piano forte; some of the most admired melodies are adapted for the voice, to poetry chiefly translated from the original Irish songs / by Thomas Campbell and other eminent poets: to which is prefixed a historical & critical dissertation on the Egyptian, British and Irish harp. Vol. 1.* London: Clementi & Comp, [1809].
M 1744 .B868 G4 1809 Rare Books XLarge

Newenham, Thomas. *A view of the natural, political and commercial circumstances of Ireland / by Thomas Newenham.* London: Printed for T. Cadell & W. Davies, 1809.
DA 975 .N49 1809 Rare Books Large

Spenser, Edmund. *The works of Spenser, Campion, Hanmer, and Marlebvrrovgh.* [Dublin: Printed for the proprietors by John Morrison, 1809].
DA 910 .Sp35w 1809 Rare Books Large

Drummond, Sir William. *An essay on a Punic inscription; found in the island of Malta.* London: Printed by A. J. Valpy [and] sold by W. H. Lunn, 1810.
DG 65 .D844 1810 Rare Books Large

Hardy, Francis. *Memoirs of the political and private life of James Caulfield: earl of Charlemont, knight of St. Patrick / by Francis Hardy.* London: T. Cadell and W. Davies, 1810.
DA 948.3 .C2 H2 1810 Rare Books Large

Stafford, Sir Thomas. *Pacata Hibernia: or, A history of the wars in Ireland, during the reign of Queen Elizabeth / Taken from the original chronicles. Illustrated with portraits of Queen Elizabeth and the Earl of Totness; and fac similies of all the original maps and plans. First published in London in 1633.* Dublin: Reprinted by the Hibernia-press co., 1810.
DA 937 .St13p 1810 Rare Books Large

Goldsmith, Oliver. *The miscellaneous works of Oliver Goldsmith. A new ed. To which is prefixed some account of his life and writings.* London: W. Otridge, 1812.
PR 3482 .O77 1812 Rare Books Medium

Letters from an Irish student in England to his father in Ireland. 2nd ed. London: A. K. Newman and co., 1812.
DA 625 .L563 Rare Books Small

Wakefield, Edward. *An account of Ireland, statistical and political / by Edward Wakefield.* London: Printed for Longman, Hurst, Rees, Orme, and Brown, 1812.
DA 975 .W35 1812 Rare Books Large

Weld, Isaac. *Illustrations of the scenery of Killarney and the surrounding country.* London: Printed for Longman, Hurst, Rees, Orme, & Brown [etc.], 1812.
DA 990 .K554 W452i Rare Books Large

Barlow, Stephen. *The history of Ireland, from the earliest period to the present time: embracing also a statistical and geographical account of that kingdom; forming together a complete view of its past and present state, under its political, civil, literary, and commercial relations / by Stephen Barlow, A.M.* London: Printed for Sherwood, Neely and Jones [et al.] [by] Law and Gilbert, 1814.
DA 910 .B249h 1814 Rare Books Medium

Clark, Richard. *The words of the most favourite pieces, performed at the Glee club, the Catch club, and other public societies.* London: Printed by the Philanthropic society, for the editor, 1814.
ML 48 .C4 W6 1814 Rare Books Medium

Connellan, Thaddeus. *An English Irish dictionary.* Dublin: Printed by Graisberry & Campbell, 1814.
PB 1291 .C752 Rare Books Small

The IRISH *Harper's legacy; being a choice collection of popular new songs, now singing with unbounded applause at the different places of public amusement.* Cork: John Connor, 1814.
PR 8860 .Ir4 1814 Rare Books Small

Mason, William Shaw. *A statistical account.* Dublin: Printed by Graisberry & Campbell, for J. Cumming; [etc., etc.], 1814–19.
DA 975 .M381s Rare Books Medium

Castlehaven, James Touchet. *The Earl of Castlehaven's Review, or his Memoirs of his engagement and carriage in the Irish wars; with Lord Anglesey's letter, containing observations and reflexions thereon.* Dublin: Printed for George Mullens, 1815.
DA 943 .T642e 1815 Rare Books Medium

Townsend, Horatio. *A General and statistical survey of the County of Cork.* Cork: Edwards & Savage, 1815.
DA 990 .C813 T664g Rare Books Medium

McCallum, Hugh. *An original collection of the poems of Ossian, Orrann, Ulin, and other bards, who flourished in the same age, collected and edited by Hugh and John McCallum.* Montrose: Printed at the Review newspaper office, for the editors, by J. Watt, 1816.
PB 1424 .M1240 Rare Books Medium

Wilson, Thomas. *A companion to the ball room*. London: Button, Whittaker, 1816.
 GV 1751 .B4 C6 1816 Rare Books Small

Leyden, John. *Historical account of discoveries and travels in Africa, by the late John Leyden, M.D. enlarged, and completed to the present time . . . by Hugh Murray*. Edinburgh: A. Constable and company [etc.], 1817.
 DT 3 .L593h 1817 Rare Books Medium

Plumptre, Anne. *Narrative of a residence in Ireland during the summer of 1814, and that of 1815 / by Anne Plumptre*. London: Printed for H. Colburn, 1817.
 DA 975 .P73 1817 Rare Books Large

Curwen, John Christian. *Observations on the state of Ireland, principally directed to its agriculture and rural population; in a series of letters, written on a tour through that country / by J. C. Curwen*. London: Baldwin, Cradock, and Joy, 1818.
 HD 625 .C9490 Rare Books Medium

Phillips, Charles. *The emerald isle: a poem / by Charles Phillips*. London: Printed for J. J. Stockdale, 1818.
 PR 5169 .P7 E5 1818 Rare Books Small

Ryan, Richard. *Biographia hibernia*. London: R. Ryan; [etc. etc.], 1819–21.
 DA 916 .R957b Rare Books Medium

Trotter, John Bernard. *Walks through Ireland in the years 1812, 1814 and 1817; described in a series of letters to an English gentleman*. London: Sir R. Phillips and col., 1819.
 DA 975 .T756w Rare Books Medium

Cromwell, Thomas. *Excursions through Ireland*. London: Printed for Longman, Hurst, Rees, Orme, and Browne; [etc., etc.], 1820.
 DA 990 .L533 C88e Rare Books Medium

MacDermot, Martin. *A new and impartial history of Ireland*. London: Printed by J. M'Gowan and G. Cowie and co.; [etc. etc.], 1820–23.
 DA 910 .M143n Rare Books Medium

Moore, Thomas. *Irish melodies / by Thomas Moore esq.; with an appendix, containing the original advertisements, and prefatory letter on music*. London: J. Power, [1821].
 PR 5054 .I8 1821 Rare Books Small

Wood, Thomas. *An inquiry concerning the primitive inhabitants of Ireland.* London: Printed for G. and W. B. Whittaker; [etc., etc.], 1821.
DA 931 .W85i 1821 Rare Books Medium

Curran, William Henry. *The life of the right honourable John Philpot Curran: late master of the rolls in Ireland / by his son, William Henry Curran.* 2nd ed. Edinburgh: A. Constable, 1822.
DA 948.3 .C936 C937L 1822 Rare Books Medium

Hamilton, William. *Letters concerning the northern coast of the county of Antrim . . . & an itinerary & guide to the Giant's causeway.* Belfast: Simms, 1822.
DA 990 .An 89 H18L Rare Books Small

O'Connor, Roger. *Chronicles of Eri: being the history of the Gaal Sciot Iber: or, the Irish people / translated from the original manuscripts in the Phoenician dialect of the Scythian language. By O'Connor.* London: Printed for Sir R. Phillips and co., 1822.
DA 930 .O18 1822 Rare Books Large

Atkinson, A. *Ireland exhibited to England.* London: Baldwin, Cradock, and Joy, 1823.
DA 975 .At541 Rare Books Medium

O'Driscol, John. *View of Ireland, moral, political, and religious.* London: Longman, Hurst, Rees, Orme and Brown, 1823.
DA 950.3 .Od6v Rare Books Medium

Cobbett, William. *A history of the Protestant "reformation" in England and Ireland; showing how that event has impoverished and degraded the main body of the people in those countries. In a series of letters addressed to all sensible and just Englishmen.* London: C. Clement, 1824–27.
BR 375 .C636h 1824 Rare Books Small

Croker, Thomas Crofton. *Researches in the south of Ireland: illustrative of the scenery, architectural remains, and the manners and superstitions of the peasantry / by T. Crofton Croker; with an appendix containing a private narrative of the Rebellion of 1798.* London: John Murray, 1824.
DA 975 .C9 1824 Rare Books Large

Moore, Thomas. *Memoirs of Captain Rock: the celebrated Irish chieftain: with some account of his ancestors / written by himself.* London: Longman, Hurst, Rees, Orme, Brown, and Green, 1824.
PR 5054 .M46 1824d Rare Books Medium

The Vocal library: being the largest collection of English, Scottish, and Irish songs, ever printed in a single volume; selected from the best authors between the age of Shakspeare, Jonson, and Cowley, and that of Dibdin, Wolcot, and Moore. London: Printed for G. B. Whittaker, 1824.
PR 1187 .V6 1824 Rare Books Small

Brewer, James Norris. *The beauties of Ireland.* London: Printed for Sherwood, Jones, & co. [etc.], 1825–26.
DA 975 .B758b Rare Books Medium

Betham, Sir William. *Irish antiquarian researches.* Dublin: W. Curry, Jun. and Company; [etc., etc., 1826]–27.
DA 905 .B465i Rare Books Medium

Kelly, Michael. *Reminiscences of Michael Kelly, of the King's theatre, and Theatre royal Drury lane: including a period of nearly half a century; with original anecdotes of many distinguished persons, political, literary, and musical.* London: H. Colburn, 1826.
ML 420 .K45 A3 R46 1826 Rare Books Medium

Kendall, Edward Augustus. *Letters to a friend, on the state of Ireland.* London: J. Carpenter & son [etc.], 1826.
DA 950.3 .K332L Rare Books Medium

Prior, Sir James. *Memoir of the life and character of the Right Hon. Edmund Burke; with specimens of his poetry and letters, and an estimate of his genius and talents.* 2nd ed. London: Baldwin, Cradock, and Joy, 1826.
DA 506 .B917 P938m 1826 Rare Books Medium

The beauties of melody: a collection of the most popular airs, duets, glees, &c., of the most esteemed authors, ancient and modern: comprising those of Arne, Handel, Haydn, Mozart . . .&c; Also a selection of the best . . . Irish melodies, with appropriate words, written exclusively for them: the symphonies and accompaniments

entirely new, and composed for this work; Interspersed with many of the beautiful Scotch melodies . . . Arranged for the voice, with an accompaniment for the piano-forte, &c; To which is prefixed, observations and instructions on music, particularly vocal and accompaniment / The whole compiled, composed, selected, and arranged by W. H. Plumstead. London: Dean and Munday, [1827].
M 1738 .P739b Rare Books Medium

Bible. Irish. Bedell. 1827. Leabhuir an Tsean Tiomna / Uilliam Bhedel. Dublin: Printed by G. & J. Grierson & M. Keene, for the British and Foreign Bible Society, 1827.
BS 251 1827 Rare Books Large

M'Carron, Rev. Alex. James. *Derry discussion: a letter, addressed to the Rev. John Hayden, containing a correct statement . . . discussion? / with a reply to the . . . religion.* By the Rev. A J. M'Carron. Belfast: T. Mairs, 1827.
BX 1779 .M126d Rare Books Small

O'Driscol, John. *The history of Ireland.* London: Printed for Longman, Rees, Orme, Brown, and Green, 1827.
DA 910 .O12 1827 Rare Books Medium

Pope, Richard T. *Authenticated report of the discussion which took place between the Rev. Richard T. P. Pope, and the Rev. Thomas Maguire . . . April 1827.* Dublin: R. Coyne, R. M. Tims, and W. Curry, Jun. & co., 1827.
BX 1780 .P81a 1827 Rare Books Medium

Real life in Ireland. 4th ed. London: W. Evans & co., [1829?].
DA 975 .R229 Rare Books Medium

Sadler, Michael Thomas. *Ireland: its evils and their remedies: being a refutation of the errors of the emigration committee and others touching that country: to which is prefixed a synopsis of an original treatise, about to be published, on the law of population, developing the real principle on which it is universally regulated / by Michael Thomas Sadler.* 2nd ed. London: J. Murray, 1829.
HC 257 .Ir2 Sa15i 1829 Rare Books Medium

Yates, G. *The ball; or, A glance at Almack's in 1829.* London: Henry Colburn, 1829.
GV 1646 .En34 Y27b 1829 Rare Books Small

Anderson, Christopher. *Historical sketches of the native Irish and their descendants; illustrative of their past and present state with regard to literature, education, and oral instruction. By Christopher Anderson.* 2nd ed., enl. Edinburgh: Oliver & Boyd; [etc., etc.] 1830.
DA 925 .An23h Rare Books Small

Gastineau, Henry. *Wales illustrated, in a series of views, comprising the picturesque scenery, towns, castles, seats of the nobility & gentry, antiquities, & c.* London: Jones & co., 1830.
DA 730 .G219w Rare Books Large

Tonna, Charlotte Elizabeth. *The Rockite: an Irish story by Charlotte Elizabeth.* 2nd ed. London: J. Nisbet, 1830.
PR 5671 .T25 R63 1830 Rare Books Small

Dublin delineated in twenty-six views of the principal public buildings. Dublin: W. F. Wakeman, 1831.
DA 995 .D852 Rare Books Medium

Hardiman, James. *Irish ministrelsy, or bardic remains of Ireland; with English poetical translations / collected and edited, with notes and illustrations, by James Hardiman.* London: J. Robins, 1831.
PB 1424 .H22i 1831 Rare Books Medium

Wright, George Newenham. *Ireland illustrated; from original drawings / by G. Petrie, R. H. A., W. H. Bartlett, & T. M. Baynes. With descriptions, by G. N. Wright.* London: H. Fisher, son and Jackson, 1831.
DA 975 .W75 1831 Rare Books Large

Dublin penny journal. Dublin: J. S. Folds, [1832–33], P. D. Hardy, [1833–36].
AP 4 .D854 Rare Books Large

Puckler-Muskau, Hermann, Furst von. *Tour in England, Ireland, and France, in the years 1828 & 1829; with remarks on the manners and customs of the inhabitants, and anecdotes of distinguished public characters. In a series of letters. By a German prince.* London: E. Wilson, 1832.
DA 625 .P961b En36 1832 Rare Books Medium

Banim, John. *The ghost-hunter and his family / by the O'Hara family [pseud.]*. New York: D. & J. Sadlier & Co., [1833].
PR 4057 .B2 G46 1833 Rare Books Small

Barrington, Sir Jonah. *Rise and fall of the Irish nation / by Jonah Barrington*. New York: D. & J. Sadlier, [1833].
DA 949.5 .B277r Rare Books Medium

Logan, James. *The Scotish Gael: or, Celtic manners, as preserved among the Highlanders, being an historical and descriptive account of the inhabitants, antiquities, and national peculiarities of Scotland; more particularly of the northern, or Gaelic parts of the country, where the singular habits of the aboriginal Celts are the most tenaciously retained / by James Logan*. 1st American ed. Boston: Marsh, Capen & Lyon, 1833.
DA 880 .H537 L828s 1833 Rare Books Medium

Moore, Thomas. *Travels of an Irish gentleman in search of a religion: with notes and illustrations / by the editor of "Captain Rock's memoirs."* London: Longman, Rees, Orme, Brown, Green, & Longman, 1833.
BX 1751 .M61 1833 Rare Books Small

Tales of my country / by the author of "Early recollections," "A visit to my birth place, The abby of Innismoyle." Dublin: William Curry, Jun. and Company; Simkin and Mashall, London; sold also by Seeley and Sons, J. Nisbet, and J. Hatchard and Son, London, 1833.
PR 5059 .B88t 1833 Rare Books Small

Taylor, William Cooke. *History of Ireland, from the Anglo-Norman invasion till the union of the country with Great Britain. With additions, by William Sampson.* New York: Harper's family library, 1833.
DA 910 .T219h Rare Books Small

Villanueva, Joaquin Lorenzo. *Phonecian Ireland. Auctore doctore Joachimo Laurentio Villanueva . . . Tr., and illustrated with notes, an additional plate, and Ptolomey's map made modern, by Henry O'Brien.* London: Longman & co. [etc.]; Dublin, R. M. Timms [etc.], 1833.
DA 920 .V712p En 36 1833 Rare Books Medium

Betham, Sir William. *The Gael and Cymbri*. Dublin: W. Curry, Jun. and Company, 1834.
    DA 140 .B465g 1834 Rare Books Medium

Blackwood, James Stevenson. *The Irish judge: a tale in four cantos / by James Stevenson Blackwood*. Dublin: Printed for the author, 1834.
    PR 4135 .B86 I7 1834 Rare Books Medium

O'Brien, Henry. *The round towers of Ireland; or the history of the tuath-de-danaans for the first time revealed by Henry O'Brien, Esq. A.B.* London: Whittaker and co., 1834.
    DA 920 .Ob6r 1834 Rare Books Medium

Wilson, James. *The musical encyclopedia: a collection of English, Scottish, and Irish songs, with appropriate music, adapted to the voice, piano forte, etc. / by James Wilson, to which is prefixed an essay on the principles of music by William Grier.* London: Allan Bell, 1834.
    M 1738 .W5 M8 1834 Rare Books Large

Wright, George Newenham. *Scenes in Ireland: with historical illustrations, legends, and biographical notices / by G. N. Wright; embellished with thirty-six engravings.* London: Printed for Thomas Tegg and son, Cheapside, 1834.
    DA 975 .W932s Rare Books Medium

Guide to the county of Wicklow: illustrated with five engravings and a map. New ed., corr. and enl. Dublin: W. Curry, 1835.
    DA 990 .W632 W932g 1835 Rare Books Small

Inglis, Henry David. *A journey throughout Ireland, during the spring, summer, and autumn of 1834 / by Henry D. Inglis.* 4th ed. London: Whittaker, 1836.
    DA 975 .In4j 1836 Rare Books Small

Journal of a tour in Ireland, during the months of October and November, 1835. London: Printed by S. Bentley, 1836.
    DA 975 .J826 Rare Books Medium

Knott, Mary John. *Two months at Kilkee, a watering place in the County Clare, near the mouth of the Shannon, with an account of a voyage down that river from*

Limerick to Kilrush, and sketches of objects of interest in the neighbourhood, which will serve as a guide to the coast scenery. Dublin: W. Curry Jun. and Company.; [etc., etc.], 1836.

DA 995 .K553 K759t 1836 Rare Books Small

Prichard, James Cowles. *Researches into the physical history of mankind.* 3rd ed. London: Sherwood, Gilbert & Piper [etc.], 1836–47.

GN 23 .P931r 1847 Rare Books Medium

Binns, Jonathan. *The miseries and beauties of Ireland.* London: Longman, Orme, Brown and co., 1837.

DA 975 .B614 Rare Books Medium

Carey, Matthew. *Vindiciae hibernicae: or, Ireland vindicated; an attempt to develop and expose a few of the multifarious errors and misrepresentations respecting Ireland, in the histories of May, Temple, Whitelack, Borlace, Rushworth, Clarendon, Cox, Carte, Leland, Warner, Macauley, Hume, and others; particularly in the legendary tales of the pretended conspiracy and massacre of 1641 / by M. Carey.* Philadelphia: R. P. Desilver, 1837.

DA 940 .C189v Rare Books Medium

Prior, Sir James. *The life of Oliver Goldsmith, M.B., from a variety of different sources / by James Prior.* London: J. Murray, 1837.

PR 3493 .P75 1837 Rare Books Medium

Ritchie, Leitch. *Ireland picturesque and romantic / by Leitch Ritchie; with twenty engravings from drawings by D. M.'clise and T. Creswick.* London: Longman, Rees, Orme, Brown, Green, and Longman, [1837].

DA 975 .R59 1837 Rare Books Medium

A topographical dictionary of Ireland: comprising the several counties, cities, boroughs, corporate, market, and post towns, parishes and villages, with historical and statistical descriptions, embellished with engravings of the arms of the cities, bishopricks, corporate towns, and boroughs; and of the seals of the several municipal corporations. With an appendix, describing the electoral boundaries of the several boroughs, as defined by the act of the 2d & 3d of William IV. London: S. Lewis, 1837.

DA 975 .L588t 1837 Rare Books XLarge

Dauney, William. *Ancient Scotish melodies: from a manuscript of the reign of King James VI: with an introductory enquiry illustrative of the history of the music of Scotland / by William Dauney*. Edinburgh, Edinburgh Print. and Pub. Co., 1838.
ML 3655 .D24 Rare Books Large

Chatterton, Henrietta Georgiana Marcia Lascelles Iremonger. *Rambles in the south of Ireland during the year 1838*. London: Saunders and Otley, 1839.
DA 975 .C392r Rare Books Medium

Croker, Thomas Crofton. *Popular songs of Ireland / collected and edited, with introductions and notes, by Thomas Crofton Croker*. London: Colburn, 1839.
PR 1187 .C7 1839 Rare Books Medium

Wills, James. *Lives of illustrious and distinguished Irishmen, from the earliest times to the present period, arranged in chronological order, and embodying a history of Ireland in the lives of Irishmen / edited by James Wills*. Dublin: MacGregor, Polson and co., 1839–47.
DA 916.4 .W685L 1839 Rare Books Medium

The ancient music of Ireland: arranged for the piano forte, To which is prefixed a dissertation on the Irish harp and harpers, including an account of the old melodies of Ireland / by Edward Bunting. Dublin: Hodges and Smith, 1840.
M 1744 .B868 G4 1840 Rare Books Large

Butts, Isaac Ridler. *Irish life: in the castle, the courts, and the country. In three volumes*. London: How and Parsons, 1840.
PR 4349 .B77 I7 1840 Rare Books Medium

Daunt, William J. O'Neill. *Innisfoyle Abbey: a tale of modern times*. London, 1840.
PR 5059 .M3 I56 1840 Rare Books Medium

Windele, John. *Historical and descriptive notices of the city of Cork and its vicinity; Gougaun-Barra, Glengariff, and Killarney. By J. Windele*. Cork: Messrs. Bolster [etc., etc.], 1840.
DA 995 .C813 W722h Rare Books Small

Alexander's select beauties for the flute. London: Published by J. Alexander, [s.n.], 1841–42.
M 60 .A4 Rare Books Large

Betham, Sir William. *Etruria-celtica: Etruscan literature and antiquities investigated.* Dublin: P. D. Hardy and sons; [etc., etc.], 1842.
PA 2402 .B465e Rare Books Medium

Hall, Anne Marie Fielding. *Sketches of Irish character / by Mrs. S. C. Hall.* Illustrated ed. London: How and Parsons, 1842.
PR 4735 .H26 S54 1842 Rare Books Large

Willis, Nathaniel Parker. *The scenery and antiquities of Ireland / illustrated from drawings by W. H. Bartlett; the literary portion of the work by N.P. Willis and J. Stirling Coyne.* London: G. Virtue, [1842].
DA 975 .W679s V818 1842 Rare Books Large

Down and Connor church accommodation society. *Fourth and final report of . . . adopted at a general meeting, held on . . . subscribers.* Belfast: the Down . . . society, 1843.
BX 5435 .D757f 1843 Rare Books Medium

Hall, Samuel Carter. *A week at Killarney / by Mr. and Mrs. S. C. Hall.* London: J. How, 1843.
DA 990 .K554 H147w 1843 Rare Books Medium

Mason, Henry Joseph Monck. *The life of William Bedell, D.D., Lord Bishop of Kilmore / by H. J. Monck Mason.* London: R. B. Seeley and W. Burnside, 1843.
BX 5596 .B39 M381L 1843 Rare Books Medium

Moore, Thomas. *The history of Ireland: commencing with its earliest period, to the great expedition against Scotland in 1545 / by Thomas Moore.* Philadelphia: Lea & Blanchard, 1843–46.
DA 910 .M778h 1843 Rare Books Large

Chambers's miscellany of useful and entertaining tracts / edited by William and Robert Chambers. Edinburgh: W. and R. Chambers, [1844].
AC 4 .C356m Rare Books Small

Graham, John. *Derriana: A history of the siege of Londonderry, and defence of Enniskillen, in 1688 and 1689.* Philadelphia: J. M. Campbell; New York, Saxton & Miles, 1844.
DA 938 .G76h 1844 Rare Books Medium

Grant, James. *Impressions of Ireland and the Irish.* London: H. Cunningham, 1844.
DA 975 .G767i 1844 Rare Books Medium

Kohl, Johann Georg. *Ireland: Dublin, the Shannon, Limerick, Cork, and the Kilkenny races, the round towers, the lakes of Killarney, the county of Wicklow . . .* New York: Harper & brothers, 1844.
DA 975 .K823i Rare Books Medium

Mac Firbis, Duald. *The genealogies, tribes, and customs of Hy-Fiachrach: commonly called O'Dowda's country. / Now first published from the Book of Lecan, in the library of the Royal Irish academy, and from the genealogical manuscript of Duald MacFirbis, in the library of Lord Roden; with a translation and notes, and a map of Hy-Fiachrach, by John O'Donovan.* Dublin: Irish archaeological society, 1844.
DA 990 .Od5 M 169 1844 Rare Books Large

The Parliamentary gazetteer of Ireland: adapted to the new poor-law, franchise, municipal and ecclesiastical arrangements, and compiled with a special reference to the lines of railroad and canal communication as existing in 1843–44; illustrated by a series of maps, and other plates; and presenting the results, in detail, of the census of 1841, compared with that of 1831. Dublin: A. Fullarton, 1844.
DA 979 .P236 1844 Rare Books Large

The Spirit of the Nation. By the writers of the Nation Newspaper. 2nd ed., rev. Dublin: J. Duffy, 1843–44 [pt 1, 1844].
PR8861 .P759 Sp48 D874 Rare Books Small

Carleton, William. *Denis O'Shaughnessy going to Maynooth / by William Carleton.* London: G. Routledge, 1845.
PR 4416 .D416 1845 Rare Books Small

Carleton, William. *Parra Sastha; or, The history of Paddy Go-Easy and his wife Nancy / by William Carleton.* Dublin: J. Duffy, 1845.
PR 4416 .P247 D875 1845 Rare Books Small

Hemans, Felicia Dorothea Browne. *Poems / by Felicia Hemans with an essay on her genius by H. T. Tuckerman; edited by Rufus W. Griswold.* Philadelphia: Sorin and Ball, 1845.
PR 4780 .A2 G74 1845 Rare Books Small

Kane, Robert. *The industrial resources of Ireland.* 2nd ed. Dublin [etc.]: Hodges and Smith [etc.], 1845.
HC 257 .Ir2 K131i 1845 Rare Books Medium

Mac-Geoghegan, Abbe James. *The history of Ireland, ancient and modern, taken from the most authentic records, and dedicated to the Irish brigade.* New York: D. & J. Sadlier, 1845.
DA 910 .M173h 1845 Rare Books Large

MacNevin, Thomas. *The history of the volunteers of 1782. By Thomas MacNevin.* Dublin: Published James Duffy, 1845.
DA 948.4 .M234h Rare Books Small

Murray, Richard. *Ireland and her church.* London: Seeley, Burnside, and Seeley, 1845.
BR 793 .M966i 1845 Rare Books Medium

Petrie, George. *The ecclesiastical architecture of Ireland, anterior to the Anglo-Norman invasion; comprising an essay on the origin and uses of the round towers of Ireland; which obtained the gold medal and prize of the Royal Irish academy / by George Petrie.* Dublin: Hodges and Smith, 1845.
NA 5484 .P448e 1845 Rare Books Large

Shirley, Evelyn Philip. *Some account of the territory or dominion of Farney: in the province and earldom of Ulster / by Evelyn Philip Shirley.* London: W. Pickering, 1845.
DA 990 .F 233 S55 1845 Rare Books Large

The Spirit of the nation. Ballads and songs by the writers of "The Nation," with original and ancient music, arranged for the voice and piano-forte. Dublin: J. Duffy, 1845.
PR 8861 .L8 S6 1845 Rare Books Medium

Wilkinson, George. *Practical geology and ancient architecture of Ireland / by George Wilkinson; illustrated with seventeen plates and seventy-two woodcuts.* London: J. Murray; [etc., etc.], 1845.
NA 984 .W55 1845 Rare Books Large

Davis, Thomas Osborne. *National and historical ballads, songs, and poems / by Thomas Davis, M.R.I.A.* A new and rev. ed. Dublin: J. Duffy, [1846].
ML 54.6 .D33 1846 Rare Books Small

Finden, Edward. *The beauties of Moore: a series of portraits of his principal female characters, from paintings by eminent artists, executed expressly for the work / Engraved by, or under the immediate superintendence of, Mr. Edward Finden.* London: Chapman and Hall, 1846.
NE 1723 .F56 1846 Rare Books XLarge

French, Nicholas, Bishop of Ferns. *The historical works of the Right Rev. Nicholas French . . .* Dublin: J. Duffy, 1846.
DA 940 .F888h 1846 Rare Books Small

O'Connell, Daniel. *The life and speeches of Daniel O'Connell, M.P.* Dublin: J. Duffy; [etc., etc.], 1846.
DA 950.22 .A3L 1846 Rare Books Medium

Pearce, Robert Rouiere. *Memoirs and correspondence of the noble Richard Marquess Wellesley . . .* London: R. Bentley, 1846.
DA 536 .W459 P315m 1846 Rare Books Medium

Bible. N.T. Irish. O'Donnell. *An Tiomna Nuadh ar Dtighearna agus ar Slanuightheora Iosa Criosd / air na tharraing go firinneach as a nGreigis ughdarach ris Uilliam O'Domhnuill.* London: Printed by Richard Clay for the British and Foreign Bible Society, 1847.
BS 2020 .G118 1847 Rare Books Small

Flanagan, Thomas. *A manual of British & Irish history.* London: T. Jones; [etc., etc.] 1847.
DA 30 .F613m 1847 Rare Books Medium

Foster, Thomas Campbell. *Letters on the condition of the people of Ireland. By Thomas Campbell Foster. Reprinted, by permission with additions and copious notes, from "The Times" newspaper.* 2nd ed. London: Chapman and Hall, 1847.
DA 975 .F817L Rare Books Medium

The land we live in: a pictorial and literary sketch-book of the British Empire / [Charles Knight . . . et al.]. London: Charles Knight, [1847–50].
DA 600 .L229 Rare Books Large

Leabhar na g-ceart, or, The Book of rights, now for the first time edited, with translation and notes, by John O'Donovan. Dublin: Printed for the Celtic society, 1847.
DA 905 .L464 Rare Books Medium

Castlereagh, Robert Stewart, Viscount. *Memoirs and correspondence of Viscount Castlereagh, second Marquess of Londonderry. Edited by his brother, Charles Vane, Marquess of Londonderry.* London: H. Colburn, 1848–53.
DA 950.23 .L846 A3m Rare Books Medium

Lover, Samuel. *Legends and stories of Ireland. By Samuel Lover.* New ed. London: H. G. Bohn, 1848.
PR 4892 .L523 B634 1848 Rare Books Small

Martin, Selina. *Summary of Irish history: from the reign of Henry II, to the beginning of the present century, with an introductory chapter / by Selina Martin.* London: Simpkin, Marshall, and co.; Dublin: D. Batten [etc.], 1848–1848.
DA 910 .M365s 1847 Rare Books Small

Nennius. *Leabhar Breathnach annso sis: the Irish version of the Historia Britonum of Nennius. Edited, with a translation and notes, by James Henthorn Todd. The introd. and additional notes by Algernon Herbert.* Dublin: Irish Archaeological Society, 1848.
DA 135 .N349h Ir 1848 Rare Books Large

Pim, Jonathan. *Condition and prospects of Ireland and the evils arising from the present distribution of landed property.* Dublin: Hodges and Smith, 1848.
DA 950.2 .P648c Rare Books Medium

Trevelyan, Sir Charles Edward. *The Irish crisis, by C. E. Trevelyan.* London: Longman, Brown, Green & Longmans, 1848.
DA 950.7 .T728i 1848 Rare Books Small

Wakeman, William Frederick. *A handbook of Irish antiquities, pagan and Christian; especially of such as are easy of access from the Irish metropolis.* Dublin: Mc-Glashan, 1848.
DA 920 .W149 1848 Rare Books Small

Butler, Richard. *The annals of Ireland, by John Clyn and Thady Dowling. Together with the Annals of Ross. Edited, from MSS. in the library of Trinity College, Dublin, with introductory remarks, by Richard Butler.* Dublin: Irish Archaeological Society, 1849.
DA 905 .C629a 1849 Rare Books Medium

Dalyell, Sir John Graham. *Musical memoirs of Scotland, with historical annotations and numerous illustrative plates, by Sir John Graham Dalyell . . .* Edinburgh: T. G. Stevenson, 1849.
ML 501 .D3 1849 Rare Books Large

Conran, Michael. *The national music of Ireland: containing the history of the Irish bards, the national melodies, the harp, and other musical instruments of Erin / by Michael Conran.* 2nd ed. London: J. Johnson, 1850.
ML 3654 .C764n 1850 Rare Books Small

Crotty, Michael, Rev. *A narrative of the reformation . . . Ireland: of which the author was the . . . country / by the Rev. Michael Crotty.* 2nd ed. London: Thomas Hatchard, 1850.
BX 5136 .C884n 1850 Rare Books Medium

Murray, Patrick. *The Irish annual miscellany.* Dublin: G. Bellew, 1850.
PR 5101 .M47 1850 Rare Books Medium

Phillips, Charles. *Curran and his contemporaries / by Charles Phillips.* Edinburgh and London: W. Blackwood and sons, 1850.
DA 948.3 .C936 P541c 1850 Rare Books Medium

History of the Cromwellian survey of Ireland, A.D. *1655–6: commonly called the Down survey*, A.D. *1655–6 / by William Petty; edited, from a manuscript in the library of Trinity College, Dublin, with another in the possession of . . . the Marquis of Lansdowne, and one in the library of the King's Inns, Dublin, by Thomas Aiskew Larcom.* Dublin: For the Irish Archaeological Society, 1851.
DA 944.4 .P456h Rare Books Medium

History of Ireland: from the beginning of the Christian era to the present time. New and popular ed. London: John Cassell, 1851.
DA 910. H.67 1851 Rare Books Small

Lover, Samuel. *Songs and ballads. Including those sung in his "Irish Evenings" and hitherto unpublished.* New York: D. & J. Sadlier, 1851.
PR 4892. S66 1851 Rare Books Small

The poets and poetry of Munster: a selection of Irish songs by the poets of the last century with poetical translations by the late James Clarence Mangan, now for the first time published with the original music and biographical sketches of the authors, by John O'Daly. 3rd ed. Dublin: John O'Daly, 1851.
PB 1395 .M928 M313p 1851 Rare Books Small

Drummond, William Hamilton. *Ancient Irish minstrelsy.* Dublin: Hodges and Smith, 1852.
PB 1424 .D844a Rare Books Medium

The emerald wreath / by the author of the Boudoir melodies, Illustrations of Irish minstrelsy, etc. etc. Dublin: J. McGlashan, 1852.
ML 287 .E4 Rare Books Small

Head, Sir Francis Bond. *A fortnight in Ireland.* London: J. Murray, 1852.
DA 975 .H34f Rare Books Medium

O'Connell, Catherine M. *Excursions in Ireland during 1844 and 1850.* London: R. Bentley, 1852.
DA 975 .Oc5e Rare Books Medium

Stocqueler, J. H. [Joachim Hayward]. *The life of Field Marshal the Duke of Wellington.* London: Ingram, Cooke, and co., 1852–53.
DA 68.12 .W46Si13L Rare Books Medium

Forbes, Sir John. *Memorandums made in Ireland in the autumn of 1852.* London:
Smith, Elder and co., 1853.
DA 975 .F744m Rare Books Medium

Lake Lore, or, an antiquarian guide to some of the ruins and recollections of Killarney
/ by A.B.R. Dublin: Hodges and Smith, 1853.
DA 990 .K45 L34 Rare Books Small

Moore, Thomas. *Memoirs, journal, and correspondence of Thomas Moore / Edited*
by the Right Honourable Lord John Russell, M.P. London: Longman, Brown,
Green, and Longmans, 1853–56.
PR 5056 .A5 Rare Books Medium

Moore, Thomas. *Moore's Irish Melodies. / Illustrated by D. Maclise, R.A.* New ed.
London: Longman, Brown, Green, and Longmans, 1853.
PR 5054 .Ir4 Rare Books Large

Sheil, Richard Lalor. *The speeches of the Right Honorourable Richard Lalor Sheil. /*
With memoir, by Thomas MacNevin. Dublin: J. Duffy, 1853.
PR 5379 .S2 Z48 Rare Books Medium

Smith, John. *A treatise on the theory and practice of music: with the principles of har-*
mony and composition, and an approved method of learning to sing by note and
in parts: intended as a class-book for academies. Dublin: J. McGlashan; New
York: J. A. Novello, 1853.
MT 6 .S67 Rare Books Large

M'Sparran, Archibald. *The Irish legend; or M'Donnell, and the Norman de Borgos:*
a biographical tale / by Archibald M'Sparran; with an original appendix, con-
taining historical and traditional records of the ancient families of the north of
Ulster. Coleraine: Printed from the author's improved American edition, at the
Chronicle Office, by J. M'Combie, 1854.
PR 4971 .M249 I7 1854 Rare Books Medium

Quigley, Hugh. *The prophet of the ruined abbey, or, A glance of the future of Ireland:*
a narrative founded on the ancient "Prophecies of Culmkill," and on other predic-
tions and popular traditions among the Irish. By the author of "The cross and the
shamrock" . . . New York: E. Dunigan and brother, [1854?].
PR 5193 .Q6 P9 Rare Books Small

Fitzpatrick, William John. *The life, times, and contemporaries of Lord Cloncurry / by William John Fitzpatrick*. Dublin: J. Duffy, 1855.
DA 950.23 .C622 F582L Rare Books Medium

Howard, John Eliot. *The island of saints: or, Ireland in 1855 / by John Eliot Howard*. London: Seeleys, 1855.
DA 975 .H834i 1855 Rare Books Small

O'Conor, Matthew. *Irish brigades; or, Memoirs of the most eminent Irish military commanders who distinguished themselves in the Elizabethan and Williamite Wars in their own country, and in the service of France, Spain, etc.: with an appendix containing memoirs of Gen. Thomas Preston, Owen Roe O'Neill, etc*. Dublin: J. Duffy, 1855.
DA 914 .Oc5i 1855 Rare Books Medium

The Petrie collection of the ancient music of Ireland: arranged for the piano-forte / edited by George Petrie. Dublin: Printed at the University Press for the Society of the Preservation and Publication of the Melodies of Ireland by M. H. Gill, 1855–82.
M 1744 .P448 1855 Rare Books XLarge

Sheil, Richard Lalor. *Sketches, legal and political, by the late Right Honourable Richard Lalor Sheil. Edited, with notes, by M. W. Savage*. London: Published for H. Colburn by his successors, Hurst & Blackett, 1855.
DA 916 .Sh42s Rare Books Medium

Annals of the Four masters. *Annals of the kingdom of Ireland, by the Four masters, from the earliest period to the year 1616. Edited from mss. in the library of the Royal Irish academy and of Trinity College, Dublin, with a translation and copious notes, by John O'Donovan*. 2nd ed. Dublin: Hodges, Smith, 1856.
DA 905 .An 75 1856 Rare Books Large

The Bunsby paper: (2d series) Irish echoes / by John Brougham . . . With designs by McLenan. New York: Derby & Jackson; Cincinnati: H. W. Derby & Co., 1856.
PS 1124 .B6 B86 1856 Rare Books Medium

[McCullam, R.]. *Sketches of the Highlands of Cavan, and of Shirley Castle, in Farney, taken during the Irish famine / by a Looker-On [R. McCullam].* Belfast: J. Reed, 1856.
DA 990 .C314 Sk29 1856 Rare Books Small

O'Brien, William Smith. *Principles of government.* Boston: P. Donohoe, 1856.
JC 223 .Ob6p 1856 Rare Books Small

O'Byrne, Daniel. *The history of the Queen's county: containing an historical and traditional account of its foundries, duns, and other antiquities: also an account of some noble families of English extraction.* Dublin: J. O'Daly, 1856.
DA 990 .Q31 Ob9h Rare Books Medium

O'Reilly, Andrew. *The Irish abroad and at home; at the court and in the camp.* New York: D. Appleton and co., 1856.
DA 910 .Ir4 1856 Rare Books Medium

Savage, John. *'98 and '48, the modern revolutionary history and literature of Ireland.* New York: Redfield, [c. 1856].
DA 949 .Sa92n 1856 Rare Books Medium

Edgeworth, Maria. *Tales and novels, with engravings on steel.* London: Simpkin, Marshall, 1857.
PR 4640 .Si57 1857 Rare Books Small

Mooney, Thomas. *A history of Ireland: from its first settlement to the present time, including a particular account of its literature, music, architecture, and natural resources, with upwards of two hundred biographical sketches of its most eminent men, interspersed with a great number of Irish melodies, original and selected, arranged for musical instruments, and illustrated by many anecdotes of celebrated Irishmen, and a series of architectural descriptions / by Thomas Mooney.* 4th ed. Boston: Patrick Donahoe, 1857.
DA 910 .M779h 1857 Rare Books Medium

Weld, Charles Richard. *Vacations in Ireland.* London: Longman, Brown, Green, Longmans, & Roberts, 1857.
DA 975 .W45v Rare Books Medium

Hall, S. C. (Samuel Carter). *A week at Killarney.* London: Virtue, 1858.
    DA 990 .K554 H147w 1858 Rare Books Medium

Marmion, Anthony. *The ancient and modern history of the maritime ports of Ireland / by Anthony Marmion . . .* 3rd ed. London: Printed for the author, by W. H. Cox, 1858.
    DA 975 .M345a Rare Books Medium

One hundred Irish airs: arranged for the piano forte. New York: P. M. Haverty, [1858–59].
    M1 .O4 1858 Rare Books XLarge

O'Sullivan, Timothy. *Timothy O'Sullivan's (commonly called Tadhg Gaelach) Pious miscellany; containing also a collection of poems on religious subjects, by Adnghus O'Daly the Divine, Taghg MacDaire MacBrody, John Hore; together with Patrick Denn's appendix.* Edited by John O'Daly. Dublin: John O'Daly, 1858.
    PR 8856 .Os8p 1858 Rare Books Small

Poems of Ireland / selected, edited, and annotated by Samuel Lover; to which is added Lover's "Metrical tales." London, New York: Ward, Lock & Bowden, [1858].
    PR 8850 .L68 1858 Rare Books Small

Moore, Thomas. *Irish melodies, with symphonies and accompaniments by Sir John Stevenson; and characteristic words by Thomas Moore.* New ed. Dublin: James Duffy, [1859].
    M 1744 .M786 I7 Rare Books Large

Annals of Ireland: Three fragments, copied from ancient sources by Dubhaltach Mac-Firbisigh; and edited, with a translation and notes, from a manuscript preserved in the Burgundian Library at Brussels, by John O'Donovan. Dublin: Dublin Archaeological and Celtic Society, 1860.
    DA 905 .Od5a Rare Books Medium

Moore, Thomas. *Memoirs, journal and correspondence of Thomas Moore / ed. and abridged from the 1st ed., by the Right Hon. Lord John Russell . . .* London: Longman, Green, Longman, and Roberts, 1860.
    PR 5056 .A5 1860 Rare Books Medium

O'Donoghue, John. *Historical memoir of the O'Briens. With notes, appendix, and a genealogical table of their several branches. Comp. from the Irish annalists. By John O'Donoghue* . . . Dublin: Hodges, Smith & co., 1860.
DA 916.3 .Ob6 Od5h Rare Books Medium

Prior, Sir James. *Life of Edmond Malone, Editor of Shakespeare with selections from his manuscript anecdotes / by Sir James Prior.* London: Smith, Elder & Co., 1860.
PR 2972 .M3 P75 1860 Rare Books Medium

Poste, Beale. *Celtic inscriptions on Gaulish and British coins.* London: J. R. Smith, 1861.
CJ 506 .P845c 1861 Rare Books Medium

Smith, Goldwin. *Irish history and Irish character.* Oxford: J. H. and J. Parker, 1861.
DA 910 .Sm57i Rare Books Small

Fitz-Gerald, John. *Legends, ballads, and songs of the lee, by John FitzGerald.* Cork: Henry & Coghlan, 1862.
PR 4705 .F576L Rare Books Small

Poste, Beale. *A vindication of the Celtic inscriptions on Gaulish and British coins; with vignettes, and a plate of facsimiles of characters used in Roman writing in the first century, from Pompeii.* London: T. Richards, 1862.
CJ 506 .P845v Rare Books Medium

Morphy, J. (John). *Recollections of a visit to Great Britain and Ireland in the summer of 1862.* Quebec: W. Palmer, 1863.
DA 625 .M829r 1863 Rare Books Medium

O'Neill, Henry. *The fine arts and civilization of ancient Ireland / illustrated with chromo and other lithographs, and several woodcuts. By Henry O'Neill* . . . London: Smith, Elder, and company; Dublin: G. Herbert, 1863.
N 6240 .O54 F56 Rare Books Large

Sadlier, Mary Anne Madden. *The fate of Father Sheehy.* New York, Boston [etc.]: D. & J. Sadlier & co., [1863?].
PS 2749 .Sa15f 1863 Rare Books Small

Whiteside, James. *The life and death of the Irish Parliament, a lecture.* [N.p., n.pub. 1863].
JN 1463 .W588L Rare Books Small

Banim, John. *The denounced.* New ed. New York: D. & J. Sadlier & co., [1865].
PR 4057 .B2 D46 1865 Rare Books Small

An historical narrative, of the origin and constitution of "The society of the Governor and Assistants, London: of the new plantation in Ulster, within the realm of Ireland," commonly called The Honourable the Irish Society; together with memoranda of principal occurrences. London: Printed only for the use of the members of the Courts of Assistants, [1865].
DA 990 .UL7 Ir4 h Rare Books Medium

Banim, John. *Peter of the castle; and The Fetches / by the O'Hara family, [pseud.].* A new ed. with introduction and notes, by Michael Banim. New York: D. & J. Sadlier & Co., [1866].
PR 4057 .B2 P48 1866 Rare Books Small

Graves, Charles. *Eloge on the late George Petrie . . .; delivered at a meeting of the Royal Irish Academy, on the 12th February, 1866 / by the Very Rev. Charles Graves, . . .* Dublin: Printed at the Univesity Press, by M. H. Gill., 1866.
DA 948.3 .P448 G783e Rare Books Medium

Keating, Geoffrey. *The history of Ireland, from the earliest period to the English invasion; tr. from the original Gaelic, by John O'Mahony.* New York: Kirker, 1866.
DA 930 .K221h En36om Rare Books Medium

Kennedy, Patrick. *Legendary fictions of the Irish Celts / collected and narrated by Patrick Kennedy.* London: Macmillan and Co., 1866.
GR 147 .K3 1866 Rare Books Medium

Fitzpatrick, William John. *Ireland before the union; with extracts from the unpublished diary of Joh Scott, LL. D., earl of Clonmell, chief justice of the King's bench, 1774–1798.* Dublin: W. B. Kelly, 1867.
DA928.5 F582i 1867 Rare Books Small

Godkin, James. *Ireland and her churches.* London: Chapman and Hall, 1867.
BR 792 .G546i Rare Books Medium

Keane, Marcus. *The towers and temples of ancient Ireland; their origin and history discussed from a new point of view. Illustrated with one hundred and eighty-six engravings on wood, chiefly from photographs and original drawings.* Dublin: Hodges, Smith, 1867.
DA 920 .K43 1867 Rare Books Large

MacCarthy, Daniel. *The life and letters of Florence MacCarthy Reagh: tanist of Carbery, MacCarthy Mor, with some portion of "The history of the ancient families of the south of Ireland," / compiled solely from unpublished documents in Her Majesty's State Paper Office by Daniel MacCarthy.* London: Longmans, Green, Reader, and Dyer; Dublin: Hodges and Smith, 1867.
DA 937.5 .M127 M127L Rare Books Medium

Pope, Richard Thomas Pembroke. *The authentic report of the discussion which took place at the lecture-room of the Dublin Institution between the Rev. Thomas Maguire and the Rev. Richard T. P. Pope.* New York: D. & J. Sadlier, 1867.
BX 1765 .M213 1867 Rare Books Medium

Buckley, Michael Bernard. *The life and writings of the Rev. Arthur O'Leary. By the Rev. M. B. Buckley.* Dublin, London: J. Duffy, 1868.
BX 4705 .OL2 B856L 1868 Rare Books Medium

Fitzgibbon, Gerald. *Ireland in 1868, the battle-field for English party strife; its grievances, real and factitious; remedies, abortive or mischievous.* London: Longmans, Green, Reader, and Dyer [etc., etc.], 1868.
DA 957 .F577i 1868 Rare Books Medium

O'Donovan Rossa, Mary Jane Irwin. *Irish lyrical poems / by Mrs. O'Donovan (Rossa).* New York: P. M. Haverty, 1868.
PR 5112 .O2 I7 1868 Rare Books Small

A Saxon's remedy for Irish discontent. London: Tinsley Brothers, 1868.
DA 910 .Sa98 1868 Rare Books Medium

Wood, J. G. (John George). *The natural history of man: being an account of the manners and customs of the uncivilized races of men / by the Rev. J. G. Wood . . . with new designs by Angas, Danby, Wolf, Zwecker, etc., etc., engraved by the brother Dalziel . . .* London: G. Routledge and Sons, 1868–70.
GN 735 .W85n 1868 Rare Books Large

Bennett, George. *The history of Bandon, and the principal towns in the West Riding of county Cork.* Cork: F. Guy, 1869.
DA 995 .B223 B439h Rare Books Medium

Gaskin, James J. *Varieties of Irish history: from ancient and modern sources and original documents.* Dublin: W. B. Kelly; [etc., etc.], 1869.
DA 990 .D852 G212v Rare Books Medium

Giles, Henry. *Lectures and essays on Irish and other subjects / by Henry Giles.* New York: D. & J. Sadlier, 1869.
PS 1744 .G392 A16 1869 SA15 Rare Books Medium

Church of Ireland. General Convention. *Statutes passed at the first session of the General Convention, 1870: with standing orders, the draft of the charter as approved by the General Convention, and resolutions with reference to finance.* Dublin: Hodges, Foster & Co., 1870.
BX 5430 1870 .C473 Rare Books Medium

Kelley, John. *A practical grammar of the ancient Gaelic or, language of the Isle of Man, usually called Manks. Edited, together with an introd. by William Gill.* London: B. Quaritch, 1870.
PB 1813 .K297p 1870 Rare Books Medium

LeFanu, Joseph Sheridan. *The fortunes of Colonel Torlogh O'Brien: a tale of the wars of King James / with illustrations on steel by H. K. Browne.* London, New York: G. Routledge and Sons, [1870].
PR 4879 .L7 F6 1870 Rare Books Medium

Mac-Geoghegan, abbe (James). *The history of Ireland, ancient and modern, taken from the most authentic records, and dedicated to the Irish brigade / by the Abbe MacGeoghegan; with a continuation from the Treaty of Limerick to the present time by John Mitchel.* New York: D. & J. Sadlier, [1870?].
DA 910 .M33 Rare Books Large

Meehan, Charles C. P. (Charles Patrick). *The fate and fortunes of Hugh O'Neill, earl of Tyrone, and Rory O'Donel, earl of Tyrconnel; their flight from Ireland, their vicissitudes abroad, and their death in exile. By the Rev. C. P. Meehan.* 2nd ed. Dublin [etc.]: J. Duffy, 1870.
DA 937.5 .T984 M47f 1870 Rare Books Medium

Sequr, Louis Gaston Adrien de. *Plain talk about Protestantism of to-day.* Boston: Patrick Donahoe, 1870.
BX 4820 .S4 1870 Rare Books Small

Sheridan, Thomas. *Some revelations in Irish history: or Old elements of creed and class conciliation in Ireland. Edited by Saxe Bannister.* London: Longmans, Green, Reader and Dyer, 1870.
DA 910 .Sh53s 1870 Rare Books Medium

Smythe, Charles R. *Letters on public schools, with special reference to the system as conducted in St. Louis. By the Hon. Charles R. Smythe.* St. Louis: G. Knapp & co., 1870.
LB 1569 .Sm98L Rare Books Medium

Trench, William Steuart. *Realities of Irish Life / by W. Steuart Trench.* 5th ed. London: Longmans, Green, 1870.
DA 975 .T79 1870 Rare Books Medium

Waring, J. B. (John Burley). *Stone monuments, tumuli and ornament of remote ages: with remarks on the early architecture of Ireland and Scotland / by J. B. Waring.* London: J. B. Day, 1870.
GN 805 .W3 1870 Rare Books XLarge

Amra Choluim Chilli. *The Amra Choluim Chilli of Dallan Forgaill: now printed for the first time from the original Irish in a ms. in the library of the Royal Irish academy; with a literal translation and notes, a grammatical analysis of the text, and copious indexes / by J. O'Beirne Crowe.* Dublin: McGlashan and Gill; [etc.], 1871.
PB 1398 .D35 1871 Rare Books Large

Wills, James. *The Irish nation: its history and its biography / by James Wills, completed by Freeman Wills.* Edinburgh, New York: A. Fullarton, 1871–75.
DA 916.4 .W55 1871 Rare Books Large

Donovan, Cornelius Francis. *Anecdotes of Ireland.* Hamilton [Ont.]: Evening Times publishing house, 1872.
DA 911.2 .D719a 1872 Rare Books Small

Fergusson, James. *Rude stone monuments in all countries: their age and uses / James Fergusson*. London: John Murray, 1872.
GN 791 .F381r 1872 Rare Books Medium

Lever, Charles James. *The works of Charles Lever*. New York: P. F. Collier, [1872].
PR 4884 .A1 Rare 1872 Books Large

Meehan, C. P. (Charles Patrick). *The rise and fall of the Irish Franciscan Monasteries: and memoirs of the Irish hierarchy in the seventeenth century: With appendix, containing numerous original documents / by Rev. C. P. Meehan*. Dublin: J. Duffy, [1872].
BX 3619 .M47r 1872 Rare Books Small

Moore, Thomas. *Literature, art and song: Moore's melodies and American poems; a biography, and a critical review of lyric poets, by Dr. R. Shelton MacKenzie . . . and a collection of choice melodies, arranged as solos, duets, trios, and quartets, with piano accompaniment, by Sir John Stevenson, and others. Illustrated by Daniel Maclise . . . and William Riches . . .* New York: International Pub. Co., [1872?].
PR 5056 .M66 1872 Rare Books Large

O'Connell, Daniel. *Life and speeches of Daniel O'Connell . . . Including many speeches not in other collections*. New York: J. A. McGee, 1872.
DA 950.22 .A3L 1872 Rare Books Medium

Conwell, Eugene Alfred. *Discovery of the tomb of Ollamh Fodhla (Ollav Fola), Ireland's most famous monarch and law-maker upwards of three thousand years ago / by Eugene Alfred Conwell, M.R.I.A., M.A.I., F.R.Hist. Soc., &c.* Dublin: McGlashan & Gill; [etc., etc.], 1873.
DA 920 .C769d 1873 Rare Books Medium

Macaulay, James. *Ireland in 1872: a tour of observation*. London: H. S. King & co., 1873.
DA 975 .M119i Rare Books Medium

McGee, James E. (James Edward). *Sketches of Irish soldiers in every land*. New York: J.A. McGee, 1873.
DA 915 .A1 M172s Rare Books Medium

Molloy, James Lyman. *The songs of Ireland: including the most favourite of Moore's Irish melodies and a large collection of old songs and ballads with new symphonies and accompaniments / by J. L. Molloy.* London, New York: Boosey, [1873].
M 1744 .M738 S 6 Rare Books Large

O'Curry, Eugene. *On the manners and customs of the ancient Irish.* London [etc.] Williams and Norgate; New York: Scribner, Welford & co.; [etc., etc.], 1873.
DA 930.5 .Oc80 Rare Books Medium

Thebaud, Augustus J. *The Irish race in the past and the present.* By the Rev. Aug. J. Thebaud . . . New York: D. Appleton & co., 1873.
DA 910 .T34i 1873 Rare Books Medium

The Wonders of the world: comprising man, quadrupeds, birds, fishes, trees, plants, mountains, caves, volcanoes, rivers, cities, remarkable edifices, ruins, antiquities, &c., &c.: with several hundred illustrative embellishments. Chicago: Published by L. W. Yaggy, 1873.
AC 5 W 845 1873 Rare Books Large

The world of wonders: a record of things wonderful in nature, science, and art. Philadelphia: New world pub. co., 1873.
AC 5 .W892 1873 Rare Books Large

Bernard, William Bayle. *The life of Samuel Lover, R.H.A.: artistic, literary, and musical, with selections from his unpublished papers and correspondence / by Bayle Bernard.* New York: D. Appleton & Co., 1874.
PR 4893 .B4 1874 Rare Books Medium

Brash, Richard Rolt. *The ecclesiastical architecture of Ireland, to the close of the twelfth century; accompanied by interesting historical and antiquarian notices of numerous ancient remains of that period / With fifty-four plates. By Richard Rolt Brash.* Dublin: W. B. Kelly: [etc., etc.], 1875.
NA 5484 .B736e Rare Books Large

Craig, John Duncan. *Real pictures of clerical life in Ireland / by J. Duncan Craig.* London: James Nisbet, 1875.
BX 1503 .C844r 1875 Rare Books Medium

Cusack, Mary Francis. *A history of the city and county of Cork / by M. F. Cusack . . . Kenmare publications.* Dublin: McGlashan and Gill; [etc., etc.], 1875.
DA 990 .C813 C951 1875 Rare Books Large

Kenney, Charles Lamb. *A memoir of Michael William Balfe.* London: Tinsley brothers, 1875.
ML 410 .B196 K395 M433 1875 Rare Books Medium

Loftie, W. J. (William John). *Views in Wicklow and Killarney from original drawings by T. L. Rowbotham . . .: with archaeological, historical, poetical and descriptive notes / compiled by the Rev. W. J. Loftie.* New York: Scribner, Wilford & Armstrong, London, M. Ward & co., 1875.
DA 990 .K554 L827v Rare Books Medium

Marcoy, Paul. *Travels in South America: from the Pacific Ocean to the Atlantic Ocean / by Paul Marcoy.* London: Blackie and Son, 1875.
F 3423 .Sa22t Rare Books Large

Donovan, Daniel, Jr. *Sketches in Carbery, county Cork; its antiquities, history, legends, and topography, by Daniel Donovan, jun.* New ed. Dublin: M. H. Gill and son, 1876.
DA 990 .C177 D719s 1876 Rare Books Small

Joyce, Robert Dwyer. *Deirdre.* Boston: Roberts Brothers, 1876.
PS 2153 .J855d 1876 Rare Books Small

Mahony, Francis Sylvester. *The final reliques of Father Prout* . . . London: Cha Ho and Windus, 1876.
PR 4972 .M33 R45 1876 Rare Books Medium

Blackburne, E. Owens. *Illustrious Irishwomen: Being memoirs of some of the most noted Irish women from the earliest ages to the present century / by E. Owens Blackburne [pseud.].* London: Tinsley brothers, 1877.
DA 916.7 .C268i Rare Books Medium

Clancy, James J. *Ireland: as she is, as she has been, and as she ought to be.* New York: T. Kelly, 1877.
DA 975 .C527i 1877 Rare Books Medium

Hoffman, F. *Ancient music of Ireland from the Petrie collection: arranged for the pianoforte.* Dublin: Pigott, 1877.
M 1 .H65 A5 1877 Rare Books Large

Irish wit and humor: anecdote biography of Swift, Curran, O'Leary and O'Connell. 25th thousand. New York: J. A. McGee, [1877?].
PN 6178 .Ir4 Ir43 1878 Rare Books Medium

Irish wit and wisdom: containing all the articles published in Haverty's Irish-American illustrated almanacs for the years 1871, 1872, 1873, 1874, and 1875. New York: P. M. Haverty, 1877.
PN 6178 .Ir4 H2991 1877 Rare Books Small

Murray, John O'Kane. *The prose and poetry of Ireland: a choice collection of literary gems from the masterpieces of the great Irish writers, with biographical sketches / by John O'Kane Murray.* 2nd ed. New York: P. F. Collier, 1877.
PR 8835 .M8 1877 Rare Books Medium

Brennan, James Joseph. *A catechism of the history of Ireland.* New York: T. Kelly, 1878.
DA 912 .B75c 1878 Rare Books Small

Dwyer, Philip. *The Diocese of Killaloe from the Reformation to the close of the eighteenth century with an appendix / by Philip Dwyer.* Dublin: Hodges, Foster, and Figgis, 1878.
BX 5505 .K554 D978d 1878 Rare Books Medium

Hogan, Edmund. *The description of Ireland: and the state thereof as it is at this present in anno 1598 / Now for the first time published from a manuscript preserved in Clongowes-Wood College, with copious notes and illustrations by Edmund Hogan.* Dublin: M. H. Gill, 1878.
DA 970 .H7 1878 Rare Books Large

John Murray (Firm). *Handbook for travelers in Ireland.* 4th ed. rev. With maps and plans. London: J. Murray, 1878.
DA 980 .M964h 1878 Rare Books Small

Moore, Thomas. *Prose and verse: humorous, satirical, and sentimental / by Thomas Moore. With suppressed passages from the memoirs of Lord Byron, chiefly from the author's manuscript . . . with notes and introduction by Richard Herne Shepherd.* New York: Scribner, Armstrong, 1878.
PR 5052 .S5 1878 Rare Books Medium

The tutor for the highland bagpipe; with a selection of marches, quicksteps, strathspeys, reels and jigs amounting to one hundred tunes by William McKay in 1841; 1843 corrected and improved by Angus McKay. 7th ed. Edinburgh: David Glen, 1878.
M 145 .T8 1878 Rare Books Small

Brash, Richard Rolt. *The Ogam inscribed monuments of the Gaedhil in the British islands / with a dissertation on the Ogam character, etc. Illustrated with fifty photo-lithographic plates, by the late Richard Rolt Brash . . . Ed. by George M. Atkinson.* London: G. Bell and sons, 1879.
DA 920 .B73 1879 Rare Books Large

The Monitor. Dublin, Ireland: Joseph Dollard, 1879. Monthly.
AP 4 .M749 Rare Books Medium

Sause, Judson. *The art of dancing, embracing a full description of the various dances of the present day, together with chapters on etiquette, the benefits, and history of dancing, by M. Judson Sause.* New York: Sause's dancing academy, [1879?].
GV 1751 .Sa87a Rare Books Small

Thackeray, William Makepeace. *The Irish sketch book: and Critical reviews / by William Makepeace Thackeray; with illustrations by the author, George Cruikshank, John Leech, and M. Fitzgerald.* London: Smith, Elder, 1879.
PR 5613 .I7 1879 Rare Books Medium

Thebaud, Augustus J. *The Irish race in the past and the present / by the Rev. Aug. J. Thebaud.* New York: P. F. Collier, 1879, 1878.
DA 910 .T34i 1879 Rare Books Medium

Fitzpatrick, William John. *The life, times, and correspondence of the Right Rev. Dr. Doyle, bishop of Kildare and Leighlin.* Dublin: J. Duffy, 1880.
BX 4705 .D775 F582L 1880 Rare Books Medium

Sherlock, Peter T. *The case of Ireland stated historically.* Chicago: P. T. Sherlock, 1880.
DA 910 .Sh54c 1880 Rare Books Medium

Carleton, William. *The works of William Carleton / by William Carleton.* New York: Collier, 1881.
PR 4416 .A1 1881 Rare Books Large

Cusack, Mary Francis. *The present case of Ireland plainly stated: a plea for my people and my race / by M. F. Cusack.* 4th ed. New York: P. J. Kenedy, [1881?].
DA 950 .C951p 1881 Rare Books Medium

Duffy, Sir Charles Gavan. *Young Ireland: a fragment of Irish history, 1840–1850 / by Sir Charles Gavan Duffy.* New York: Appleton, 1881.
DA 950 .D874y Rare Books Medium

Mahony, Francis Sylvester. *The works of Father Prout (the Rev. Francis Mahony). Edited with biographical introduction and notes by Charles Kent.* London, New York: G. Routledge and Sons, 1881.
PR 4972 .M279 A1 R765 Rare Books Small

McGee, James E. (James Edward). *The men of '48, being a brief history of the repeal association and the Irish confederation: with biographical sketches of the leading actors in the latter organization, their principles, opinions, and literary labors / by James E. McGee; in one volume.* Boston: D. O'Loughlin, Irish National Publishing House, c. 1881.
DA 950.2 M172m 1881 Rare Books Small

Ryan, Abraham Joseph. *Poems: patriotic, religious, miscellaneous / by Abram J. Ryan, (Father Ryan).* Baltimore: John B. Piet, 1881.
PS 2745 .A2 P64 1881 Rare Books Medium

Sullivan, Margaret Buchanan. *Ireland of to-day; the causes and aims of Irish agitation.* Philadelphia: J. M. Stoddart & co., 1881.
DA 910 .Su551 1881 Rare Books Medium

Williams, Alfred M. *The poets and poetry of Ireland: with historical and critical essays and notes / by Alfred M. Williams.* Boston: James R. Osgood, [1881?].
PR 8850 .W67p 1881 Rare Books Medium

Bagenal, Philip H. (Philip Henry). *The American Irish and their influence on Irish politics / by Philip H. Bagenal.* Boston: Roberts Brothers, 1882.
E 184 .Ir4 B146a 1882 Rare Books Small

Barrington, Sir Jonah. *Personal sketches of his own times.* Chicago: Union Catholic Publishing company, 1882.
DA 948.3 .B277 A3p 1882 Rare Books Small

Mair, James Allan. *The book of Irish readings in prose and verse: from the works of popular Irish authors / edited by James Allan Mair.* Glasgow, London: Cameron and Ferguson, 1882.
PR 8835 .M35 1882 Rare Books Small

McIntosh, John. *Songs of liberty, and other poems / by Dr. John McIntosh: Dedicated to the Land Leagues of the world.* Chicago: Woodward & O'Leary, publishers, 1882.
PR 4989 .M8 S6 1882 Rare Books Medium

Savage, John. *'98 and '48: the modern revolutionary history and literature of Ireland / by John Savage.* Chicago: Belford, Clarke & Co., 1882.
DA 949 Sa92n 1882 Rare Books Small

Songs of Old Ireland: a collection of fifty Irish melodies / the words by Alfred Perceval Graves. London, New York: Boosey, [1882].
M 1744 .S71 S6 1882 Rare Books Large

Conyngham, David Power. *Ireland past and present.* New York, Philadelphia [etc.]: J. Sheehy, 1883.
DA 910 .C769i Rare Books Large

Irish popular songs / with English and metrical translations, and introductory remarks and notes by Edward Walsh. 2nd ed. rev. and corr. / with original letters never before published. Dublin: W. H. Smith, 1883.
PB 1353 .W224 1883 Rare Books Small

Egan, P. M. *The illustrated guide to the city and county of Kilkenny / by P. M. Egan.* Kilkenny: P. M. Egan, [1884?].
DA 990 .K553 Eg14i Rare Books Medium

Fitzpatrick, William John. *The life of Charles Lever / by W. J. Fitzpatrick.* New ed. rev. London: Ward, Lock, [pref. 1884].
PR 4885 .F58 1884 Rare Books Medium

Mackenzie, R. Shelton (Robert Shelton). *Bits of Blarney / edited by R. Shelton Mackenzie.* Chicago: Belford, Clarke, 1884.
PR 4971 .M199b 1884 Rare Books Small

O'Brien, James. *Irish Celts: A cyclopedia of race history.* Detroit: L. F. Kilroy & company, 1884.
DA 916 .Ob6i 1884 Rare Books Medium

The poets and poetry of Munster: a selection of Irish songs by the poets of the last century. With poetical translations by the late James Clarence Mangan, and the original music; biographical sketches of the authors; and Irish text revised by W. M. Hennessey. M.R.I.A. Edited by C. P. Meehan, C.C. 4th ed. Dublin: J. Duffy [1884].
PB 1395 .M928 M313p 1884 Rare Books Small

Read, Charles Anderson. *The cabinet of Irish literature: selections from the works of the chief poets, orators, and prose writers of Ireland, with biographical sketches and literary notices / by Charles A. Read.* London: Blackie & Son; New York: Samuel Hall, 1884.
PR 8833 .R43 1884 Rare Books Large

Savage, John. *Picturesque Ireland: a literary and artistic delineation of the natural scenery, remarkable places, historical antiquities, public buildings, ancient abbeys, towers, castles, and other romantic and attractive features of Ireland. / Illustrated in steel and wood, by eminent native and foreign artists.* Ed by John Savage. New York: T. Kelly, 1884.
DA 975 .S28 1884 Rare Books Large

Banim, John. *The bit o'writin' [and other tales] / by the O'Hara family [pseud.] A new edition, with introduction and notes.* New York: Sadlier & Co., [1885?].
PR 4057 .B2 B58 1885 Rare Books Small

Banim, John. *The mayor of Wind-Gap; and Canvassing / by the O'Hara Family; a new edition, with introduction and notes, by Michael Banim.* New York: D. & J. Sadlier, 1885.
PR 4057 .B2 M38 1885 Rare Books Small

Maginn, William. *Miscellanies: prose and verse / by William Maginn, edited by R. W. Montagu.* London: S. Low, Marston, Searle, & Rivington, 1885.
PR 4972 .M3 A6 1885 Rare Books Medium

McGee, Thomas D'Arcy. *A popular history of Ireland, from the earliest period to the emancipation of the Catholics.* Rev. and continued to the present time, by D. P. Conyngham. New York: D. & J. Sadlier & Co., [1885].
DA 910 .M172p 1885 Rare Books Medium

Melodies of Ireland: a collection of the famous airs of the Emerald Isle, expressly arr. for the piano or organ. Boston: White-Smith, [1885?].
M 38.5 .M45 1885 Rare Books XLarge

Walsh, Thomas. *Ecclesiastical history of Ireland, by Rev. Thomas Walsh and D. P. Conyngham.* New York: P. J. Kenedy, [1885?].
BX 1503 .W168e 1885 Rare Books Medium

The Ballad poetry of Ireland. New York: Fords' national library, 1886.
PR 8860 .B3 1886 Rare Books Small

Duffy, Sir Charles Gavan. *The league of north and south. An episode in Irish history, 1850–1854.* London: Chapman and Hall, limited, 1886.
DA 955 .D874L Rare Books Medium

Griffin, Gerald. *Poems by Gerald Griffin.* Dublin: M. H. Gill and Son, 1886.
PR 4728 .G875 A17 G41 1886 Rare Books Small

Higgins, Charles. *Home rule: or the Irish land question / Facts and arguments by Charles Higgins.* Chicago: Rand, McNally, [1886?].
DA 950 .H535h 1886 Rare Books Medium

O'Connor, T. P. (Thomas Power). *Gladstone-Parnell, and the great Irish struggle. A graphic story of the injustice and oppression inflicted upon the Irish tenantry,*

and a history of the gigantic movement throughout Ireland, America and Great Britain for "home rule," with biographies of the great leaders. By. Hon. Thomas Power O'Connor, M.P., and Robert McWade, esq. General introduction by Hon. Charles Stewart Parnell, M. P. Canadian introduction by A. Burns, American introduction by Prof. R. E. Thompson. [S.I.]: Edgewood Pub. Co., [1886?].
DA 950 .Oc56g 1886 Rare Books Medium

O'Connor, T. P. (Thomas Power). The Parnell movement: with a sketch of Irish parties from 1843 / by T. P. O'Connor. London: K. Paul, Trench & Co., 1886.
DA 951 .Oc5p 1886 Rare Books Medium

O'Reilly, Bernard. The cause of Ireland pleaded before the civilized world. New York: P. F. Collier, [1886].
DA 910 .Or13c 1886 Rare Books Large

Wood-Martin, W. G. (William Gregory). The lake dwellings of Ireland; or, Ancient lacustrine habitations of Erin, commonly called crannogs / by W. G. Wood-Martin. Dublin: Hodges, Figgis & Co.; [etc.], 1886.
GN 786 .Ir2 W859L 1886 Rare Books Large

Craik, Dinah Maria Mulock. An unknown country, by the author of "John Halifax, gentleman." New York: Harper & brothers, 1887.
DA 975 .C845u 1887 Rare Books Medium

Ferguson, Sir Samuel. Hibernian nights' entertainments / by Sir Samuel Ferguson. Dublin: Sealy, Bryers & Walker; [etc., etc.] 1887.
PR 4699 .F381h 1887 Rare Books Small

Ferguson, Sir Samuel. Ogham inscriptions in Ireland, Wales, and Scotland. Edinburgh: D. Douglas, 1887.
DA 920 .F381o Rare Books Medium

The Irish problem, as viewed by a citizen of the empire. London: Hatchards, 1887.
DA 951 .Ir4 1887 Rare Books Small

Lawless, Emily. Ireland / by Emily Lawless; with some additions by Mrs. Arthur Bronson. New York: T. F. Unwin; New York: G. P. Putnam's, [1887].
DA 910 .L424i Rare Books Medium

Mandat-Grancey, E. (Edmond), baron de. *Paddy at home: "Chez Paddy" / Tr. By A. P. Morton.* London: Chapman and Hall, 1887.
DA 975 .M312c En36 Rare Books Medium

McCarthy, Justin H. (Justin Huntly). *Ireland since the union; sketches of Irish history from 1798 to 1886.* Chicago, New York: Belford, Clarke and co., 1887.
DA 950 .M127i Rare Books Medium

Sparling, Henry Halliday. *Irish minstrelsy. Being a selection of Irish songs, lyrics, and ballads; original and translated.* London [etc.]: W. Scott, 1887.
PR 8851 .Sp26i 1887 Rare Books Small

Upton, George P. (George Putnam). *The standard cantatas; their stories, their music, and their composers; a handbook, by George P. Upton.* 7th ed. Chicago: A. C. McClurg, [1887?].
MT 110 .Up8s 1887 Rare Books Small

Walpole, Charles George. *A short history of the kingdom of Ireland from the earliest times to the union with Great Britain: with five maps and appendices / by Charles George Walpole.* London: K. Paul, Trench, 1887.
DA 910 .W165s 1887 Rare Books Medium

Banim, John. *Father Connell: a tale / by the O'Hara family.* A new ed. with introd. and notes by Michael Banim. New York: D. & J. Sadlier, [etc.], [1888?].
PR 4057 .B2 F38 1888 Rare Books Small

Cole, Alan S. *A Renascence of the Irish art of lace-making* . . . London: C. & H., 1888.
NK 9446 .C674r Rare Books Medium

Davidson, John Morrison. *The book of Erin; or, Ireland's story told to the new democracy.* London: W. Reeves, [1888?].
DA 910 .D283b Rare Books Small

Graves, Charles L. (Charles Larcom). *The Blarney ballads / by Charles L. Graves; with illustrations by G. R. Halkett.* London: Swan Sonnenchein, 1888.
PR 4728 .G18 B5 1888 Rare Books Medium

Hipkins, Alfred James. *Musical instruments, historic, rare and unique.* Edinburgh:
A. and C. Black, 1888.
ML 462 .H611m 1888 Rare Books Oversize

McAnally, David Rice. *Irish wonders; the ghosts, giants, pookas, demons, leprechawns,*
banshees, fairies, witches, widows, old maids, and other marvels of the Emerald
Isle: popular tales as told by the people / by D. R. McAnally, Jr. Illustrated by
H. R. Heaton. Boston: Houghton Mifflin, [1888].
PR 4964 .M3 I7 1888b Rare Books Medium

Wright, Robert Creighton. *Echoes from the Blarney stone and other rhymes. By W. C. R.*
Chicago: C. H. Kerr & company, [1888?].
PS 3364 .W935e Rare Books Small

[Banim, John]. *The peep o'day: or, John Doe by the O'Hara family. A new ed. / with*
introduction and notes by Michael Banim . . . New York: D. & J. Sadlier & co.,
[1889?].
PR 4057 .B2 P4 1889 Rare Books Small

Downey, Edmund. *From the green bag / by F. M. Allen [pseud.].* London: Ward and
Downey, 1889.
PR 4613 .D48 F76 1889 Rare Books Medium

Froude, James Anthony. *The two chiefs of Dunboy: or, An Irish romance of the last*
century / by J. A. Froude. New York: C. Scribner's Sons, 1889.
PR 4706 .T86 1889 Rare Books Small

Mac-Geoghegan, abbe (James). *The history of Ireland, ancient and modern: taken*
from the most authentic records and dedicated to the Irish Brigade / by the Abbe
Mac-Geoghegan; [translated from the French by Patrick O'Kelly]; with a con-
tinuation from the Treaty of Limerick to the year 1868 by John Mitchell; rev. and
continued to the present time by D. P. Conyngham. New York: D. & J. Sadlier,
[1889?].
DA 910 .M173h 1889 Rare Books Large

McCarthy, Justin. A *history of our own times / by Justin McCarthy.* Chicago, New
York: Belford, Clarke & co., 1889.
DA 550 .M127h B411 Rare Books Medium

O'Grady, Standish. *Red Hugh's captivity. A picture of Ireland, social and political, in the reign of Queen Elizabeth. By Standish O'Grady.* London: Ward and Downey, 1889.
DA 937 .Og7r 1889 Rare Books Small

O'Reilly, John Boyle. *The poetry and song of Ireland / Ed. by John Boyle O'Reilly . . . With the publisher's supplement to the 2d ed. The whole forming a standard encyclopaedia of Erin's poetry and song; and a biographical portrait gallery of her poets. Illustrated with over one hundred choice engravings.* New York: Gay brothers & co., [1889?].
PR 8851 .O7 1889 Rare Books Large

Phallic objects, monuments and remains; illustrations of the rise and development of the phallic idea (sex worship) and its embodiment in works of nature and art. [N.p.]: Priv. print., 1889.
BL 460 .P5 1889 Rare Books Medium

Scotch-Irish Congress. *The Scotch-Irish in America: proceedings of the Scotch-Irish Congress / published by order of the Scotch-Irish Society of America.* Cincinnati, Ohio: Robert Clarke & Co., 1889.
E 184 .Sco811 Sco81p Rare Books Medium

Yeats, W. B. (William Butler). *Representative Irish tales. Compiled with an introd. and notes by W. B. Yeats. 1st [–2d] ser.* New York: G. P. Putnam's Sons, [189–].
PR 88785 .Y34r Rare Books Small

Ancient Irish music: comprising one hundred Irish airs hitherto unpublished, many of the old popular songs, and several new songs / collected and edited by P. W. Joyce; the harmonies by Professor Glover. Dublin: M. H. Gill, 1890.
M 1744 .J854 1890 Rare Books Large

Davis, Thomas Osborne. *Prose writings of Thomas Davis. Edited, with an introd., by T. W. Rolleston.* London: W. Scott, [1890?].
PR 4525 .D298 A16 R649p Rare Books Small

Hyde, Douglas. *Beside the fire: a collection of Irish Gaelic folk stories / Ed., tr., and annotated by Douglas Hyde . . . with additional notes by Alfred Nutt.* London: D. Nutt, 1890.
GR 147 .H9 1890 Rare Books Medium

Leamy, Edmund. *Irish fairy tales.* Dublin: M. H. Gill, 1890.
PS 2235 .L475i 1890 Rare Books Small

Murray, Patrick Joseph. *The life of John Banim: the Irish novelist / with extracts from his correspondence, general and literary. Also selections from his poems.* New York: D. & J. Sadlier, [1890?].
PR 4057 .B2 Z5 1890 Rare Books Small

O'Brien, William. *When we were boys: a novel by William O'Brien, M.P.* London: Longmans, Green, and Co. and New York: 15 East 16th Street, 1890.
PR 5112 .O19 W44 1890 Rare Books Medium

O'Rorke, Terence. *History of Sligo, town and country.* Dublin: J. Duffy, [1890].
DA 990 .SL35 Or6h Rare Books Medium

Wilde, Lady. *Ancient cures, charms, and usages of Ireland: contributions to Irish lore / by Lady Wilde.* London: Ward and Downey, 1890.
GR 147 .W644a 1890 Rare Books Small

French, Henry Willard. *Our boys in Ireland / by Henry W. French.* New York: Worthington, [1891?].
DA 975 .F74 1891 Rare Books Large

The Glen collection of Scottish dance music; strathspeys, reels, and jigs, selected from the earliest printed sources or from the composer's works / arranged with new accompaniments for the pianoforte by John Glen. Edinburgh: [J. Glen], 1891–95.
M 1746 .G55 1891 Rare Books XLarge

Harding's collection of jigs, reels, etc. S. L.: Frank Harding, 1891.
M 32 .H3 1891 Rare Books XLarge

Kennedy, Patrick. *Legendary fictions of the Irish Celts.* London and New York: Macmillan and co., 1891.
GR 147 .K3 1891 Rare Books Medium

Lovett, Richard. *Ireland illustrated with pen and pencil / by Richard Lovett. Revised by E. P. Thwing.* New York: Hurst, 1891.
DA 975 .L947i 1891 Rare Books Large

Roche, James Jeffrey. *Life of John Boyle O'Reilly / by James Jeffrey Roche. Together with his complete poems and speeches, ed. by Mrs. John Boyle O'Reilly. Introduction by His Eminence, James cardinal Gibbons.* New York: Cassell Pub. Co., [1891?].
PS 2493 .R6 1891b Rare Books Medium

Zimmer, Heinrich. *The Irish element in mediaeval culture, by H. Zimmer; tr. by Jane Loring Edmands.* New York [etc.] G. P. Putnam's Sons, 1891.
DA 932 .Z65e En36 Rare Books Small

Irish pleasantry and fun: a selection of the best humorous tales by Carleton, Lover, Lever and other popular writers / with sixteen illustrations by J. F. O'Shea. Dublin: M. H. Gill, 1892.
PN 6178 .Ir4 Ir42 Rare Books Large

O'Donoghue, D. J. (David James). *The poets of Ireland: a biographical dictionary with bibliographical particulars / by D. J. O'Donoghue.* [London]: [Paternoster Steam Press], 1892.
PR 8706 .O5 1892 Rare Books Medium

Ward and Lock's pictorial and descriptive guide to Connemara and the western highlands of Ireland . . . including a guide to the Midland great western railway and its branches . . . London: New York [etc.]: Ward, Lock, Bowden and Co., [1892].
DA 990 .C762 W21 Rare Books Small

Barlow, Jane. *Irish idylls.* New York: Dodd, Mead & company, 1893.
PR 4063 .B3 I757 1893 Rare Books Medium

Chappell, W. (William). *Old English popular music / by William Chappell, F.S.A. A new ed. with a preface and notes, and the earlier examples entirely revised by H. Ellis Wooldridge.* London: Chappell; New York: Novello, Ewer, 1893.
M 1740 .C368 O43 1893 Rare Books Large

Crowley, Denis Oliver. *Irish poets and novelists / profusely illustrated and embracing complete biographical sketches of those who at home and abroad have sustained the reputation of Ireland as the land of song and story, with copious selections from their writings. Introd. by Thomas R. Bannerman.* 3rd ed. San Francisco, Calif.: [P.J. Thomas], 1893.
PR 8835 .C7 1893 Rare Books Medium

Curtin, Jeremiah C. *The story of Ireland: her struggles for self-government with the lives and times of her great leaders, giving a graphic account of the services, devotion, and sacrifices of her patriot sons.* New York: Gay Brothers & co., [1893?]. DA 910 .C94s 1893 Rare Books Large

Healy, William. *History and antiquities of Kilkenny: (county and city) with illustrations and appendix / comp. from inquisitions, deeds, wills, funeral entries, family records, and other historical and authentic sources.* [Kilkenny: P. M. Egan, 1893]. DA 990 .K553 H349h Rare Books Medium

Larminie, William. *West Irish folk-tales and romances; collected and translated by William Larminie. With introduction and notes, and appendix containing specimens of the Gaelic originals phonetically spelt.* London: E. Stock, 1893. GR 141 .L326w 1893 Rare Books Medium

Lecky, William Edward Hartpole. *A history of Ireland in the eighteenth century.* New ed. New York: D. Appleton and company, 1893. DA 947 .L495h 1893 Rare Books Small

LeFanu, William. *Seventy years of Irish life, being anecdotes and reminiscences, by W. R. LeFanu.* New York: Macmillan, 1893. DA 952 .L4 1893 Rare Books Medium

Prentice, Jessie Eloise. *Musical moments: short selections in prose and verse for music lovers.* New and enl. ed. Chicago: A. C. McClurg and company, [1893?]. PN 6071 .M973 P918 1893 Rare Books Medium

Smith, Charles. *The ancient and present state of the county and city of Cork.* Cork: Guy & co., 1893–94. DA 990 .C813 S65 Rare Books Large

Stanford, Sir Charles Villiers. *Irish songs and ballads / the words by Alfred Percival Graves, the music arranged by C. Villiers Stanford.* London: Novello, 1893. M 1744 .S7 I7 Rare Books Large

Foote, Arthur. *An Irish folk-song / Arthur Foote; the poem by Gilbert Parker.* Boston: (146 Boylston St., Boston): Arthur P. Schmidt, [1894?]. M 1744 .F66 Rare Books 1894 XLarge

O'Donoghue, D. J. (David James). *The humor of Ireland: selected, with introduction, biographical index and notes / by D. J. O'Donoghue: the illustrations by Oliver Paque.* London: Walter Scott; New York: Scribner, 1894.
PN 6178 .I6 O37 1894 Rare Books Medium

Poetry and legendary ballads of the south of Ireland / by various writers, with biographical notes, etc. First series. Cork: Guy, 1894.
PR 8851 .P64 1894 Rare Books Large

Barlow, Jane. *Bog-land studies.* 3rd ed. New York: Dodd, Mead, 1895.
PR 4063 .B3 B64 1895 Rare Books Medium

Downey, Edmund. *The merchant of Killogue: a munster tale, by F. M. Allen [pseud.].* A new ed. London: Downey & Co., 1895.
PR 4613 .D48 M47 1895 Rare Books Medium

The Irish song book: with original Irish airs / edited, with an introduction and notes by Alfred Perceval Graves. 2nd ed. London: T. F. Unwin; New York: P. J. Kennedy, 1895.
M 17444 .G783 I7 1895 Rare Books Small

Murphy, Con. T. *The miller of Glanmire: an Irish story / by Con T. Murphy.* Chicago: G. W. Baker, 1895.
PR 5101 .M424 M55 1895 Rare Books Medium

Daunt, William J. O'Neill. *A life spent for Ireland. Being selections from the journals of the late W. J. O'Neill Daunt. Ed. by his daughter.* London: Unwin, 1896.
DA 950.23 .D267 A3L Rare Books Medium

Mathew, Frank James. *The wood of the brambles / by Frank Mathew.* London: Lane, 1896.
PR 4984 .M87 W66 1896 Rare Books Medium

Moffat, Alfred. *The minstrelsy of Scotland: 200 Scottish songs, adapted to their traditional airs / arranged for voice with pianoforte accompaniment, and supplemented with historical notes, by Alfred Moffat.* 2nd ed. London: Augener, 1896.
M 1746 .M695 M5 1896 Rare Books Large

White-Smith Music Publishing Co. *White's Excelsior collection of jigs, reels, and hornpipes, clogs, highland flings, strathspeys and a miscellaneous selection of favorite tunes old and new: Arranged for the violin with bowing and fingering.* Boston: White-Smith Publishing Co., 1896.
M 43 .W4 1896 Rare Books Large

Borlase, William Copeland. *The dolmens of Ireland: their distribution, structural characteristics, and affinities in other countries; together with the folk-lore attaching to them; supplemented by considerations on the anthropology, ethnology, and traditions of the Irish people. With four maps, and eight hundred illustrations, including two coloured plates / by William Copeland Borlase* . . . London: Chapman & Hall, ld., 1897.
DA 920 .B6 D65 1897 Rare Books Large

Brown, James Duff. *British musical biography.* Birmingham: S. S. Stratton, 1897.
ML 106 .G798 B813 1897 Rare Books Large

Macalister, Robert Alexander Stewart. *Studies in Irish epigraphy: a collection of revised readings of the ancient inscriptions of Ireland, with introduction and notes / by R. A. Stewart Macalister.* London: D. Nutt, 1897–1907.
DA 920 .M117s Rare Books Medium

Moffat, Alfred. *The minstrelsy of Ireland / Alfred Moffat.* London: Augener, [1897].
M 1744 .M695 M51 1897 Rare Books Large

Molloy, J. Fitzgerald (Joseph Fitzgerald). *The romance of the Irish stage; with pictures of the Irish capital in the eighteenth century, by J. Fitzgerald Molloy.* New York: Dodd, Mead and company, 1897.
PN 2601 .M738r 1897 Rare Books Medium

O'Connell, Jeremiah D. *The "Scotch-Irish" delusion in America.* Washington, D. C.: American-Irish publication, 1897.
E 184 .Sco811 Oc5s Rare Books Medium

Joyce, P. W. (Patrick Weston). *Irish music and song: a collection of songs in the Irish language set to music / edited for the Society for the Preservation of the Irish Language by P. W. Joyce.* Dublin: M. H. Gill, 1898.
M 1744 .J854 1898 Rare Books Large

Maclise, Daniel. *The Maclise portrait-gallery of illustrious literary characters, with memoirs biographical, critical, bibliographical, and anecdotal illustrative of the literature of the former half of the present century.* New ed. London: Chatto & Windus, 1898.
PR 457 .M268m 1898 Rare Books Medium

Purcell, W. J. *The tourist's Ireland: a guide book. A picturesque sketch of a journey through Ireland containing valuable information to Americans about to visit Ireland / by W. J. Purcell* . . . Chicago: J. S. Hyland & co., [1898?].
DA 980 .P971t Rare Books Medium

Tynan, Katharine. *The dear Irish girl / by Katharine Tynan.* Chicago: A. C. McClurg, 1899.
PR 4790 .H593 D43 1899 Rare Books Medium

Fox, C. Milligan. *Four Irish songs / by C. Milligan Fox; words by Edith Wheeler and Alice Milligan; the Connacht Caoine (in Irish) by Tadhg O Donnchadha; illustrated by Seaghan MacCathmhaiol.* Dublin: Maunsel, [19—].
M 1755 .F6 Rare Books Large

Gems of Irish song: containing 124 favourites, including Killarney and a number of others. Glasgow: M. Allan, [19—?].
M 1744 .G467 1900z Rare Books Small

Lawrence, W., photographer. *Pictures in colour of the lakes of Killarney and south of Ireland / with descriptive notes.* Norwich [Eng.]: Jarrold & Sons, [19—.].
DA 990 .K554 L439p Rare Books Medium

The minstrelsy of Ireland: 206 Irish songs adapted to their traditional airs: arranged for voice with pianoforte accompaniment, and supplemented with historical notes / by Alfred Moffat. 3rd enl. ed. London: Augener, [19—?].
M 1744 .M695 M51 Rare Books Large

The Well-known songs of Ireland / edited and arranged by Hubert E. Rooney. Dublin: James Duffy & Co., [19—?].
M 1744 .R674 W4 Rare Books Large

Young Ireland song book. Dublin: Irish Book Bureau, [19—].
  M 1744 .Y686 1900z Rare Books Large

Atlas and cyclopedia of Ireland. New York: Murphy & McCarthy, [1900?].
  DA 910 .J854a 1904 Rare Books Large

Haweis, H. R. (Hugh Reginald). *Music and morals.* New York and London: Harper
  & brothers, 1900.
  ML 60 .H389 1900 Rare Books Small

Maguidhir, E. *Seoidini Ceoil. / Magui ir do cuir i gcir agus i n-eagar.* Baile A a Clia
  [i.e., Dublin]: Oideacais na hEirann, Teor., [between 1900 and 1928].
  M 1744 .M358 S46 1900z Rare Books Small

Barlow, Jane. *From the land of the shamrock.* London: Metheun [1901].
  PR 4063 B3 .F76 1901 Rare Books Medium

Frazer, Lilly Grove. *Dancing . . .* London: Longmans, Green, 1901.
  GV 1601 .F869d Rare Books Medium

Gregory, Lady. *Ideals in Ireland.* London: At the Unicorn, 1901.
  DA 913 .G862i 1901 Rare Books Medium

*Hyland's mammoth Hibernian songster: a collection of over 500 songs that are dear to
  the Irish heart, including sheets of selected music and numerous toasts and sentiments / edited by "The Blackbird."* Chicago: J. S. Hyland & Co., [1901?].
  PR 8860 .H 997m Rare Books Medium

Johnston, Charles. *Ireland.* New York: Merrill and Baker, [1901?].
  DA 910 .J642i 1901 Rare Books Medium

Joyce, P. W. (Patrick Weston). *Irish music and song: a collection of songs in the Irish
  language / set to music [and] edited for the Society for the Preservation of the Irish
  Language by P. W. Joyce.* New ed. Dublin: M.H. Gill and Son, 1901.
  M 1744 .J854 1901 Rare Books Large

Manson, William Laird. *The Highland bagpipe: its history, literature, and music.*
  Paisley: London, A. Gardner, 1901.
  ML 980 .M318h Rare Books Medium

O'Conor, Manus. *Irish com-all-ye's: a repository of ancient Irish songs and ballads— comprising patriotic, descriptive, historical and humorous gems, characteristic of the Irish race* / compiled and arranged by Manus O'Conor. New York: Popular Pub. Co., [1901?].
PR 8860 .O3 1901 Rare Books Large

Stanford, Sir Charles Villiers. *An Irish Idyll: in six miniatures for voice with pianoforte accompaniment, op. 771.* London: Boosey & Co., [1901?].
M 1621 .S736 I66 1901 Rare Books Large

Stanford, Sir Charles Villiers. *Songs of Erin: a collection of fifty Irish folk songs.* / The words by Alfred Perceval Graves, the music arranged by Charles Villiers Stanford. Op. 76. London and New York: Boosey & Co., 1901. Pub. pl. no. H.2870.
M 1744 .S7 S6 1901 Rare Books Large

MacCowan, Roderick. *The men of Skye / by Roderick MacCowan.* Glasgow: John Macneilage; Edinburgh: Norman Macleod, 1902.
BX 5390 .M137m 1902 Rare Books Medium

O'Keefe, James George. *A handbook of Irish dances, with an essay on their origin and history,* by J. G. O'Keefe and Art O'Brien. Dublin: O'Donoghue, [1902?].
GV 1646 .I2 Ok2h Rare Books Small

Petrie, George. *The complete collection of Irish music / as noted by George Petrie; edited from the original manuscripts, by Charles Villiers Stanford.* London: Published for the Irish Literary Society of London by Boosey; New York: Steinway Hall, [1902–5?].
M 1744 .P448 1902 Rare Books Large

An Cruitire: eoghan laoide do hlear. 1 mBaile Atha Cliath [Dublin]: Chonnradh na Gaedhilge, 1903.
M 142 .C44 C7 1903 Rare Books Large

Henebry, Richard. *Irish music: being an examination of the matter of scales, modes, and keys, with practical instructions and examples for players / by Richard Henebry.* Dublin: The Printing Assoc., [1903?].
ML 287 .H4 Rare Books Large

Hughes, Herbert. *Songs of Uladh, collected and arranged by Padraig MacAodh O'Neill, with words by Seosamh Mac Cathmhaoil and designs by Seaghan Mac Cathmhaoil.* Belfast: [W. Mulan], 1903.
M 1 .H8 S6 Rare Books 1903 XLarge

Lecky, William Edward Hartpole. *Leaders of public opinion in Ireland by William Edward Hartpole Lecky.* New ed. New York, London [etc.]: Longmans, Green, and co., [1903?].
DA 948 .A5 L495L 1903 Rare Books Small

MacManus, Seumas. *A lad of the O'Friels, by Seumas MacManus.* New York: Mc-Clure, Phillips & Co., [1903?].
PR 6025 .Ac64L 1903 Rare Books Small

O'Neill's music of Ireland: eighteen hundred and fifty melodies: airs, jigs, reels, horn-pipes, long dances, marches, etc., many of which are now published for the first time / collected from all available sources, and edited by Capt. Francis O'Neill; arranged by James O'Neill. Chicago: Lyon & Healy, 1903.
M 1 .O5 O5 1903 Rare Books XLarge

Armstrong, Robert Bruce. *Musical Instruments / Robert Bruce Armstrong.* Edinburgh: D. Douglas, 1904–8.
ML 501 .A76 1904 Rare Books XLarge

Finerty, John Frederick. *Ireland; the people's history of Ireland.* New York, London: The Co-operative publication society [1904].
DA 910 .F494i Rare Books Medium

Gael (Brooklyn, New York, N.Y.). *The Gael: a monthly journal devoted to the preserva-tion and cultivation of the Irish language and the autonomy of the Irish nation = An Gaodhal: leabhar-aithris miosamhal tabhartha chum an teanga Ghaedhilge a chosnad agus a shaorthughadh agus chum fein-riaghla cinidh na h-Eireann.* Brooklyn, N.Y.: M. J. Logan, [–1904].
AP 73 .G118 Rare Books Large

Irish Folk Song Society, London. *Journal of the Irish Folk Song Society.* Dublin: [S.n.], 1904.
ML 5 .I7 J6 Rare Books Large

Irish literature / Justin McCarthy, M.P., editor in chief. Maurice F. Egan, LL.D., Douglas Hyde, LL.D., Lady Gregory, James Jeffrey Roche, LL.D., associate editors. Charles Welsh, managing editor. Philadelphia: J. D. Morris & Co., [1904].
PR 8833 .Ir4 Rare Books Medium

Lane, Timothy O'Neill. *Lane's English-Irish dictionary, comp. from the most authentic sources. By T. O'Neill Lane.* Dublin: Sealy, Bryers and Walker; London: D. Nutt, 1904.
PB 1291 .L244e 1904 Rare Books Medium

Mangan, James Clarence. *Irish and other poems / by James Clarence Mangan, with a selection from his translations.* New edition. Dublin: M.H. Gill & Son, Ltd., 1904.
PR 4973 .A17 G41 Rare Books Small

Mansfield, Milburg Francisco. *Romantic Ireland, by M.F. and B. McM. Mansfield . . . illustrated by Blanche McManus Mansfield.* Boston: L. C. Page & company, [1904?].
DA 977 .M317r 1904 Rare Books Small

McCarthy, Justin. *An Irishman's story.* New York: Macmillan, 1904.
DA 565 .M127 1904 A3i Rare Books Medium

O'Farrelly, Agnes. *The O'Growney memorial volume / [by] Agnes O'Farrelly.* Dublin: M. H. Gill; London, D. Nutt, [1904].
PB 1109 .O4 O4 1904 Rare Books Large

Flood, William Henry Grattan. *The story of the harp.* London: The Walter Scott publishing co., ltd.; New York: C. Scribner's sons, 1905.
ML 1005 .F659s 1905 Rare Books Small

Hogan, Andrew. *Importance of Irish history.* Chicago: J. S. Hyland Co., 1905.
DA 913 .H678i 1905 Rare Books Small

Mathew, Frank James. *Ireland.* London: A. & C. Black, [1905].
DA 977 .M421i Rare Books Medium

The minstrelsy of England: a collection of English songs adapted to their traditional airs: for voice with pianoforte accompaniment / supplemented with historical notes by Edmonstowne Duncan. London: Augener, [pref. 1905].
M 1740 .M54 Rare Books Large

Fitz-Gerald, S. J. Adair (Shafto Justin Adair). *Stories of famous songs.* London: J. B. Lippincott Co., 1906.
PN 1381 .F576s Rare Books Small

Flood, William H. Grattan (William Henry Grattan). *A history of Irish music / by Wm. H. Grattan Flood.* Dublin [etc.]: Browne and Nolan, limited, 1906.
ML 287 .F659h Rare Books Small

Hyde, Douglas. *A literary history of Ireland from earliest times to the present day. 4th impression.* London: T. F. Unwin, 1906.
PB 1306 .H992L Rare Books Medium

O'Brien, R. Barry (Richard Barry). *Studies in Irish history, 1603–1649; being a course of lectures delivered before the Irish literary society of London.* Dublin, Belfast & Cork: Browne & Nolan, limited; [etc., etc.], 1906.
DA 940 .Ob6s ser. 2 1906 Rare Books Medium

[Whyte, Henry]. *The Celtic lyre; a collection of Gaelic songs with English translations, by Fionn [pseud.]; music in both notations.* Edinburgh: J. Grant, 1906.
M 1744 .W5 C4 1906 Rare Books Medium

Bards of the Gael and Gall: examples of the poetic literature of Erinn; done into English after the metres and modes of the Gael / by George Siegerson . . . 2nd ed., rev. and enl., with a new frontispiece. London: T. F. Unwin, 1907.
PR 8863 .E5 B37 1907b Rare Books Medium

Casey, John K. (John Keegan). *The rising of the moon; and other ballads, songs, and legends, by John K. Casey . . .* Dublin: M H. Gill & Son, Ltd., 1907.
ML 54.6 .C273 1907 Rare Books Medium

Fraser, Alexander Duncan. *Some reminiscences and the bagpipe.* Edinburgh: W. J. Hay; [etc., etc., 1907].
ML 980 .F862s Rare Books Medium

The Golden treasury of Irish songs and lyrics / edited by Charles Welsh. New York: Dodge Pub. Co., [1907?].
PR 8861 .L8 W4 1907 Rare Books Medium

Haltigan, James. *The Irish in the American revolution, and their early influence in the colonies, by James Haltigan.* Washington, D.C.: P.J. Haltigan, [1907?].
E 269 .Ir4 H169i 1908 Rare Books Medium

Irish songs: a collection of airs old and new / edited and the piano accompaniments arranged by N. Clifford Page. Boston: Oliver Diston Co.; New York: Ditson & Co., [1907?].
M 1744 .P344 1907 Rare Books Large

O hUiginn, Brian. *Glimpses of Glen-na-Mona: stories and sketches* / by Brian O hUiginn ("Brian na Banban"). Dublin: Gill, 1907.
PR 6003 .R351g 1907 Rare Books Small

O'Neill, Francis. *The dance music of Ireland: 1001 gems: Double jigs, single jigs, hop or skip jigs, reels, hornpipes, long dances, set dances, etc.* / Collected and selected from all available sources, and edited by Capt. Francis O'Neill; arranged by Sergt. James O'Neill. Chicago: Lyon & Healy, 1907.
M 1744 .D36 1907 Rare Books XLarge

The piobaireachd: as MacCrimmon played it / with instructions how to read and understand music by J. McLennan. Edinburgh: J. McLennan, [1907].
MT 530 .M3 1907 Rare Books Large

Williams, John Lloyd. *Sixteen Welsh melodies: with traditional and original Welsh words and English lyrics* / by Alfred Perceval Graves; the music edited and arranged by J. Lloyd Williams and Arthur Somervell. London, New York: Boosey, [1907–9?].
M 1742 .W4 1907 Rare Books Large

Collisson, William Alexander Houston. *Dr. Collisson in and on Ireland: a diary of a tour, with personal anecdotes, notes autobiographical and impressions.* London: R. Sutton, [1908].
DA 977 .C697d Rare Books Medium

Craig, J. P. (James Patrick). *An craobin ceoil: a collection of songs / written and composed by J. P. Craig.* Derry: D. G. Craig & Co., 1908.
M 1744 .C735 1908 Rare Books XLarge

O'Donnell, Frank Hugh Macdonald. *Paraguay on Shannon: the price of a political priesthood; remarks on policy and proceedings of a ribbonman board and a royal arranged commission.* London: P. S. King, 1908.
BX 1495 .Od5p 1908 Rare Books Medium

Patriotic and folk-lore songs / arranged by the special teachers of singing in the Chicago public schools; edited by Frederick H. Pease. Chicago: Rand, McNally, [1908].
M 1627 .P322 Rare Books Medium

Robinson, Stanford Frederick Hudson. *Celtic illuminative art in the gospel books of Durrow, Lindisfarne, and Kells.* Dublin: Hodges, Figgis, & co., limited, 1908.
ND 2940 .R63 1908 Rare Books XLarge

Hennessy, Swan. *Blaithfhleasg bheag =: Petite suite irlandaise: d'fhonnaibh Arsa Gaedhealacha as leabhar Petrie = d'apres des Airs anciens de la colletion Petrie / cheithre lamhada da seinm ar phiano—pour piano a quatro mains par Swan Hennessy.* Paris: E. Demet, [1909?].
M 203 .H432 1909 Rare Books XLarge

Old Irish folk music and songs; a collection of 842 Irish airs and songs, hitherto unpublished / edited, with annotations, for the Royal society of antiquaries of Ireland, by P. W. Joyce. London, New York: Longmans, Green, and co.; [etc., etc.], 1909.
M 1744 .J854 1909 Rare Books Large

Sonneck, Oscar George. *Report on "The Star-Spangled Banner," "Hail Columbia," "America," "Yankee Doodle" / comp. by Oscar George Theodore Sonneck . . .* Washington: Govt. Print. Off., 1909.
ML 3561 .S762 1909 Rare Books Large

Gems of melody: a collection of traditional Irish melodies: with accompaniments for piano or harp. Dublin: Pigott, [191–?].
M 1744 .G46 Rare Books Large

Bolton, Charles Knowles. *Scotch Irish pioneers in Ulster and America.* Boston: Bacon and Brown, 1910.
E 184 .Sco811 B639s Rare Books Medium

Fox, Charlotte Milligan. *Songs of the Irish harpers / collected and arranged for harp and piano by C. Milligan Fox.* London: Bayley & Ferguson; New York: Schirmer, [1910].
M 272 .F6 S6 1910 Rare Books XLarge

Hogan, Edmund. *Onomasticon goedelicum locorum et tribuun Hiberniae et Scotiae: an index, with identifications, to the Gaelic names of places and tribes / by Edmund Hogan* . . . Dublin: Hodges, Figgis & Co., Limited; [etc., etc.], 1910.
DA 979 .H643 1910 Rare Books Large

O'Dwyer, Robert. *Eithne: romantic opera founded upon the Irish folk-story Ean an ceoil binn / libretto by Thomas O'Kelly.* Dublin: Cramer, Wood; New York: J. W. Stern, [c. 1910].
M 1503 .O39 E5 1910 Rare Books Large

O'Neill, Francis. *Irish folk music: a fascinating hobby, with some account of allied subjects incl. O'Farrell's Treatise on the Irish or union pipes and Touhey's Hints to amateur pipers / by Capt. Francis O'Neill.* Chicago: The Regan Printing House, [1910].
ML 3654 .On2i Rare Books Medium

O'Reilly, Edward. *An Irish-English dictionary: with copious quotations from the most esteemed ancient and modern writers, to elucidate the meaning of obscure words, and numerous comparisons of Irish words with those of similar orthography, sense, or sound in the Welsh and Hebrew languages / by Edward O'Reilly. A new ed., carefully rev. and cor. with a supplement . . . by John O'Donovan.* Dublin: James Duffy and Co., Limited, [1910].
PB 1291 .Or3i 1910 Rare Books Large

Popular selections from O'Neill's dance music of Ireland: double jigs, single jigs, hop or slip jigs, reels, hornpipes and long dances / arranged by Selena A. O'Neill. Chicago: Pub. by Request of the Gaelic Junior Dancing Clubs, 1910.
M 1744 .O54 D36 Rare Books Large

Barlow, Jane. *Irish ways / by Jane Barlow . . . with illustrations in colour and black and white by Warwick Goble.* 2nd ed. London: George Allen & Sons, 1911.
PR 4063 .B3 I77 1911 Rare Books Medium

Flood, William H. Grattan. *The story of the bagpipe.* London: Walter Scott publishing co., ltd.; New York: C. Scribner's sons, 1911.
ML 980 .F659st 1911 Rare Books Small

Galpin, Francis William. *Old English instruments of music: their history and character.* London: Methuen, 1911.
ML 501 .G1390 Rare Books Medium

Hall, S.C. (Samuel Carter). *Ireland: its scenery, character and history, by Mr. and Mrs. S. C. Hall, illustrated from paintings by F. S. Walker and photographs.* Boston: Nichols, 1911.
DA 975 .H147i N546 Rare Books Medium

Irish tunes for the Scottish and Irish war-pipes / compiled by William Walsh; arranged by David Glen. Edinburgh: D. Glen, [1911].
M 145 .I75 1911 Rare Books Small

O'Donoghue, D. J. *The humour of Ireland; selected, with introduction, biographical index and notes, by D. J. O'Dooghue.* London: Walter Scott Publishing Co., ltd.; New York: C. Scribner's Sons, 1911.
PN 6178 .Ir4 Od5h Hesburgh Library Music — O'Neill (2nd floor)

O'Sheel, Shaemas. *The blossomy bough: poems / by Shaemas O Sheel.* New York: Published by the Franklin Press for S. O Sheel, 1911.
PS 3529 .S5 B68 1911 Rare Books Medium

O'Sullivan, Patrick. *Irish songs in English and Gaelic / arranged and harmonized for two voices with piano accompaniment by Patrick O'Sullivan. Irish-American patriotic songs / composed and adapted to American airs / by A. J. Seabrook.* Chicago: O'Sullivan & Seabrook, [1911].
M 1744 .O8 I7 1911 Rare Books Large

Rice, Edw. LeRoy (Edward LeRoy). *Monarchs of minstrelsy, from "Daddy" Rice to date / by Edw. LeRoy Rice . . .* New York City, N.Y.: Kenny Pub. Col., [1911?].
ML 106 .U3 R5 Rare Books Large

Roche, Frank. *Collection of Irish airs, marches & dance tunes / compiled and ar-ranged for violin, mandoline, pipes and flute, with an introduction by Charles J. Brennan.* Dublin: Pigott & Co., Ltd., 1911–.
M 1 .R6 C6 1911 Rare Books Large

Fox, Charlotte Milligan. *Annals of the Irish harpers / by Charlotte Milligan Fox.* New York: Dutton, 1912.
ML 3654 .F69 1912 A56 Rare Books Medium

MacGill, Patrick. *Songs of the dead end.* London: Year Book Press, 1912.
ML 54.6 .M17 1912 Rare Books Medium

O'Mahony, John. *A history of the O'Mahony septs of Kinelmeky and Ivagha and the Kerry branch / by Rev. Canon O'Mahony.* Crookstown, Co. Cork: Guy & Co., Ltd., 1912.
CS 499 .Om1 Om1h 1912 Rare Books Large

Bigger, Francis Joseph. *An piob mor.* Ardrigh, Belfast: Le Feile Padraiz, 1913.
ML 980 .B592 Rare Books Medium

Craig, Anne Abbott Throop. *Book of the Irish historic pageant; episodes from the Irish pageant series "An dhord fhiann," by Anna Throop Craig . . .* New York, Printed by Francis & Loutrel, [1913?].
PN 3206 .C844a Rare Books Medium

Feis under auspices of Gaelic League of Ireland: Comiskey Park [Chicago], Aug. 3, 1913. [s.n.].
GT 294.5 .F45 1913 Rare Books Large

Hughes, Herbert. *Songs from Connacht: nine poems of Padraic Colum / set to music by Herbert Hughes.* London; New York: Boosey, 1913.
M 1621 .H83 S6 1913 Rare Books XLarge

Lecky, William Edward Hartpole. *A history of Ireland in the eighteenth century.* New impression. London, New York: Longmans, Green, and Co., 1913.
DA 947 .L46 1913 Rare Books Small

Maginnis, Thomas Hobbs. *The Irish contribution to America's independence.* Philadelphia: The Doire publishing company, 1913.
E 184 .Ir4 M272i Rare Books Medium

O'Neill, Francis. *Irish minstrels and musicians: with numerous dissertations on related subjects / by Capt. Francis O'Neill.* Chicago: The Regan Printing House, [1913].
ML 287 .O5 I86 1913 Rare Books Large

Seymour, St. John D. (St. John Drelincourt). *Irish witchcraft and demonology.* Dublin: Hodges, Figgis & co. ltd.; [etc., etc.], 1913.
BF 1581 .Se96i 1913 Rare Books Medium

Weygandt, Cornelius. *Irish plays and playwrights / by Cornelius Weygandt.* Boston; New York: Houghton Mifflin, 1913.
PR 8789 .W545i Rare Books Medium

Begbie, Harold. *The happy Irish.* New York: Hodder and Stoughton, George H. Doran company, [1914].
DA 977 .B393h Rare Books Medium

Coffey, Diarmid. *O'Neill & Ormond, a chapter in Irish history / by Diarmid Coffey.* Baltimore: Norman Remington Co., 1914.
DA 940 .C645o 1914 Rare Books Medium

Darley, Arthur Warren. *Feis ceoil collection of Irish airs: hitherto unpublished / edited by Arthur Darley & P. J. McCall.* Dublin: Feis Ceoil Association, 1914.
M 1744 .D28 1914 Rare Books Large

Davis, Thomas Osborne. *Thomas Davis, selections from his prose and poetry, with an introduction by T. W. Robinson, M.A.* London: T. F. Inwin, [1914].
PR 4535 .D298 A16 R649t Hesburgh Library General Collection

Le Fanu, William Richard. *Seventy years of Irish life: being anecdotes and reminiscences / by W.R. Le Fanu.* London: Arold, [1914].
PR 4879 .L521s Hesburgh Library Music—O'Neill (2nd floor)

Phibbs, Harry C. *Sweet olde Irish songs: a selection of famous Celtic airs and ballads.*
／*Edited by Robert J. Cole and Harry C. Phibbs.* New York: The Log Cabin Press,
1914.
M 1744 .C6 S9 1914 Rare Books Large

Wilson, Philip, M.A. *The beginnings of modern Ireland / by Philip Wilson.* Dublin;
London: Maunsel, 1914.
DA 935 .W696b Rare Books Medium

Breatnach, Padraig A. *Songs of the Gael: a collection of Anglo-Irish songs and bal-
lads wedded to old traditional Irish airs / by an t-A air Padruig Brea nac.* Dublin:
Browne and Nolan, [1915].
PR 8860 .S058 1915 Rare Books Small

Breatnach, Padraig A. *Songs of the Gael; a collection of Anglo-Irish songs and bal-
lads, wedded to the old traditional Irish airs.* First series. Revised and enlarged.
Dublin: Browne and Nolan, Limited, 1915.
M 1744 .B7 1922 Rare Books Small

*O'Neill's Irish music: 400 choice selections arranged for piano or violin: airs, jigs,
reels, hornpipes, long dances, etc., most of them rare, many of them unpublished
/ collected and edited by Francis O'Neill; arranged by Selena O'Neill.* Enl. ed.
Chicago: Lyon & Healy, [1915].
M 1 .O5 O51 Rare Books XLarge

*Irish songs and ballads for medium voice / pianoforte accompaniments by Charles R.
Baptie.* Concert ed. Glasgow: J. S. Kerr, [1916?].
M 1744 .B37 1916 Rare Books XLarge

1916 song book. Dublin: Irish Book Bureau, [1916].
PR 8860 .S66 1916 Rare Books Medium

Stanford, Sir Charles Villiers. *Four Irish dances / composed by C. Villiers Stanford;
arranged for piano by Percy Grainger.* New York: J. Fischer, [1916?].
M 35 .S76 F6 1916 Rare Books XLarge

O'Casey, Sean. *Songs of the wren, humorous and sentimental to well known airs.*
Dublin: F. O'Connor, [1918?].
M 744 .O328 A56 1918 Rare Books Medium

O'Donnell, Manus. *Betha Colaim chille.* Urbana, Ill.: The University of Illinois under the auspices of the Graduate school, 1918.
PB 1398 .Od5b Rare Books Large

Rooney, Hubert E. *An Smolac: Irish songs / edited and arranged by Hubert E. Rooney.* Dublin: Maunsel, 1918.
M 1744 .R674 S4 1918 Rare Books Large

Cork: its trade & commerce: official handbook of the Cork Incorporated Chamber of Commerce & Shipping. Cork, Ireland: Guy & Co., 1919–.
HC 258 .C813 1919 Rare Books Large

Coisir a mhoid: the mod collection of gaelic part songs. Glasgow: A. Maclaren, [192–?].
M 1746 .C65 Rare Books Large

Flood, Wm. H. Grattan (William Henry Grattan). *John Field of Dublin: inventor of the nocturne: a brief memoir / written by W. H. Grattan Flood . . .* Dublin: M. Lester, limited, [1921].
ML 410 .F545 F56 J64 1921 Rare Books Medium

Waifs and strays of Gaelic melody: comprising forgotten favorites, worthy variants, and tunes not previously printed / collected and edited by Francis O'Neill; arranged by Selena O'Neill. 2nd ed., enl. Chicago: Lyon & Healy, 1922.
M 1 .O5 W3 1922 Rare Books XLarge

Mason, Redfern. *Rebel Ireland.* San Francisco: The author, [1923?].
DA 963 .M381r Rare Books Small

The violin made easy and attractive: this Gaelic collection of Irish airs, jigs, reels, hornpipes, marches, etc. / Selected, arranged and fingered with bowing marked by Batt Scanlon. San Francisco: B. Scanlon, [c. 1923].
M 43 .S3 V5 1923 Rare Books Small

Burchenal, Elizabeth. *Rinnce na Eirann: National dances of Ireland, containing twenty-five traditional Irish dances collected from original sources in Ireland by J.M. Lang . . . and national dance music including an original composition by Arthur Darley. With full directions for performance and numerous illustrations and diagrams / Edited and described by Elizabeth Burchenal . . . piano*

arrangements by Emma Howells Burchenal. New York: A. S. Barnes and Co., 1924.
GV 1646 .Ir2 B8 1924 Rare Books XLarge

Londubh an chairn: being songs of the Irish Gaels in staff ansd sol-fa with English metrical translations / edited by Maighread Ni Annagain agur Seamus de Chalanndioluin. Dublin, Cork; Educational Company of Ireland, [1925].
M 1744 .L63 Rare Books Large

Rainn agus amhrain: cnusasacht rann agus amhran o Chonndae na Midhe, o Chonndae Lughmhaidh agus o Chonndae Ardmhacha / Eamonn O Tuathail Ard-Mhaighistir Cholaiste Laighean, do thiomsuigh agus do chuir i n-eagar. l mBaile Atha Cliath: Brun agus O Nolain, 1925.
M 1744 .R23 1925 Rare Books Medium

Ulster songs and ballads of the town and the country / collected and set down by H. Richard Hayward; with an introduction by St. John Ervine. London: Duckworth, 1925.
PR 8860 .H38 1925 Rare Books Small

O'Dwyer, Robert. *Se U la: as "U la de'n Craoi" / do can An Craoi in; do cuir ceol leo Riobard O Du ir.* Dublin: O'Dwyer, 1926.
M 1744 .O39 U2 1926 Rare Books Large

Bornschein, Franz C. (Franz Carl). *Home: a bird fantasy: a one act cantata with old celtic folkmusic / harmonized by F. C. Bornschein; lyrics and play by Francis P. Donnelly.* New York: J. Fischer, [1927].
M 1513 .B6 H6 1927 Rare Books Large

Siegerson, George. *Songs and poems.* Dublin: James Duffy & Co., 1927.
ML 54.6 .S45 1927 Rare Books Small

Archibald, James. *Longing: old Gaelic folk song / words and adaptation by James Archibald; transcribed and arr. by Harry Bell,* 1928.
M 1744 .A7 L6 Rare Books XLarge

The Celtic song book: being representative folk songs of the six Celtic nations / chosen by Alfred Perceval Graves. [London]: E. Benn, limited, 1928.
M 1744 .G783c 1928 Rare Books Medium

Henebry, Richard. *A handbook of Irish music.* Dublin: Cork University Press, 1928.
ML 287 .H4 1928 Rare Books Large

Gill's Irish reciter: a selection of gems from Ireland's modern literature / edited by J. J. O'Kelly. 6th ed., rev. and enl. Dublin: M. H. Gill & Son, 1929.
PR 8835 .O54 1929 Rare Books Small

O'Higgins, Brian. *Songs of Glen na Mona / Brian O'Higgins.* Dublin: B. O'Higgins, [1929–]. (Dublin: Printed at the Sign of the Three Candles.)
PR 6029 .H5 S6 1929 Rare Books Medium

Lloyd, David de. *Tir na n-og: an opera in three acts / Welsh libretto by T. Gwynn Jones: music by David de Lloyd.* [London]: Oxford Univ. Press, [1930?].
M 1503 .L75 T57 1930 Rare Books Large

The dance music of Ireland / arranged by R. M. Levey. London: Frederick Harris, [1931?].
M 1744 .D36 1931 Rare Books XLarge

Goodman, P. *The school and home song-book; a collection of songs for use in Irish schools. Selected and arr. by P. Goodman.* Dublin: James Duffy, [n.d.].
M 1992 .G653 Rare Books Small

SOUTH *of Ireland. Illustrated and described: Souvenir of Killarney: its lakes, woods, islands, and mountains.* Cork: Guy & co., ltd., [n.d.].
DA 990 .K554 S087 Rare Books Medium

O'Neill's letter of inquiry to Notre Dame president Reverend Charles L. O'Donnell, C.S.C., about the disposition of his Irish library confirms that at age eighty-three he was still a "magnificent penman." *(Reproduced from the original held by the Department of Special Collections, University Libraries of Notre Dame)*

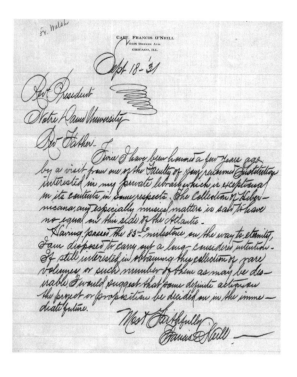

With characteristic generosity, O'Neill donated his valuable library of Hibernicana to the University of Notre Dame in 1931 "with no obligation imposed but that of their removal with no expense to the donor." The Francis O'Neill Collection draws scholars of Irish music and history from around the world. *(Reproduced from the original held by the Department of Special Collections, University Libraries of Notre Dame)*

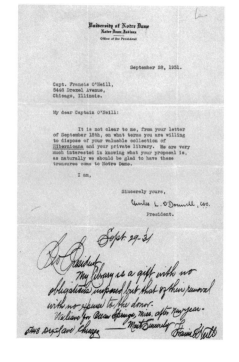

REPORT OF THE GENERAL SUPERINTENDENT OF POLICE OF THE CITY OF CHICAGO TO THE CITY COUNCIL FOR THE FISCAL YEAR ENDING DECEMBER 31, 1903

Office of the General Superintendent of Police,
Chicago, Illinois, February 1, 1904

To the Honorable the Mayor and City Council of the City of Chicago.

Gentlemen:—I have the honor to submit herewith the annual report of the Department of Police for the year ending December 31, 1903.

The outlook for an increase of revenue for the maintenance of this department for the year 1903 was so encouraging that in the month of February your honorable body passed an order authorizing me to fill the vacancies which had been accumulating in the Police Department during the years 1901 and 1902. As a result of your action, 122 probationary patrolmen were appointed and a few promotions were made in the higher ranks. Before the vacancies in the Sergeants' lists could be filled a blight fell on our financial prospects and the contemplated promotions had to be abandoned.

The increase of the salaries of patrolmen from $1,000 to $1,100 per year in the appropriation bill for the year 1903, has been much appreciated by the rank and file of the service. At one time or another the salaries of all grades of commanding officers as well as patrol drivers, operators, mechanics, etc., had been increased, but the salaries of patrolmen for a third of a century, remained the same up to last year.

An appropriation of but $3,492,488.07 was made for this department where $3,750,659.27 was necessary. The shortage of $258,171.20 was, by the exercise of rigid economy, reduced to $115,981.94 at the end of the year. This shortage was met by special appropriation from general receipts.

All vacancies caused by death, resignation and dismissal have remained unfilled since the city's shortage of revenue for the year 1903 was realized, about the first of March.

The year 1903 has been one of strife and turmoil, and the necessity for large police details at the scene of labor troubles has dissipated the strength and efficiency of the service as far as traveling post, and suppressing lawlessness and crime in the residence districts is concerned.

As a whole the Department is growing old and while many patrolmen, by reason of long service and the ills incident to police duties, are not as active and efficient on post as desired, they would be fairly satisfactory in the performance of certain lines of duty, such as at street and railway crossings, public play grounds, public baths, schools in congested neighborhoods, and so on, where men are actually necessary if younger men were available for active police work. If this city is to be adequately policed, an increase of at least one thousand patrolmen is a crying necessity.

It may not be out of place to direct attention to the fact that the police of this city have been given few opportunities to enjoy the days off duty to which they are entitled, during the past two years. When not on active police duty they have been kept in reserve at their respective stations most of the time.

In addition to their regular nine hours of patrol duty they attend police courts, justice courts, coroner's inquests, grand jury sessions and criminal courts, besides being subject to call for any special duty required.

Instead of the eight hour system which is in operation in New York City, with sixteen hours off, the case is sometimes reversed in Chicago. Notwithstanding their long and uncertain hours on duty, the police have shown patience and endurance which is highly creditable to them under the circumstances.

Since the capture of the car barn bandits and their imitators, Chicago has been comparatively free from crime. The incarceration of nearly a score of desperate criminals, half of whom can scarcely hope to escape the gallows, has put an end to an epidemic of crime, which for a time was alarming.

Safe blowers have abandoned Chicago as a profitable field of operations since some of the craft whose prior experience had led them to believe they would be immune from serious punishment, were arrested and convicted and actually compelled to serve their terms.

Confidence men who were driven out of Chicago over two years ago have remained away, so that swindling by the confidence game is rarely heard of. The streets have been free of beggars and "hard luck touchers" while a depraved class of women who infested the streets in certain portions of the city, have been completely suppressed in all except a limited district, by the persistent work of the police; and even in this limited area, conditions have been much improved.

The wine-room ordinance has been well enforced and observed during the year 1903, only three cases of clear violation of said ordinance have been discovered and in each case the saloon license was revoked by His Honor, the Mayor, on my recommendation. In nothing has reform and improvement been so marked as in the management and control of saloons. This is so evident to all citizens of Chicago that details are unnecessary. The strict enforcement of the midnight closing ordinance during the last months of the year was an innovation which required both educational and coercive measures. This action, as compared with the tolerant methods of nearly a third of a century, during which time the law was practically a dead letter, seemed almost revolutionary. The enforcement of the midnight closing ordinance, however, was found to be practicable and after a short period of uncertainty the law has been pretty generally observed.

Chicago is now as free from gambling as it is possible for a large city to be. Neither faro nor roulette exist; stud poker is extremely rare, while draw poker and craps are sporadic. Betting on the horse races, however, continues to be a popular mode of diversion and is indulged in notwithstanding the efforts of the police to suppress it. The old fashioned style of pool rooms and hand books are things of the past and have been succeeded by other and more secret methods of catering to the large number of people who desire by this means, excitement and entertainment. Telephones have taken the place of the tickers, suppressed by an ordinance introduced by His Honor, Mayor Harrison. Now verbal agreements, nods, winks and signals serve in lieu of written memoranda. Under these circumstances the evidence necessary to secure conviction in court is extremely difficult to procure. The resources of the police department have not yet been exhausted and it is quite probable that means will be found, capable of overcoming this evil.

Suppression of policy has been for some time directed by Mr. Shelby M. Singleton, Secretary of the Citizens' Association, who is assisted by six police officers of his own selection. Evidence sufficient to indict has been easily secured, as it has been repeatedly secured in the past by the police, but the first conviction for conducting a policy shop under existing laws has yet to be won, although the efforts of the police have considerably curtailed its operations.

In no branch of police effort were the results so uniformly satisfactory as in the suppression of so-called "get rich quick" concerns. The year 1903 was one of uninterrupted disaster to the schemes concocted by fertile brains to delude the credulous and unwary of both sexes. The special detail under charge of Officer Clifton R. Wooldridge, operating from the office of the General Superintendent, has punished and put out of business scores of matrimonial bureaus and agencies, turf investment concerns, home building associations, bucket shops, lotteries, wire tappers, fake promoters, book agencies and miscellaneous concerns. The readiness with which the United States Courts have co-operated with the Police Department has been very gratifying and deserves special commendation.

THE CAR BARN BANDITS

Extra editions of the Sunday morning papers of August 30 gave to the Chicago public the story of a murderous hold-up, which, before the capture of the perpetrators, was destined to become the most sensational crime with which the department ever grappled. I refer to the raid on the City Railway Company's barn at Sixty-first and State streets, in which two men were killed and another seriously wounded.

Around 3 o'clock on the morning of the robbery the four employees in the office of the cashier were startled by the breaking of a window pane, which was immediately followed by a volley of revolver shots. Frank Stewart, the night receiver, fell mortally wounded with a bullet in the abdomen, which caused death in a few minutes. John Johnson, a motorman, was instantly killed, one of the bandits encountering him in the doorway of the waiting room. The robbers quickly secured the money which was in Stewart's care, amounting to about $2,400 and fled, leaving no clew whatever to the police to work on.

Learning of the rapidity with which the shots were fired, as described by William Edmon, who was wounded, the officers came to the conclusion that the desperadoes were armed with a new make of gun known as the automatic. This information was given to every officer on the force, and the man-hunt was taken up for the most desperate band of criminals that ever infested Chicago, and who were evidently the perpetrators of several crimes of a similar character committed during the previous three months.

The usual roundup of hoodlums and other suspicious characters resulted fruitlessly, and for weeks this department was absolutely at sea as to the identity of the daring bandits. All of the old-time desperate criminals were looked up and accounted for, and the reckless bravado with which the crime was committed suggested that it was the work of old hands at the game who had come from some other city and were unknown in Chicago, instead of youthful novices. Day and night with unflagging zeal the search for the robbers was continued, and dozens of clews were run down that came to naught. Even the reward of $5,000 offered by the Chicago City Railway Company failed to elicit any information of value.

About two months after the raid on the car barns Officers John Quinn and William Blaul of the Forty-first Precinct were given information that one Gustave Marx, who lived in that police district, had exhibited an automatic revolver in a saloon and was possessed of considerable money. Both knew Marx and they spent several days looking for him. Shortly before 11 o'clock on Saturday night of November 21 Quinn and Blaul saw Marx in a saloon at Addison avenue and North Robey street. He was standing at the bar drinking with a crowd of young men.

Quinn entered through the front door of the saloon and Blaul by a side entrance. "I want you," Quinn said to Marx, and before he could place his hands on the suspect's shoulder, he had received his death wound. Marx had whipped out a revolver and fired several shots, the first of which struck Quinn in the stomach. He died soon after being taken to a hospital.

Officer Blaul, who had witnessed the shooting of his partner, closed in on Marx and showed him no more mercy than the latter had shown Quinn. Marx was wounded twice, once in the shoulder and another bullet striking him in the hip. As he fell Blaul leaped upon him with the ferocity of a tiger and disarmed him of two revolvers.

The prisoner was taken to the Sheffield Avenue Station and his air of bravado convinced Assistant Chief Schuettler, who talked with him, that he was one of the gang that committed the murderous raid on the City Railway Car barns. Sunday, Monday and Tuesday he was subjected to a rigid examination, and finally late in the afternoon of the last day, he broke down and confessed that he had been a party to several murders, among them the car barn job. He gave the names of his companions in crime—Harvey Van Dine, Peter Niedermeier, and Emil Roeski. As soon as he had weakened, the machinery of the entire police department was set in motion to circumvent the capture of the other members of the gang.

Right here I wish to remark that there are carping critics of this department who maintain that to "sweat" or persistently interrogate a prisoner is barbarous and that such a practice should be abolished. All I care to say in reply is, that if the "stomach pump," as it is sometimes called, had not been applied to Marx he never would have confessed to complicity in the raid on the car barn; neither would he have "squealed" on his accomplices in that and several other crimes.

Photographs of Van Dine and Niedermeier were secured and circulars with their pictures, were sent broadcast on the day following Marx's confession. The pictures were also printed in the Chicago newspapers, and in this way a wide circulation was gained.

During the time that Marx was locked up and before he "squealed" his partners, who knew of his arrest, remained in Chicago, but kept under cover. When they read Marx's confession in the Wednesday morning papers they decided that flight was the only thing left for them, and consequently they fled from the city that night, going to Indiana.

It developed later that the rescue of Marx from the Sheffield Avenue Police Station was planned by Van Dine and Niedermeier. They rented a building in the vicinity, which was to be set on fire. The patrol wagon and crew would respond and so would any commanding officers in the station expect the desk sergeant. To take the latter and lock-up keeper unawares and shoot them if necessary was the program, and liberate their confederate during the progress of the fire. The publication of Marx's confession effected a sudden transformation in their sentiments, and their desire to destroy him was more intense than their desire to effect his liberation. The assassination of Officer Blaul at this time by Van Dine and Niedermeier was frustrated merely by the officer's absence from the city until after Marx's confession.

On the following day, Thanksgiving, they stopped at a little grocery near Pine, Ind., where they bought something to eat. A country school teacher, who that day had seen the pictures of Van Dine and Niedermeier in a Chicago newspaper, recognized them as the hunted bandits and he informed his department by telegraph of his suspicions.

Acting under instructions from the Superintendent's office the following men were despatched that night to Indiana: Detective Sergeants Mathew Zimmer and James Gleason, and Officers Martin J. Qualey, Joseph Baumer, John Sheehan, Joseph Hughes and John Driscoll.

At a late hour that night the seven officers arrived at Pine, having driven ten miles across the country from Indiana Harbor. They conferred with the school teacher and took up the trail.

At 5 o'clock the next morning the officers saw smoke curling from a dug-out alongside the railroad tracks some distance from Pine. Suspecting that they had found their quarry they approached the hut with drawn revolvers and commanded those inside to surrender. A slanting door was thrown open and one of the bandits showed himself, discharging his revolver at the same time. Driscoll was mortally wounded in the first volley of shots that belched from Niedermeier's automatic gun, and Zimmer was the next to fall a victim with dangerous wounds in the head and right shoulder.

The officers withdrew to care for their injured companions, and Sheehan ran to Calumet Heights, where he secured a handcar that conveyed him to Miller's Station, the nearest telegraph point. He sent a message to police headquarters informing me of the wounding of Driscoll and Zimmer and asking for reinforcements.

In less than half an hour fifty officers equipped with rifles and ammunition, in charge of Assistant Superintendent Schuettler and Secretary James Markham, were on board a special train speeding for Indiana.

While Sheehan was gone on this errand Van Dine and his two companions emerged from their hiding place, and a lively exchange of shots took placed between them and the officers still on guard. The desperadoes succeeded in getting away, although one of them, Roeski, was hit by a bullet in the leg. They made their escape through clumps of underbrush and over snow-crusted marshes to the sand pits at

East Tolleston, where there was a locomotive on a sidetrack. Here they saw a chance to escape by taking possession of the engine. Brakeman Sovea was standing near the locomotive and on his refusal to climb into the cab, was shot and killed by Niedermeier. This, perhaps, was the most cold-blooded murder that they had committed.

The trio climbed aboard the engine, and with their revolvers held at his head, compelled the fireman to run it down the tracks to Liverpool, where it was fortunately derailed. Unable to proceed further they abandoned the locomotive and sought safety in flight across the country, and eventually took refuge in a corn field, on seeing that they were being gradually surrounded by Chicago policemen. In the language of Van Dine: "The country was alive with policemen."

The shooting of the brakeman back at the sand pits aroused the other employees that worked there, and some of them having shotguns, started in pursuit of the engine. They were joined by farmers who were shooting rabbits, and it was not long before the posse came to Liverpool, and by footprints in the snow, trailed the bandits to a corn shock in which they were hiding. The farmers and the men from the sand pits blazed away at the corn shock, peppering the faces of those inside with shot. Roeski, although suffering severe pain from the wound in his leg, inflicted in his encounter with the police at the dug-out, made a dash for liberty and escaped to the Calumet, which stream he followed for miles, partly on the ice, until captured at Aetna by a policeman while waiting for a train to Chicago. Van Dine and Niedermeier begged for mercy and threw their weapons, five revolvers and 250 rounds of cartridges, out of the shock.

After the escape of the bandits from the dug-out, a second telegram calling for more men to surround them in the Indiana wilderness was promptly responded to with a second expedition of forty men armed with rifles, in charge of Lieutenant Harding and Sergeant Mooney.

The incessant tramping through the snow, trailed by the policemen, who, coming from all directions were steadily closing in, so fatigued and alarmed the bandits that they gladly surrendered to the Indiana hunters in preference to falling into the hands of Secretary Markham's company of police, who were less than one thousand yards behind them.

Van Dine and Niedermeir were brought to the office of the Superintendent of Police, where they confessed to the car barn robbery and murders and several other crimes preceding that. Roeski arrived later in charge of the officers who captured him in the Aetna depot. The latter was not implicated in the car barn raid, but he had been in former hold-ups with the gang and killed his man.

Without doubt this quartet of youthful desperadoes was the most reckless and daring that ever operated in Chicago or vicinity. None of them was over 23 years old, and up to the time of their identity being discovered through the arrest of Marx, they were never suspected of being criminally inclined.

Their initial crime was committed July 9, when they held up a saloon at 1820 North Ashland avenue. Otto Bauder, a young boy who was in the place when the robbers invaded it, was shot and killed in attempting to run away. This was followed August 2 by the robbery of a saloon at 2120 West North avenue, in which B. C. La Grosse, the proprietor, was shot and killed. Adolph Jensen, a customer, also was shot, dying the next day from his wound. Then came the raid on the car barn, which later resulted in their capture. Several other lesser crimes than those mentioned were committed by them and to which they confessed. They were speedily indicted, and as this report goes to the press their trial is in progress.

In the hunt for the slayers of Stewart and Johnson an arrest was made by Patrol Sergeant James L. Mooney, assisted by officers of the Harrison Street station, that proved to be of great importance. This was the capture of John Healy, who had fled Chicago 17 years before, after committing a murder in the Seventh Precinct, or old Deering Street district. His identity did not become known for nearly two weeks after his arrest as he had grown from a boy to mature manhood. By clever detective work his identity was established, and before the end of the year he was placed on trial for the old murder. He is now serving a 14 years' sentence in the Joliet penitentiary. When arrested he had returned to the life of a western desperado and was heavily armed.

Other important captures of the year were those of the Aurora electric car robbers, the murderers of Saloonkeeper Patrick Barrett and the "Northwest Trio." Three men held up the motorman and conductor near Aurora on the night of October 8. In an exciting chase that followed by Aurora police officers, one of the bandits was shot and killed. The other two escaped.

A week later Lieutenant Healy and Officers McSwiggen and Conroy of the Thirty-second Precinct arrested two men for passing bogus checks. They were identified as James and Thomas Conway, brothers. Detective Sergeant Patrick Hamilton, of police headquarters, called to see the prisoners at the West Chicago Avenue Station, and observed that James Conway answered the description of one of the men who held up the Aurora street car. The brothers were taken to Aurora, where they were fully identified by the conductor and motorman. They have since been convicted.

Patrick Barrett, a saloon keeper at 4216 Wallace street, was shot and killed by three robbers who entered his place of business at 11:30 o'clock on the night of May 26. As in the case of the car barn bandits there was no clew for the police to work on. Captain (now inspector) John L. Revere, detailed several of his best officers on the case, and on June 20 they captured James Sammons, who had recently been released from the Pontiac Reformatory. A few days later Hugh Riley, an all-around crook, who associated with Sammons and John Lynch, also recently out of Pontiac, was arrested. Lynch was captured after a desperate struggle, in which he fired several shots at the officers who apprehended him. They were indicted for the murder and are now in jail awaiting trial.

On the same night of the Barrett murder Alderman Peter Wendling was held up and robbed by four men in the Third Police Precinct. He notified the Twenty-second Street Station, and Patrol Sergeant Phil Miller with several officers, hurried to the scene of the robbery. They encountered the bandits, who suddenly opened fire upon them, seriously wounding Sergeant Miller. One of the men was captured and proved to be Steve Keleher, a notorious thief. Keleher was not with the others when they killed Barrett. For the shooting of Sergeant Miller he was indicted, but has not yet come to trial.

The "Northwest Trio," as they styled themselves, was composed of Frank Krawczynski, Frank Czepek and Joe Dolinski, all of them mere youths. They were cheap imitators of the car barn bandits, and started in on their career of crime after the capture of Van Dine, Niedermeier and Roeski in Indiana. They committed a dozen or more robberies, in one instance killing their victim, Mathew Daniels, a saloon keeper at 1005 North Hoyne avenue, and wounding Otto Loser, the porter.

Krawczynski was arrested a few nights after the Daniels holdup by Lieutenant Healy, of the Thirty-second Precinct, and Detective Sergeant Patrick Hamilton. He thrust a revolver in Hamilton's face, but a blow from Lieutenant Healy knocked the weapon from his hand before it was discharged.

After a "sweat box" investigation he confessed to the Daniels robbery and murder and gave the names of his two companions, Czepek and Dolinski. They were identified by several of their victims and they are now in jail awaiting trial for the murder of Daniels.

The killing of Edward Lucas, a desperate thief, by Officer John W. Norton, of the Thirty-second Precinct, on May 22, deserves mention in this report. Although the taking of a human life is a serious matter, I commend Officer Norton for ridding Chicago of this notorious burglar, who half an hour before he was killed committed a robbery on the west side. The shooting was unavoidable.

IMPORTANT STRIKES OF THE YEAR

Labor disturbances that severely tried the forbearance, intelligence, and, I might add, the bravery of the members of this department, marked the past year. The most serious of these troubles was the strike of the Chicago City Railway employees, which was inaugurated November 12 and continued two weeks. This strike, in which about 2,000 men were involved, was the most serious that Chicago had experienced in years.

It is not my purpose to go into the merits or causes or this strike. Efforts to arbitrate the differences between the company and the men were futile, and as a result of a vote of the Union employees in mass meeting assembled, the strike was ordered. Nor was this action taken in haste. The men, through their representative, W. D. Mahon, International President of the Amalgamated Association of Street Railway Employees, had exhausted all means in their power to avert the tie-up, and after balloting on the proposition they decided that strike they must, a large majority favoring that course.

Strikes of all kinds entail extra work and hardship upon the police, but a street railway strike is the one that is most feared and the most difficult to control. With over 300,000 people depending daily upon the Chicago City Railway lines for transportation, the suspension of business on account of a strike meant a serious proposition for the municipality to deal with.

Having in mind the street car strikes of former years that were marked by violence and even death, it was anything but a pleasant outlook for this department to contemplate. The riots in St. Louis attending the street car strike of 1900 in which 23 persons were killed and 238 injured, forcibly reminded this department what might be expected in Chicago unless the law was enforced with a firm hand.

After the last night-cars had been run into the barns on the morning of November 12 the strike went into effect. A delegation representing the Union called upon His Honor, the Mayor, and myself the first day of the strike and assured us of their pacific intentions. Their earnest efforts, however, to keep in check the most rabid of the strikers and their sympathizers proved unavailing.

Between 8 and 9 o'clock of that day the company started four cars on the Wentworth avenue line and five cable trains on the Cottage Grove avenue line, police being stationed along the streets on both routes. The cars were manned by non-union crews. Strike sympathizers and teamsters blocked the tracks and attacked the operatives with stones and bricks. The violence was so great that at noon the attempt to run the cars was abandoned. One cable train was wrecked by a mob of rioters and another was abandoned by the crew. The electric cars met a similar fate.

At a conference held at my office that afternoon, Assistant Chief Schuettler, Inspectors Hunt, Lavin, Wheeler, Campbell and myself being present, plans were formulated and a line of action mapped out which was strictly followed until the termination of the strike.

Several cars on the Wentworth Avenue line were taken out of the Seventy-ninth street barn the second morning of the strike, and with from 10 to 12 policemen on each car and a cordon of officers along the street, the trip was made to the Washington street terminus. This, however, was not accomplished with ease. Mobs of men and women lined the thoroughfare traversed by the cars, and not only were obstructions placed on the tracks, but teamsters blocked the way, making it necessary for the cars to creep along slowly.

Inspector Hunt, with a force of 400 men brought the cars to Thirty-ninth street where he delivered them to Inspector Lavin who had a like number of men, distributed from there to the down-town terminus, where he was aided by Captain Gibbons, with a force of 250 men, who cleared the streets and kept the crowds moving north of Van Buren street. Assistant Chief Schuettler was in charge of the movement of the cars, and kept in close touch with the inspectors and captains under them; as well as communicating with police headquarters at frequent intervals. The police had frequent clashes with strikers and their sympathizers, being compelled to use their clubs frequently in order to open a passage way for the cars, especially at railway intersections. Several arrests were made this day, as well as the days following. After completing the round-trip the cars were run into the barns, and that ended the disorder of the second day. No attempt was made that day to operate cars on any other line.

The question having arisen as to the right of policemen to escort cars, or to ride on them in preserving the peace and protecting property, Mayor Harrison asked for an opinion on the matter from the corporation counsel. The opinion follows:

"There is no statute nor any principle of the common law, nor any decision of any court, holding that the police may not escort a street car nor ride thereon for the purpose of preserving the peace or preventing the destruction of property. Street cars operating upon the public street partake of the public character of such streets. Such cars are public places within the meaning of the term as used in the law. If the Mayor deems it necessary to put the police force on street cars operating on the public street, the existence of the necessity affords him a power as broad as the need."

The same conditions as described on the second day of the strike existed on succeeding days, only that the violence became greater and policemen on one occasion were compelled to use their revolvers. No one was killed, however, as the shots were fired in the air to frighten the rioters and create a stampede.

On advice of the aldermanic body at a meeting the City Council held on November 16, His Honor, the Mayor, appointed a peace commission to confer with the officers of the railway company and the strikers, and offer means toward a settlement of their differences. This commission was composed of Aldermen Palmer, Finn, Jackson, Scully, Bradley, Eidman, Maypole and Ruxton. The commission held a 12-hour session on the day following its appointment. Both sides to the controversy were given a hearing and mediation was offered, but as the street railway and union officials could not "get together" on certain points, naught came of the meeting. In the end, however, the commission succeeded in having the strike called off.

On the day following this first conference the company opened up the Cottage Grove avenue cable line by running ten trains under a guard of several hundred policemen. A large number of these reinforcements were brought from the North and West divisions of the city, because the Wentworth avenue line, which had been in operation several days, had to be protected as usual. The Indiana avenue electric line was opened November 18, and the Halsted street line the following day. Sixty-two cars were being operated on the tenth day of the strike. The number of cars in operation daily before the strike began was over 1,000.

It was in opening the State street cable line on November 23 that the police found it necessary to use their revolvers to disperse a riotous mob at Forty-first street that had thrown obstructions of iron girders across the tracks. Inspectors Hunt and Lavin were in charge of the forces, under direction of the Assistant Superintendent. In the conflict that day Inspector Lavin was struck in the head by a brick. Although the wound was serious he refused to quit, returning to his post after the injury was dressed.

The strike had now been in progress twelve days and the outlook was becoming more grave. On November 24 Mayor Harrison and the Aldermanic Mediation Committee were in conference until after midnight with the representatives of the company and the union, straining every nerve to reach an agreement by which the men could honorably return to work. It was nearly 2 o'clock in the morning of November 25 when an agreement was reached which was submitted by President Mahon to the members of the union at a meeting held that forenoon. The men ratified the action of the president and the strike was at once declared off.

Cars were put in operation the next morning, Thanksgiving day, the same as before the inauguration of the strike, but as a few of the crews, known as "strike breakers," were retained by the company, police officers rode with them for protection. This was continued several days until their presence was no longer required.

Before concluding this subject I wish to say that the members of this department never performed better work than in the manner the law was upheld by them during the troublous days of the street railway strike. It would be unfair to single out any one officer for praise—they all performed their duties faithfully and won the respect of all good citizens. The two "flying squadrons" of twelve men each, selected by Inspector Lavin to do duty on the Wentworth avenue and Halsted street lines, performed notable service.

Many of the men detailed for this duty from the Third, Fourth and Fifth Divisions were obliged to leave their homes early in the morning before street cars were running and had to be conveyed in patrol wagons to their respective places of assignment, long before the Chicago City Railway cars were taken out of the barns.

All day they remained "riding cars" or standing on the street exposed to the chilly weather and were obliged to take their chances in getting a lunch in the vicinity. As a consequence many of them contracted ailments from the hardships and exposure. Eleven hundred men were detailed at the strike.

Second in importance of the labor troubles of the year was the strike of the employees of the Kellogg Switchboard Supply company, in which seven hundred men and women were involved. Although the strike went into effect May 4 there was no serious disturbance until near the middle of July. Union pickets had interfered with the non-union workmen, and Judge Holdom had issued an injunction restraining them from loitering around the plant or committing overt acts, such as hampering the delivery and shipment of goods by the Kellogg company.

On the morning of July 11 two truck loads of goods under a police guard, accompanied by a patrol wagon, left the company's plant at Green and Congress streets for the terminal transfer freight house at Ogden avenue and Rockwell street. A crowd of strikers, sympathizers and idlers met the wagons and police a short distance from the Kellogg establishment and missiles were hurled at the officers. There were several tilts between the police and the mob, but the results were not serious. On arriving at the freight house an unlooked for interference presented itself. More than 100 teamsters, all of whom were in sympathy with the strikers who had followed the police, blocked the way so that the Kellogg wagons could not be driven up to the freight house doors. As fast as the police would jerk one recalcitrant driver out of the way, another would pull in, and in that way the blockade was effectually kept up for hours. Extra details of police were summoned and they finally succeeded in breaking through the barrier.

On the return trip to the company's barn the police were again besieged by a howling mob, and a lively skirmish ensued. A wagon load of reinforcements was dispatched to the scene from the Des Plaines Street Station and the police were victorious. A large number of teamsters and strikers were arrested that day, which marked the beginning of a week's rioting.

The late Inspector John D. Shea took personal charge of the delivery of goods on the succeeding days, and the clashes between the mobs and the police at times bordered on what Chicago experienced preceding the throwing of the bomb in Haymarket Square. For several days the rioting was desperate, but the police performed their duty bravely and in a manner that challenged the admiration of the critics of this department. At one time during the strike 600 policemen were required to preserve the peace. As a tribute to the memory of Inspector Shea, whose death, hastened by overwork, was an irreparable loss to this department, I desire to say as a part of this report that I received many commendatory letters from leading citizens, as well as from the secretary of the company, concerning his able handling of the Kellogg strike.

Other strikes of the year worthy of notice were the Elevator Men and Janitors, Restaurant and Hotel Waiters and Cooks, the Laundry Workers, Stationary Engineers and the strike of Franklin Union, No. 4, of Printing Press Feeders. This department was given considerable trouble by the strike of the restaurant and hotel employees in August, but nothing occurred that could be dignified as a riot. The strike entailed much extra work on the police force, but the men performed their duties faithfully and uncomplainingly.

THE IROQUOIS THEATRE DISASTER

The most terrible calamity that ever visited this city was the burning of the Iroquois theatre December 30, in which nearly 600 persons perished. The horrors of that day will never be effaced from the memory of those who took part in the rescues, and to this department great credit is due for the heroism displayed. Some of us, as policemen, had gone through the fire of 1871 when Chicago was laid in ashes, but that conflagration was insignificant compared to the awful holocaust that cost so many precious lives.

"Mr. Bluebeard, Jr.," a spectacular production, that was in the sixth week of a successful run, held the stage on the day of the fatal matinee. The playhouse was crowded with an audience of two thousand, most of them women and children. A few minutes after the curtain had ascended on the second act the scenery caught fire in the flies, and owing to its inflammable nature the flames leaped from one set of the scenery to another in an incredibly short time.

The stage was equipped with an asbestos curtain, but it failed to work successfully and fall to the stage floor. Immediately there was a wild panic. Tongues of flame shot out in the auditorium of the theater and licked the proscenium arch.

In the terrible panic that ensued scores of lives were crushed out and many others met a more horrible death in the flames. More than 250 persons were injured, some of whom died later.

It was about half past three o'clock when the alarm of fire came in; and on learning its location I immediately ordered every available officer in the down-town district to the scene. Companies of men were also hurriedly called from the First, Third and Fifth divisions. Within half an hour, several hundred policemen responded, having been rushed to the theatre in patrol wagons.

The sight that met the gaze of those who were first on the scene is one that will never be forgotten. Men, women and children were madly struggling to escape from the burning building, and the weakest of them fell and were trampled to death. In the gallery, where the greatest number of lives were lost, the tragic scene presented to the rescuers will haunt them for years to come. Piled eight and ten deep lay the bodies of women and children who were suffocated by the blast of hot air and smoke that swept over the gallery, carrying death to all.

The number of lives saved by members of this department is not known as no record was kept by rescuers, but many more undoubtedly would have perished but for the prompt service rendered.

Comparatively few lives were lost on the main floor. In the aisles and stairways of the first and second balconies the bodies were piled up promiscuously and almost inextricably. The removal of the bodies by the police from the second balcony was in charge of Assistant Superintendent Schuettler, while the work of removal from the first balcony was under my personal supervision.

With only lanterns to partially dispel the gloom amid smoke and steam the police and firemen worked together steadily and solemnly, and accomplished a work in less than three hours which experienced men thought would take ten times as many.

This department was taxed to the utmost, every ambulance and dozens of patrol wagons being called to remove the injured to hospitals. In addition a few business trucks were pressed into service. The promptness and method with which the injured were cared for and bodies removed to the different morgues, showed what the Chicago Police Department can do in an exigency of that kind and furnished an object lesson in discipline of which we may feel justly proud.

The dead were removed to undertaking establishments where officers specially detailed took charge of the valuables found on bodies as well as all other means of identification. These valuables were placed in envelopes and numbered to correspond with the number of the body, thereby avoiding confusion and greatly aiding in the identification. The envelopes were turned over to the coroner with an accurate description of each body from which they were taken, and the result was that more than 400 dead were identified before midnight. As the bodies were extricated from the mass, all property which fell to or was found on the floor was immediately taken charge of by Secretary Mayer.

All property found in and about the theatre was brought to the office of the Assistant Superintendent of Police and to the Custodian's office, where it remained until other quarters could be secured.

The goods recovered, all of which were water-soaked or otherwise damaged, consisted of 4,530 articles. They were classified and displayed to the public for identification and delivery, under the supervision of Police Custodian De Witt C. Cregier.

The debris scraped and collected from the theatre floors was carefully examined, a rocking sluice box, such as is used in mining camps was constructed, and through this the dirt was carefully sieved. More than $1,000 worth of diamonds and other precious stones were found, all of which were identified and delivered. Two hundred and seventy-six dollars in coin and currency also came from the debris.

Among the articles found in the theater were 195 pocket books containing $884.33. There were 33 sealskin coats and a miscellaneous lot of astrakhan, otter, mink, Persian lamb, bear skin and other fur garments taken from the ill-fated playhouse. Fifty diamond rings were found, also ear rings, stick pins, a sun burst, and other articles of jewelry too numerous to mention. Besides the articles enumerated there were 259 ladies' and misses' cloth coats, 93 men's and boys' overcoats, 263 ladies' hats, 100 girls' hats, 66 men's hats, 240 pairs of rubbers, 30 pairs of shoes and 50 opera glasses.

The articles of little value that were not claimed at the expiration of a month were given to the Salvation Army. The property identified and claimed amounted to about $50,000.

It is gratifying to state that the systematic and thorough work of this department was appreciated by the friends of the dead and injured as well as the community at large. Only in one case was property mislaid by an officer, and in that one the claimant received the value of the goods from the officer responsible for the loss.

IN CONCLUSION

To digress for a moment. Some twenty years ago a comic opera, the "Pirates of Penzance," was produced in this city. In it was sung a rollicking ditty the burden of which was "A policeman's lot is not a happy one." What with strikes, investigations and espionage by reform bodies, the old song is peculiarly applicable to the present day Chicago bluecoat.

Unjustly in many instances the members of this department have been assailed on every hand, but with very few exceptions, I am proud to say, they passed through the ordeal of investigation unscathed.

Looking retrospectively over one of the most eventful years in local police history, I am constrained to say that this department performed its duty well, and that, at times, under the most trying circumstances. It is also a pleasure to add that the utmost harmony prevails and that the personnel of the force is better than ever in of history and will compare favorably, I think, with that of any similar organization of the world.

An event out of the ordinary in which this department participated with much credit to itself, was the visit to Chicago of the President of the United States. Nothing was left undone to safeguard the city's distinguished guest during his brief stay here, and his visit is one of the few pleasant memories of the year. It is a source of gratification to be able to mention that the distinguished gentlemen complimented the Police department on the excellence of its arrangements on that occasion.

Respectfully submitted,

Francis O'Neill,

General Superintendent of Police

NOTES

EARLY YEARS

3   **My birth on August 28, 1848**   Francis O'Neill was born on August 28, 1848, in Tralibane, County Cork, and baptized Daniel Francis in the parish of Caheragh on August 30, 1848. Thanks to Nicholas Carolan for setting the record straight in his classic study, *A Harvest Saved: Francis O'Neill and Irish Music in Chicago* (Cork, Ireland: Ossian Publications, 1997). O'Neill first enrolled in the Dromore national school and completed his education at the Bantry national school.

5   **parish priest, Canon Sheehan**   Thanks to Emmet Larkin for identifying Canon George Sheehan, a curate in Cork City in the 1850s, as O'Neill's parish priest and for sharing his insights on the significance of the Cork School of Design. For a comprehensive account of the early years of the Cork School of Design, see http://www.crawfordartgallery.com/1851-1875.html. Thomas Hovenden, one of the school's graduates and a contemporary of Francis O'Neill, achieved great success as a painter in the United States. According to the *New York Times*, Hovenden's *Breaking Family Ties* "has been engraved or reproduced in large numbers and is a familiar object on the walls of thousands of homes in the United States." *New York Times*, August 15, 1895; see also *Chicago Tribune*, August 15, 1895; August 18, 1895.

5   **I decided to challenge the Fates in a wider field of human endeavor**   Francis O'Neill's decision to leave Ireland may also have been related to "His elder brother's persistence . . . in appropriating his salary for investment in stock and cattle dealing," cited by Charles Ffrench, ed., *Biographical History of the American Irish in Chicago* (Chicago: American Biographical Publishing, 1897), 311.

8   **Bishop Delaney**   The Right Reverend William M. Delany (1804–86) served as bishop of Cork from August 15, 1847, until his death on November 14, 1886. He is buried in the Ursuline Convent in Blackrock. Thanks to Claretian archivist Malachy McCarthy and to Julie Satzik at the Archdiocese of Chicago Archives and Records Center for verifying this information.

8   **barque Anne** The "Cork Harbor Shipping News," a regular feature in the *Cork Examiner,* published information on arrivals and departures in the 1860s. Thanks to Jeanne M. Follman for calling our attention to articles digitized by Ireland Old News, http://irelandoldnews.com.

15   **Emerald Isle**   Our gratitude to Richard D. Barrett for locating the *Emerald Isle*'s ship's manifest in the National Archives in Washington, D.C., that documents the arrival of O'Neill's future wife, Anna Rogers (b. 1849), in New York City on August 6, 1866, along with her mother, Mary; a sister, Julia (b. 1847); and a brother, John (b. 1859). Because he was an assistant steward on the *Emerald Isle*, O'Neill's name does not appear on the ship's manifest, lending credence to his claim that he was "paid for coming to America, and therefore not an emigrant." For information on the *Emerald Isle* and its role in transporting Mormon emigrants from Liverpool to New York, see http://www.xmission.com/~nelsonb/ship_desc.htm#eisle.

15   **we never met again**   This is a classic illustration of the difference between memory and history. Writing in his eighties, O'Neill remembered leaving "Fred the Belgian" in Liverpool in 1866. However, in the memoir, Fred reappears as a crew member on the *Minnehaha* two years later.

SAILING UNDER THE AMERICAN FLAG

17   **sailors' boardinghouses**   For a contemporary perspective on sailors' boardinghouses in New York City, see "Jack Ashore," *Harper's* 47 (July 1873): 161–70. Near O'Neill's boardinghouse on Oliver Street was Old Saint James Church, the birthplace of the first American branch of the Ancient Order of Hibernians in 1836.

20   **Minnehaha of Boston**   The *New York Times* of March 24, 1856, reported that the poet Henry Wadsworth Longfellow was a featured speaker at the "collation"

that followed the launch of the *Minnehaha*, "a new three deck ship, of 1,800 tons" from the yard of Boston shipbuilder Donald McKay.

23   **which I contrived to save through many hazards**   While still a teenager, Francis O'Neill began collecting beautiful objects, and this interest continued after his marriage to Anna Rogers. They surrounded themselves in their home on Drexel Boulevard with fine linen, crystal, china, and silverware — including scorched dishes from the Great Chicago Fire — that remain prized family possessions.

24   **a cargo of guano**   *Webster's Third New International Dictionary* (1996) describes guano, a popular fertilizer in the nineteenth century, as the "partially decomposed excrement" of seafowl that is "rich in phosphates, nitrogenous matter, and other material for plant growth." See "Life on a Guano Island," *New York Times,* June 20, 1869. In her 1881 fact-finding report, *Ireland of To-Day: The Causes and Aims of Irish Agitation,* Margaret Buchanan Sullivan discovered that Irish peasants "had not a single article of bedclothing except guano-sacks" to keep them warm. Sullivan's book, published by J. M. Stoddart, Philadelphia, is part of the O'Neill Collection at the University of Notre Dame.

QUIT SEA LIFE AFTER FOUR YEARS' EXPERIENCE

37   **my oldest brother, Philip**   O'Neill was the youngest of seven children born to John O'Neill and Catherine O'Mahony. His oldest brother, Philip, was baptized on January 17, 1835; Mary, who was also known as Nancy, was baptized on July 6, 1836; John was baptized on July 17, 1838; Michael was baptized on January 15, 1841, and died in his childhood years; Catherine was baptized on September 19, 1843; and another child named Michael was baptized on October 1, 1845. Using the name of a deceased child again in the same family seems unusual in the twenty-first century, but this appears to have been a common practice in the Irish culture. Francis and Anna used the name John Francis for two of their children. Carolan, *Harvest Saved,* 66.

37   **Boston Pilot**   The *Boston Pilot* in 1869 was "Irish America's leading weekly newspaper" with nearly 100,000 subscribers. See Charles Fanning's excellent analysis of the *Pilot* under editor John Boyle O'Reilly, "Respectability and

Realism," in *The Irish Voice in America: 250 Years of Irish-American Fiction* (Lexington: University Press of Kentucky, 1990, 2000), 161–66.

39   **barque Sunnyside commanded by Captain Patrick Myers**   O'Neill probably sailed with Captain Patrick Myers on the barque *Pensaukee*, not the *Sunnyside*. According to John Brandt Mansfield, *History of the Great Lakes*, vol. 1 (Chicago: J. H. Beers, 1899), 302–4, in 1870, Myers "was appointed master of the barque Pensaukee, a very smart boat, and sailed her five consecutive seasons." See *Chicago Tribune*, May 16, 1870, and June 25, 1870, for news of the barque *Pensaukee*'s shipments between Chicago and Buffalo. Born in County Clare, Ireland, in 1827, Myers was one of thirty-two "lake captains" in Chicago in the 1860s and 1870s mentioned by Thomas M. Mulkerins in *History of Holy Family Parish: Priests and People* (Chicago: Universal Press, 1923), 474–760.

40   **I married the handsome Anna Rogers on November 30, 1870**   The new elegant brick church of Holy Trinity in Bloomington, Illinois, was nearing completion when it was destroyed by a cyclone on April 18, 1869, so it is likely that Anna Rogers and Francis O'Neill exchanged their wedding vows in makeshift quarters, possibly the frame church that had originally belonged to the Methodist congregation. "Holy Trinity Church," in *Historical Encyclopedia of Illinois and History of McLean County*, ed. Newton Bateman and Paul Selby (Chicago: Munsell, 1908), 872. See also the history of Holy Trinity parish in *New World*, March 14, 1900.

42   **a controlling influence**   Advancement in the John V. Farwell Dry Goods Company may have been along religious lines. Farwell was a leader of the Young Men's Christian Association in Chicago and founder of the Illinois Street Mission for "saloon boys" that had developed into a "large church and Sunday school." See the Farwell biography in David Ward Wood, ed., *Chicago and Its Distinguished Citizens* (Chicago: M. George, 1881), 465–67. For a description of the new John V. Farwell building at Franklin and Monroe streets, see *Chicago Tribune*, February 25, 1872.

46   **box, occupied as our first home**   The *Lakeside Annual Directory of the City of Chicago* listed Frank O'Neill as living at 2702 Wallace from 1880 through 1889. The Recorder of Deeds of Cook County files showed that Francis O'Neill purchased the property at 2702 Wallace in April 1878. The 1880

census card and census report indicated their address to be 2712 Wallace, but this must have been a clerical error. Because of the strength of evidence of ten years of the *Lakeside Directory* and the Recorder of Deeds documents, the house that O'Neill described building had to be the property at 2702 Wallace. The O'Neill family moved to 5448 South Drexel Boulevard in 1890, but they continued to own the house on Wallace, which they converted to two apartments. O'Neill the landlord charged fifty cents a week for each unit. According to Mary Wade, O'Neill's granddaughter, his daughters argued with one another about who would have the privilege of collecting the rent.

48   ***Alderman Tracey, master mechanic for the Union Stock Yards and Transit Company***   In 1870, Sixth Ward aldermen William Tracey and Michael Schmitz represented 22,918 Chicagoans living west of Clark Street between Sixteenth Street and Egan Avenue [Thirty-ninth Street]. *Chicago Census Report; and Statistical Review* (Chicago: Richard Edwards Printer and Book Manufacturer, 1870), 1238. For background information on the reform-minded "Committee of Seventy" and the Police Board, see *Chicago Tribune*, February 5, 1873, and November 9, 1873.

50   ***the bullet plugged me in the left breast***   The *Chicago Tribune* and *Chicago Inter Ocean* of August 18, 1873, confirm that burglar John Bridges shot O'Neill on August 17, 1873. Although we have been unable to corroborate the exact date O'Neill joined the force, on July 22, 1873, the Police Board awarded the Chicago Engraving Works a contract for "500 stars for the police force." See especially the *Chicago Tribune* editorial "Shooting Policemen," August 21, 1873.

51   ***Alderman Gilbert, then acting mayor***   Alderman James H. Gilbert was elected acting mayor on August 12, 1878, during the absence of Mayor Monroe Heath. *Chicago Tribune*, August 13, 1878.

53   ***my style of writing***   M. L. Ahern described Francis O'Neill as "a magnificent penman." *Political History of Chicago* (Chicago: Donohue and Henneberry, 1886), 221. And according to John J. Flinn, he "has never been fined, suspended or reprimanded while connected with the police department." *History of the Chicago Police* (Chicago: Police Book Fund, 1887), 463.

53   ***Mayor Carter H. Harrison, the elder***   During his career on the Chicago Police Department, Francis O'Neill worked with both Mayor Harrisons, Carter Sr.

(1879–87, 1893) and Carter II (1897–1905, 1911–15). Melvin G. Holli, "Mayors," *Encyclopedia of Chicago*, ed. James R. Grossman, Ann Durkin Keating, and Janice L. Reiff (Chicago: University of Chicago Press, 2004), 511.

54   **Levy Mayer**   One of Chicago's most prominent attorneys, Levy Mayer (1858–1922), was a founding partner of the firm now known as Mayer, Brown, Rowe and Maw. Mayer's firm defended the owners of the Iroquois Theater that burned in 1903; Armour and Company "against the federal government's landmark 1905 antitrust case"; and Charles A. Comiskey, "whose 'Black Sox' threw the 1919 World Series." See "Another New Era in the Practice of Law," http://www.mayerbrownrowe.com; and poet Edgar Lee Masters's biography, *Levy Mayer and the New Industrial Era* (printed under the direction of Yale University Press, New Haven, Conn., 1927). Northwestern University's Levy Mayer Hall (1926) is named in his honor.

55   **Alderman McAbee**   James B. McAbee served as alderman of the Twenty-fourth Ward on the North Side from his election on April 1, 1890, until his death on February 9, 1892. See *Chicago Tribune*, April 2, 1890; February 10, 1892; February 13, 1892.

55   **Mr. Brennan, chief clerk**   According to Ahern, Michael Brennan, born in County Mayo, Ireland, in 1842, joined the police force on December 15, 1870 (Ahern, *Political History of Chicago*, 214). Brennan served as chief of police from 1893 to 1895. See Maureen O'Donnell, "Family Fills Up Police Ranks," *Chicago Sun-Times*, January 23, 2007.

56   **the new general superintendent, or chief of police**   See Ahern, *Political History of Chicago*, for contemporaneous views of O'Neill's colleagues: John D. Shea, 199; Joseph Kipley, 199–200; Simon O'Donnell, 196–97; and Frederick Ebersold, 194–95.

58   **living in Hyde Park I was obliged to return to the city every evening**   The village of Hyde Park, where the O'Neill family lived at 5448 South Drexel Boulevard, was not annexed to the City of Chicago until June 29, 1889. According to Ann Durkin Keating, "Between 1861 and 1889, Hyde Park Township, the area south of 39th Street and east of State Street, was an independent political unit separate from, and geographically larger than, Chicago." Ann Durkin Keating, "Hyde Park Township," in *Encyclopedia of Chicago*, 405.

58   **Robert W. McClaughry**   Major Robert W. McClaughry was warden of Joliet, Illinois. See *Chicago Tribune*, November 18, 1885, and November 10, 1920.

64   **a copy of that report**   Francis O'Neill's vivid account of the great railway strike of 1894 provides a level of detail unavailable in newspaper articles and in the official *Report on the Chicago Strike of June–July 1894* compiled by the United States Strike Commission (Washington, D.C.: Government Printing Office, 1895). O'Neill takes aim at railroad officials, especially John Newell, president of the Lake Shore and Southern Michigan Railway, and new employees "who succeeded the strikers [and] charged every mishap resulting from their own inexperience to the strikers." He was also critical of federal troops sent to Chicago by President Grover Cleveland, claiming that the "United States Regulars, Infantry and Cavalry were unequal to the task of taking a train of cattle more than half a mile from the yards."

65   **Lieutenant Fitzpatrick**   According to Ahern, John E. Fitzpatrick, "commended to promotion for bravery at Haymarket," was born in Johnstown, Pennsylvania, in 1852 and joined the Chicago police force on January 13, 1883, after working for three years at the Bridgeport Wire Works. Appointed drillmaster of the Chicago Police Department in 1885, his military experience included "the organization of the Johnstown Zouaves, and of the Sherman Guards at Springfield." Ahern, *Political History of Chicago*, 206–7.

67   **general manager Newell**   O'Neill's version of the retreat of railroad president John Newell and his son, Ashbel, includes more "local color" than the story published by the *Chicago Tribune*, July 4, 1894. See also Newell's obituary, *Chicago Tribune*, August 27, 1894.

69   **United States Regulars arrived in the Yards**   In its July 21, 1894, issue, *Harper's Weekly* portrayed the U.S. Infantry marching into the stockyards in a positive light, a characterization challenged by O'Neill's report.

69   **Inspector Hunt**   For Inspector Nicholas Hunt's testimony before the U.S. Strike Commission on August 28, 1894, see *Report on the Chicago Strike*, 385–89.

75   **the incendiaries succeeded in firing and destroying the two story frame hay warehouse at Loomis Street**   The *Chicago Tribune*, July 6, 1894, depicted the shooting as "the culmination of a series of conflicts between mobs and officials vested

with authority," and the newspaper headline blared, "Cold Lead for Edward O'Neil and Antonio Hopp."

76   **_Fire Marshal Fitzgerald urgently needed police protection_**   In his appearance before the U.S. Strike Commission on August 22, 1894, John Fitzgerald, assistant fire marshal and chief of the Eleventh Battalion of the Chicago Fire Department, corroborated O'Neill's account of the presence of "youngsters." According to Fitzgerald, when he tried to stop young boys from setting railroad cars on fire, "I got throwed in the ditch." *Report on the Chicago Strike,* 390–92.

80   **_John Jackman . . . and John alias "Engine" Burke were fatally shot_**   For information on the killing of "Engine" Burke and Thomas Jackman at Forty-ninth and Loomis streets and a list of injured, see *Chicago Tribune,* July 8, 1894. The newspaper reported, "The men shot by the troops and the police lay about like logs." *Harper's Weekly* captured the scene in an engraving published on July 21, 1894.

81   **_Lieutenant Healy of the 10th precinct_**   For information on Lieutenant Healy's handling of the first train to run out of the stockyards, see "A Big Mob is Overawed," *Chicago Daily News,* July 10, 1894.

82   **_he fatally shot one of the men, named Albert Miles, in the back_**   The *Chicago Tribune,* July 18, 1894, reported the killing of Albert Miles by Oscar Vardaman under the headline "Bullet for a Tough."

83   **_Officer William Feeley . . . was run over and instantly killed_**   According to the *Chicago Tribune,* October 24, 1894, the Committees on Police and Fire Pension favorably considered the widow Lizzie Feeley's request for aid. Patrolman William Feeley is one of seventeen thousand officers honored on the Officer Down Memorial Page, http://www.odmp.org.

83   **_Respectfully submitted_**   Although Francis O'Neill does not indicate exactly when he wrote his report on the great strike of 1894, internal evidence suggests that it was before the indictment of Oscar Vardaman on July 24, 1894, and his transfer to the Detective Bureau on December 14, 1894. See *Chicago Tribune,* December 15, 1894, for details of General Order No. 424.

84   **The civil service law**   Although the first civil service exam for patrolmen in Chicago was held on December 29, 1894, O'Neill is probably referring to the civil service act passed by the Illinois State General Assembly on March 20, 1895. For a discussion of civil service litigation, see *Chicago Tribune*, December 18, 1897. See also, "Police Commission Bill Has Few Friends," *Chicago Tribune*, December 12, 1897, for statements by Mayor Carter Harrison II, Joseph Kipley, superintendent of police, and former mayors and police superintendents.

84   **an average of 99.80 to my credit**   O'Neill's 99.80 score on the civil service exam was published in "Fit to Be Captains," *Chicago Chronicle*, February 1, 1898.

87   **the press and public supported my action**   For accounts of O'Neill's arrest of Republican aldermen Joseph A. Lammers and Joseph F. Haas, see *Chicago Daily News*, February 13, 1896; *Chicago Tribune*, February 13, 1896; *Chicago Inter Ocean*, February 13, 1896; *Chicago Tribune*, February 19, 1896; and *Chicago Inter Ocean*, February 19, 1896. Among those who sent O'Neill congratulatory letters were "Professors of the Chicago University, Judges of the courts, bankers and packers" (*Chicago Tribune*, February 19, 1896). For news of Lammers's ten-dollar fine, see *Chicago Daily Sun*, February 21, 1896; *Chicago Daily News*, February 21, 1896; *Chicago Tribune*, February 22, 1896. For news of Lammers's subsequent ouster from the city council, see *Chicago Tribune*, April 13, 1896.

90   **Debs's strike**   Eugene V. Debs (1855–1926), a native of Terre Haute, Indiana, organized the American Railway Union in Chicago in June 1893, "the first industrial union in the United States," http://www.eugenevdebs.com/pages/history.html. For Debs's role in the Pullman Strike, see "Pullman Strike," in *Encyclopedia of Chicago*, 666.

90   **I ordered an escort of police for the Ross funeral**   Alexander Ross's obituary, *Chicago Tribune*, May 13, 1901, refers to him as former assistant general superintendent.

91   **Robert E. Burke, president of the Cook County Democracy**   Honorary pallbearers at Robert E. Burke's funeral included many prominent Democratic politicians, sixteen judges, and eight aldermen, including "Hinky Dink" Kenna,

"Bathhouse John" Coughlin, and Johnny "DePow" Powers. *Chicago Tribune*, July 31, 1921. Reverend Edward A. Kelly, founder of Saint Cecilia parish at Forth-fifth and Wells streets in 1885, also served as chaplain for the Seventh Regiment of the Illinois National Guard. For information on the regiment during the Spanish-American War, see *Chicago Tribune*, June 6, 1898; September 7, 1898; September 9, 1898; and September 10, 1898. For a contemporary view of civil service in Chicago, see A. N. Waterman, ed., *Historical Review of Chicago and Cook County*, vol. 1 (Chicago: Lewis Publishing, 1908), 112–16.

92   **Yerkes' Franchise**   According to historian Harold Platt, Charles Tyson Yerkes (1837–1905), a native of Philadelphia, "played a crucial role in modernizing and integrating [Chicago's] public transit system," first by converting horse-car lines to cable and then "to electric traction . . . In 1897, he built the elevated loop around the central business district." See Platt, "Charles Tyson Yerkes and Street Railways," in *Encyclopedia of Chicago*, 793. Mayor Carter H. Harrison II recalled, "The harder I fought Yerkes' efforts to get a [railway] franchise . . . the more unpopular I became with the Gray Wolf membership [of the city council] which was eager to be debauched." Carter H. Harrison, *Growing up with Chicago:* (Chicago: Ralph Fletcher Seymour, 1944), 287.

94   **office of general superintendent of police**   Press coverage of O'Neill's appointment as superintendent was extensive, and typical was the *Chicago Chronicle* editorial, May 1, 1901, that declared: "Probably there is not an officer of police in Chicago who is better equipped by character, experience, education and temperament for the superintendency than is Captain O'Neill." See also *Chicago Tribune*, April 30, 1901, May 1, 1901; *Chicago Daily News*, April 30, 1901, May 1, 1901; *Chicago Inter Ocean*, April 30, 1901; *Chicago Record Herald*, April 30, 1901, May 1, 1901; *Chicago South Side Daily Sun*, April 30, 1901; *Chicago's American*, May 1, 1901; *Chicago Chronicle*, April 30, 1901; *Chicago Evening Post*, April 30, 1901; *Chicago Citizen*, May 4, 1901.

97   **a former inspector of police**   At the time of the Pullman Strike in 1894, John E. Fitzpatrick was an inspector of police in charge of the First Division and lived just three blocks from O'Neill at 5822 South Drexel Boulevard. For an account of his testimony on August 24, 1894, before the United States Strike Commission, see *Report on the Chicago Strike*, 389–90.

99   **the unpleasant duty of filing charges against the chief of detectives**   For information on the scandal in the Detective Bureau, see *Chicago Tribune*, August 13, 1901; August 23, 1901; August 28, 1901; and September 4, 1901. Background information on O'Neill's plans to clean up the levee appears in *Chicago Tribune*, May 13, 1901; June 23, 1901; June 30, 1901; July 7, 1901.

100   **the high-handed action of Judge Altgeld**   O'Neill did not share defense attorney Clarence Darrow's high opinion of former Illinois governor John Peter Altgeld (1847–1902), whose political career ended in 1893 when he "granted the three imprisoned [Haymarket] defendants absolute pardon, citing the lack of evidence against them and the unfairness of the trial." Christopher Thale, "Haymarket and May Day," *Encyclopedia of Chicago*, 375. At a funeral service on March 14, 1902, defense attorney Clarence Darrow praised John "Pardon" Altgeld, who "opened the prison doors and set the captive free." *Chicago Tribune*, March 15, 1902.

102   **courteous treatment at police headquarters**   In her memoir, *Living My Life* (1931), Emma Goldman recalls Francis O'Neill's "courteous treatment" of her and how her jailers' attitudes underwent a sudden transformation. "The matron and the two policemen assigned to watch my cell began to lavish attention on me. The officer on night duty now often appeared with his arms full of parcels, containing fruit, candy, and drinks stronger than fruit juice." For accounts of Emma Goldman's arrest in Chicago, see *New York Times*, September 11, 1901; *Chicago Tribune*, September 11, 1901; September 12, 1901; September 15, 1901.

102   **When President Roosevelt visited Chicago**   See *Chicago Tribune*, April 2, 1903, for President Theodore Roosevelt's itinerary, which included a carriage ride to Hyde Park and the cornerstone-laying ceremony for the University of Chicago Law School.

106   **I fell heir to the Kellogg Switchboard strike**   For background information on the reaction of Chief O'Neill to the Piper Report commissioned by the Chicago City Club, see *Chicago Tribune*, March 2, 1904; March 21, 1904; March 22, 1904. For "plain talk by O'Neill" on the Kellogg Switchboard strike, see *Chicago Tribune*, July 16, 1903; for criticism of O'Neill by Chicago Federation of Labor President John J. Fitzpatrick, see *Chicago Tribune*, July 27, 1903.

106   **The tie-up of the Chicago city railway lines**   On November 12, 1903, thirty-five hundred employees of the Chicago Railway Company went out on strike "with the intention of tying up all the north and south trunk lines of the surface railway and all the east and west lines completely." *Chicago Inter Ocean,* November 12, 1903. See also *New York Times,* November 13, 1903.

108   **Brode Davis, a fifty-dollar-a-day attorney**   Brode Bradford Davis, born in Lewis, Iowa, in 1868 and educated at Iowa State University and the University of Michigan, began his law practice in Chicago in 1890. In 1900 he became an office associate of Frank Lowden, who was elected governor in 1917. By 1911 Davis was a director of the Mahin Advertising Company as well as president of the Battle Creek Breakfast Food Company. *The Book of Chicago* (Chicago: Chicago Evening Post, 1911), 64; *Who's Who in Chicago* (Chicago: A. N. Marquis, 1926), 225, 543.

110   **With the approval of the mayor**   Carter H. Harrison II (1860–1953) was elected mayor of Chicago five times and served from 1897 to 1905 and from 1911 to 1915.

113   **Parsons, the American anarchist**   Albert R. Parsons (1848–87) produced *Alarm: A Socialist Weekly,* regarded as "the leading English-language anarchist journal in the United States." He was tried and convicted and hung with three other Haymarket defendants in Cook County Jail on November 11, 1887. *Encyclopedia of Chicago,* 985, 502.

117   **when the bomb was thrown in the midst of the police at Haymarket Square**   At the time of the Haymarket tragedy, Francis O'Neill was clerk of records at the Central Station, where he was regarded as "one of the most valuable of the staff of the Police Superintendent [Frederick Ebersold]." In 1886 his colleagues at the Central Station included "Inspector and Secretary, John Bonfield; Lieutenants, Joseph Kipley and John D. Shea; Custodian, John O'Donnell; Clerks, Joseph B. Shepard, Michael Brennan and Wm. E. Turner; Desk Sergeants, John E. Mahoney, Charles M. Day, Michael Langan [and] Photographer, Michael P. Evans." Ahern, *Political History of Chicago,* 220, 222. See also Paul Averich, *The Haymarket Tragedy* (Princeton, N.J.: Princeton University Press, 1984); Carl H. Smith, "The Dramas of Haymarket," http://www.chicagohistory.org/dramas; and James Green, *Death in the Haymarket* (New York: Random House, 2006).

118   **the assassination of President McKinley**   See especially "Emma Goldman Shocks Police: Unmoved When the Death of President Is Reported Prematurely," *Chicago Tribune*, September 14, 1901.

119   **the most recent visit of Prince Henry**   Prince Henry of Prussia visited Chicago during a whirlwind tour, March 3–4, 1902. For background information, see *Chicago Tribune*, March 2, 1902.

122   **copies of the address**   O'Neill's May 1903 address to the Annual Convention of the International Association of Chiefs of Police strikes many of the same themes in his published essay, "Why the Laws of Chicago Cannot Be Properly Enforced," *Chicago Inter Ocean*, February 8, 1903. We are grateful to John E. Corrigan for providing us with the text. O'Neill also contributed occasional pieces such as "The Detective in Fiction and in Life," *Chicago Tribune*, April 6, 1902; and "The City Boy," *New Carmelite Review*, November 1903: 24–26. Thanks to Reverend Louis P. Rogge, O.Carm., Carmelite Provincial Archives, Darien, Illinois, for making available this rare document, a copy of which O'Neill pasted into his personal scrapbook.

135   **Mayor Harrison the elder**   Carter Harrison I (1825–93) served as mayor of Chicago from 1879 to 1887. Just months after his reelection to a fifth term, he was assassinated by Patrick Eugene Prendergast on October 28, 1893, "the night before the close of the World's Fair." Edward M. Burke, "Assassination of Carter Harrison," *Encyclopedia of Chicago*, 511.

138   **my orchard out in Palos**   According to an account published in the *Chicago Tribune* on July 25, 1905, at the time of his resignation as superintendent, O'Neill claimed he planned to "go out to my farm in the town of Palos [in Cook County, Illinois] and live according to my own ideals. I have 80 acres there, part of the farm that [Detective] Jack Shea's father used to own. It has some water and natural forest on it, and I shall go into the farming business."

140   **One hasty glance was enough**   Apparently O'Neill's private secretary, James Markham, finally figured out that the police chief might be playing music at "Mecca," the name given Sergeant James O'Neill's home at 3522 South Washtenaw Avenue. See especially "Rumor Strikes Chief O'Neill," *Chicago Tribune*, February 21, 1902; and Caoimhin MacAoidh, *The Scribe: The Life*

and Works of James O'Neill (Co. Limerick, Ireland: Drumlin Publications, 2006).

143   ***Professor John P. Barrett, city electrician***   John P. Barrett, born in 1837 in Auburn, New York, moved to Chicago with his parents in 1845. He left school at age eleven and became a sailor until the age of twenty-two, finally securing a position as a telegrapher with the Chicago fire department. By 1876 he had become superintendent, and during the World's Fair of 1893 he was "chief of the electricity department . . . having been the unanimous choice of all the electricians in the country for that distinguished office . . ." Ffrench, *Biographical History of the American Irish in Chicago*, 666–67. In 1884 Barrett ordered "forty miles of insulated wire" that was laid underground for the "city fire and police alarms." *Chicago Tribune*, February 5, 1884. See also the biographical entry for Austin J. Doyle, in Ffrench, 90–92; and Joseph M. Fay, "Pull Boxes Placed in Department in 1880," *Police* "13–15," July 1927, 36–37.

146   ***Officer Whalen . . . summoned the patron wagon***   The murder of Walter Koeller by two acquaintances from Northern Illinois Normal School sent shock waves through Chicago and Dixon, Illinois, as well as their hometown of Hermann, Missouri. According to the *Chicago Tribune* of September 4, 1899, patrolman T. M. Whelan heard the report of the killing over the police telephone from the Warren Avenue Station, and in little more than two hours he had arrested Richard Honeck and Herman Hundhausen for the crime. See especially *Chicago Tribune* editorial, September 5, 1899, praising the police department for "the speed with which the murderers of young Walter Koeller were captured."

146–47 ***Captain Michael P. Evans***   Michael P. Evans, credited with installing the fingerprint system in the Chicago Police Department in 1888, continued to work in the Bureau of Identification until his death in the fall of 1931. In a touching note to Paul R. Byrne, librarian at the University of Notre Dame, on October 6, 1931, O'Neill wrote, "Must if alive attend the funeral of Capt. M. P. Evans Saturday forenoon." For brief account of Evans's funeral and burial in Mount Olivet Cemetery, see *Chicago Tribune*, October 11, 1931.

148   ***much time had elapsed between the bandits' escape and their dramatic capture***   Not only was the case of the "Car-Barn Bandits" front-page news in all the city's newspapers in the fall of 1903, but Chicagoans flocked to North Clark Street

to see Mamie Dunn, the fiancée of one of the murderers. Finally, after the death of Detective Joseph Driscoll, the eighth victim, in December 1903, Mayor Carter Harrison II asked the manager of the dime museum "in the name of civic decency, to withdraw Miss Dunn from the list of attractions." See especially *Chicago Inter Ocean*, December 2, 1903; and *Chicago Tribune*, December 2, 1903.

150 **Sergeant James L. Mooney** Having worked on the police detail at the 1893 World's Fair, James Mooney joined the Chicago Police Department in 1894. He was quickly promoted to sergeant in 1897. On January 30, 1900, James Mooney married Julia Ann O'Neill, the oldest daughter of Anna and Francis O'Neill, in Saint Thomas the Apostle Church in Hyde Park. It's likely that Anna and Francis O'Neill were already living at 5448 South Drexel Boulevard when the new church was dedicated on December 14, 1890. A delegation of eighty police officers, led by Inspector Nicholas Hunt and Captain J. E. Lloyd of the Hyde Park District police station, met Archbishop Patrick A. Feehan at Fifty-first Street and Drexel Boulevard and accompanied him to the church. *Chicago Tribune*, December 15, 1890. In November 1922, Francis O'Neill lent his name to the campaign to build the present Saint Thomas the Apostle Church designed by noted architect Barry Byrne. We are grateful to Theresa McDermott for providing us with information on the O'Neill family contributions to the parish between 1916 and 1922. As for James Mooney, when he took the civil service test in December 1905, he scored fourth highest in the city with 83.41 percent. *Chicago Tribune*, March 2, 1905. He was promoted to lieutenant in 1905 and to captain in 1921. He is remembered for protecting the Republican Steel headquarters during the May 30, 1937, strike. He had a distinguished career, retiring as captain in 1940. He died in 1960.

152 **Judge Edward F. Dunne** Judge Edward F. Dunne was elected mayor of Chicago on April 4, 1905, defeating John Maynard Harlan by 24,454 votes. See "Dunne Is Mayor; Victor by 24,454," *Chicago Tribune*, April 5, 1905.

152 **reappointment to a cabinet office in a new administration was never thought of** O'Neill's record-shattering reappointment as superintendent of police occurred on July 11, 1905, but by July 25, according to the *Chicago Daily News*, he had "refused to do what he considered the 'dirty work' of the administration and become in police parlance the 'fall guy' of the Dunne regime."

152   **The teamsters' strike**   The bitter 105-day "teamsters' strike," named in honor of delivery men who "use horses and wagons," was finally settled on July 20, 1905. Chief O'Neill lamented, "We are handicapped for want of men. At least 1,000 more will be needed in the event of any spread of the labor trouble. It is difficult to spare men from their regular police duties, and a man who is on duty all night is not fitted for strike duty during the day." *Chicago Tribune*, April 9, 1905.

INCLINED TO RETIRE

157   **Douglas Hyde**   As part of his visit to Chicago, the great Gaelic scholar Douglas Hyde lectured in the Fine Arts building on January 13, 1906.

158   **six children interred in Chicago cemeteries**   The large limestone monument in Calvary Cemetery is the resting place for five of Anna and Francis O'Neill's ten children: John Francis, another John Francis, Mary Catherine, Francis, and Philip Anthony, all of whom died between 1871 and 1885. Francis O'Neill built the mausoleum in Mount Olivet Cemetery in Chicago in memory of his son Rogers Francis, who died at the age of eighteen on February 13, 1904. The mausoleum was finished in June 1905; Rogers O'Neill's body was interred in the mausoleum on June 27, 1905. More than a thousand people attended his funeral Mass at Saint Thomas the Apostle Church, celebrated by Archbishop James E. Quigley, and students from Saint Ignatius College (now Loyola University) served as Rogers's pallbearers. *New World*, February 20, 1904.

160   **Father Bernard Murray, Dr. Bristol, and William J. Onahan**   Reverend Bernard P. Murray, born in Antrim, Ireland, founded Saint Bernard parish in Chicago's Englewood neighborhood at Sixty-sixth Street and Stewart Avenue in 1887. Dr. Bristol may have been Edward Samuel Bristol, a native of London who served in the Civil War and established an agricultural implements firm in Chicago in 1877. William J. Onahan, born in County Carlow, Ireland, and a prominent Chicagoan since 1854, donated many of his books to the University of Notre Dame and Saint Ignatius College (now Loyola University).

162   **a local history**   In 1892 O'Neill was elected to the Cork Historical and Archaeological Society, founded in 1891 "for the Collection, Preservation, and Diffusion of all available information regarding the Past of the City and County

of Cork, and South of Ireland generally." Fellow members included William Onahan of Chicago. *Journal of the Cork Historical and Archaeological Society* 6 (January–March 1900).

170   **Selena O'Neill**   In his 1913 book *Irish Minstrels and Musicians*, Francis O'Neill praised his collaborator, Selena O'Neill (not related to Francis O'Neill), asserting, "In the piano contest [in the February 1913 Feis in Philadelphia] Miss O'Neill had no real rivalry, for she alone of the competitors played Irish dance music, a feat which evidently astonished the audience." O'Neill's granddaughter Mary Wade recalls taking the streetcar with her brother Philip to take piano and violin lessons from Miss Selena O'Neill. Noel P. Rice, president of the Irish American Heritage Center and director of the Academy of Irish Music describes a Feis as a daylong competition in music and dance; at times the Feis can include baking contests, and there is always an emphasis on socializing.

171   **Irish Folk Music . . . published in 1913**   One of the great Irish cultural events in Chicago on August 3, 1913, was the Feis at Comiskey Park. Organized by the Gaelic League of Ireland and the Chicago Gaelic Society, it featured thirty-one contests in singing and storytelling as well as traditional Irish music, "jig, reel, hornpipe, figure dances," accompanied by "violin, flute, Highland Pipes and Irish Pipes" as well as Irish football and hurling competitions. O'Neill was a major supporter of the Feis, and the handsome brochure was designed by the city's leading Irish American artist, Thomas A. O'Shaughnessy, creator of the new Celtic stencils and stained-glass windows in Old Saint Patrick's at Adams and Desplaines streets, the "mother parish" of the Chicago Irish. *Chicago Citizen*, July 26, 1913; August 2, 1913.

173   **Resigned July 25, 1905**   Francis O'Neill died on January 28, 1936, and his funeral Mass was held at Saint Thomas the Apostle Church, where he had been a parishioner for more than forty years. He was buried in the O'Neill mausoleum at Mount Olivet Cemetery, the resting place for son Rogers O'Neill (who died in 1904) and for Anna O'Neill (who died in 1934). *Chicago Daily News*, January 28, 1936; *Chicago Tribune*, January 29, 1936.

INDEX

FRANCIS O'NEILL was born to a farming family in Tralibane, County Cork, Ireland, in 1848. He left Ireland in 1865 and died in Chicago in 1936.

ELLEN SKERRETT is the editor of *At the Crossroads: Old Saint Patrick's and the Chicago Irish* and has written widely on Catholicism and Chicago. Her latest book is a history of Loyola University Chicago.

MARY LESCH is Francis O'Neill's great-granddaughter. Mary's grandmother was Julia O'Neill Mooney, and her father was Frank (Francis) Mooney. She is now retired and divides her time between Chicago and Harbert, Michigan.

1903   Reappointed general superintendent of police for a second term by Mayor Carter Harrison II.

Published his first book, *O'Neill's Music of Ireland, Eighteen Hundred and Fifty Melodies,* edited by Captain Francis O'Neill; arranged by James O'Neill.

April 2: President Theodore Roosevelt visited Chicago.

May: Addressed the International Association of Chiefs of Police on the duties and difficulties of the police chief.

Designed and introduced new police badges.

November 12: Restored order during the Chicago City Railway strike.

November 27: Directed the capture of the car-barn bandits.

1904   February 13: Son Rogers died at the age of eighteen.

May: Addressed the International Association of Chiefs of Police on scientific improvements in police methods.

1905   June 25: Buried Rogers O'Neill (2-7-1886 to 2-13-1904) in the new O'Neill mausoleum at Mount Olivet Cemetery.

July 11: Reappointed general superintendent of police for a third term by Mayor Edward Dunne.

July 25: Retired from the police force following the conclusion of the teamsters strike.

1906   Visited Ireland with wife, Anna.

1907   Published his second book, *The Dance Music of Ireland, 1001 Gems,* edited by Captain Francis O'Neill; arranged by James O'Neill.

1908   Published *O'Neill's Irish Music: 250 Choice Selections Arranged for Piano and Violin.* Collected and edited by Captain Francis O'Neill; arranged by James O'Neill.

1910   Wrote and published *Irish Folk Music, a Fascinating Hobby.*

Published *Popular Selections from O'Neill's Dance Music of Ireland;* arranged by Selena O'Neill.

1913   Wrote and published *Irish Minstrels and Musicians.*